The
Prenatal
Person

The Prenatal Person

Ethics from Conception to Birth

Norman M. Ford SDB

Director
Caroline Chisholm Centre for Health Ethics
East Melbourne
Australia

Blackwell
Publishing

First published 2002 by Blackwell Publishers Ltd,
a Blackwell Publishing company.

Library of Congress Cataloging-in-Publication Data

Ford, Norman M.
The prenatal person: ethics from conception to birth / Norman M. Ford.
    p. cm.
Includes bibliographical references and index.
ISBN 0-631-23491-8 (alk. paper) – ISBN 0-631-23492-6
(pbk. : alk. paper)
1. Human reproductive technology – Moral and ethical aspects.
2. Human reproductive technology – Religious aspects – Catholic Church.
I. Title.
RG133.5. F66 2002
176 – dc21
2002066415

A catalogue record for this title is available from the British Library.

Set in 10/12½ pt Sabon
by SNP Best-set Typesetter Ltd., Hong Kong
Printed and bound in Great Britain by MPG Books Ltd,
Bodmin, Cornwall

For further information on
Blackwell Publishers, visit our website:
www.blackwellpublishers.co.uk

Contents

Preface

The human reproductive revolution, coupled with the recent therapeutic advances made from conception to birth, have raised new practical ethical questions to which health professionals and informed lay persons seek answers. This book offers some responses from an ethical perspective that is consistent with the Catholic Christian tradition. Secular ethicists may agree with some of the suggested answers but they will differ sharply on others. The underlying reasons for these differences need to be carefully explored for the benefit of Catholic and secular scholars and healthcare professionals. Philosophical reasoning will be very much part of this dialogue between the views of Christian and secular ethicists on the practical ethical issues raised. It is necessary that discussions on health ethics be held in the context of the relevant medical and scientific facts as well the basic religious and secular belief systems of the participants, be they health professionals, scientists, ethicists, or interested members of the community. It would be unrealistic to engage in debates on health ethics unaware of others' views if they are to be relevant in today's world.

The Bible has shaped Western culture over the centuries and has made significant ethical contributions to medical decision-making for the preservation of human life and restoration of health. The beliefs that Christians hold not only enlighten their understanding of the meaning of human existence but they also powerfully influence how many Christians live and behave. While the Bible provides a focal point of unity for Christians, disagreements exist on some difficult matters in the area of health ethics from conception to birth. My views derive from the

Catholic tradition but at times I make suggestions for developing and refining this living tradition. While Catholics and other Christians differ on ethical issues in areas like reproductive technology and the termination of pregnancy, there are many other areas where there is substantial agreement.

Secular thinkers may not accept the Bible as God's Word, but many admire the Bible's portrait of how a *good person* should behave and live. The Bible does not give answers to specific problems in healthcare ethics but, along with the Christian tradition, it provides a broad blueprint of what it means to be an authentic human person, in the light of which moral principles may be formulated. These may then be used as guidelines for the responses by health professionals as issues arise in clinical practice. I explain the underpinnings of ethical principles based on the Catholic Christian tradition for the consideration of health professionals and informed lay readers. The reasons for treating the human embryo as a person from conception onwards in practice are discussed in Part I of the book. Likewise the same applies to other moral values, such as the reasons given for the importance of autonomy and its ethical implications. These reasons will not be repeated in Part II of the book: they will be taken for granted. The reasons for other ethical views on many issues are also discussed. Readers in their turn will make their own ethical evaluation of positions presented. I believe these discussions and clarifications will be helpful for Christian and secular healthcare professionals who work side by side in delivering health services. It will also help them learn why their Catholic patients may hold certain practical ethical views, say, in relation to reproductive technology.

At the same time it is important to explain to Christians and other theists why it is that so many morally upright health professionals and philosophers hold ethical opinions that are quite different from typical Christian views. A metaphysical conceptual framework that only allows for material entities and a world without God profoundly alters one's concept of the human person and of ethics. A mutual understanding of the reasons underlying certain ethical views of Catholics and non-Catholics will likewise be beneficial for healthcare professionals and scientists. This avoids misleading, and possibly hurtful, stereotypes being applied to colleagues. For our mental health it is important to recall that not all ethical issues are equally important. It is also true that not all the reasons given to support the ethical positions of Christians or secular humanists carry the same weight.

Relevance of Scientific and Medical Facts

A proper discussion of the wide range of ethical issues from conception to birth could not proceed without sufficient understanding of the relevant scientific, medical, and clinical facts. This information is given to the extent that it is needed by nonclinicians for a proper ethical analysis and evaluation of the issues under consideration. The scientific and medical data given are generally relevant for the developed world whether they are taken from Europe, North America, or Australia. A health professional's ideology or ethical views should not distort scientific facts nor their proper relevance to clinical practice. This is necessary if the appropriate ethical principle is to be employed in each case. At times it is necessary to do one's utmost to preserve life, at another time it is morally permissible to withdraw treatment and simply provide comfort care. Christian and secular ethicists should agree on the scientific and medical facts of a case before making a judgment on the ethics of treatment procedures in medical practice. At other times ethical disputes boil down to differences in the interpretation of the relevant facts and their correct clinical implications for treatment options.

The use of slogans and uncritically formulated guidelines may be useful for the purposes of mass inculturation, but they are inadequate to serve as ethical guidelines for making right clinical decisions in complex cases. The documentation of sources given in endnotes enables additional information to be sought by readers and researchers. The relevant scientific and medical facts given need to be kept in mind as they are presupposed in the sections where ethical analysis and evaluations are considered.

For Whom Will This Book Be Useful?

One need not be an academic, professionally trained in philosophy, theology, the Bible, medicine, or physiology to understand, and benefit from, reading this book. All that is needed is an interest in ethical issues from conception to birth – issues discussed in the media for the benefit of interested lay people in the wider community. It will interest doctors, nurses, midwives, healthcare professionals generally, members of clinical ethics committees, medical and nursing students, health reporters, ethicists, students, hospital chaplains, moral philosophers and theologians, and government advisers.

Norman Ford SDB
Director
Caroline Chisholm Centre for Health Ethics
East Melbourne, 3002, Australia
Lecturer, Melbourne College of Divinity/
Catholic Theological College
Adjunct Professor, Australian Catholic University
Senior Honorary Research Fellow
Monash University
January 2002

Acknowledgments

I am indebted to many persons for their assistance in writing this book. I thank Catholic Theological College and Cabrini Hospital in Melbourne for the financial contribution made towards the visiting fellowship I was awarded at Clare Hall, Cambridge, UK, to research and write most of the first draft of this book from September 1993 to March 1994. I would like to thank Dr. David Allen, Rev. Bill Uren SJ, and Professor Peter Singer for their encouragement and valuable comments on an earlier draft of the entire book. I have very much appreciated the support and advice received from the following academics who read earlier drafts of at least one chapter of the book: Professor Francis Moloney SDB, Rev. Dr. Mark Coleridge, Professor John Hearn, Professor Alan Trounson, Professor Roger Short, Dr. Janet Gross-Hanning, Dr. Cormac Nagle OFM, Dr. Mackenzie Talbot, Lesley Freemann, Dr. Jane Halliday, Dr. Karen Dawson, Professor Bob MacMahon, Professor Tony d'Apice and Dr. Andrew Watkins.

I would like to thank Deirdre Fetherstonhaugh and Tracey Phelan, researchers of the Caroline Chisholm Centre for Health Ethics, for their many helpful suggestions made on several chapters. I also thank Margaret Casey, the Centre's administrative assistant, for diligently proofreading the entire text. Finally I would like to thank Laura Barry and Rebecca Harkin of Blackwell Publishers for their advice in finalizing the book for publication. In spite of all the assistance received, I assume responsibility for any errors and inelegancies that may have slipped into the text.

I am grateful to the Academic Press for permission to use modified parts of my article under the entry *Fetus* in chapters entitled "Human Embryo" and "Fetus." The article *Fetus* was published in *The Encyclopedia of Applied Ethics*, vol. 2 (San Diego: Academic Press, 1998).

I acknowledge that an earlier version of much of the chapter on "Prenatal Screening and Diagnosis" was read as a paper in a Conference on Genetics and Ethics organized by the Center for Health Care Ethics, St. Louis University, St. Louis, on October 30, 1999. This original paper has been included in the conference proceedings that will be published as follows: *Genetics and Ethics: An Interdisciplinary Study*, ed. Gerard Magill, St. Louis: Saint Louis University Press, 2002.

Part I
Foundations

1

Morality
for Persons

One who wishes to understand more deeply their own ethical views ought to consider those of their major critics. By paying attention to criticisms of one's own ethical positions, one is forced to rethink the presuppositions and foundations of those ethical beliefs. For the purposes of this book there is no need to consider the ethical views of many philosophers individually. It suffices to focus attention on a prominent philosopher like Professor Peter Singer who has been conspicuous in contemporary bioethical debates. His outspoken views are representative of many others who do not articulate their thoughts as clearly as he does. His views are important and his claims warrant critical analysis. Some of his views shock, but Singer is an honest philosopher who is consistent with his fundamental assumptions, which differ in many important ways from my own and those of the Christian tradition.

Peter Singer has recently dismissed traditional ethics: "After ruling our thoughts and our decisions about life and death for nearly two thousand years, the traditional western ethic has collapsed."[1] He goes further and bluntly says "modern medical practice has become incompatible with belief in the equal value of all human life."[2] He says "the fact that a being is human, and alive, does not in itself tell us whether it is wrong to take that being's life."[3] He adds:

> Thousands of years of lip-service to the Christian ethic have not succeeded in suppressing entirely the earlier ethical attitude that newborn infants, especially if unwanted, are not yet full members of the moral community.[4]

He is convinced that the western ethic fails because the "traditional view that all human life is sacrosanct is simply not able to cope with the array of issues that we face" and because it assumes "that we are responsible for what we intentionally do in a way that we are not responsible for what we deliberately fail to prevent."[5] He suggests secular utilitarian ethics can succeed.

In keeping with the scope of this book, I will first give a brief account of Singer's *utilitarian* ethical theory and his concept of person, held also by other secular contemporary philosophers. I will then outline my own ethical theory, beginning with the traditional concept of the human person and how this influences my own ethical and bioethical views. All this will throw some light on whether there is any justification for the criticisms made against the traditional western ethic and whether it is possible for it to survive and continue to be applied consistently in the modern world of medicine by refining, without denying, its basic philosophical and ethical principles. At least the exercise will serve to pinpoint where the real differences lie between both approaches to ethical issues from conception to birth.

1.1 Utilitarianism

Singer says that people

> who hold unconventional ethical beliefs are still living according to ethical standards *if they believe, for any reason, that it is right to do as they are doing.*[6]

I take this to mean it is enough for them to be prepared to justify what they are doing for their conduct to be ethical, in the sense opposed to non-ethical, rather than unethical. He requires, however, that justifying reasons for conduct must go beyond self-interest if it is to qualify as ethical conduct. This is because it is unanimously agreed by philosophers that ethical conduct must be acceptable from a universal point of view. Going beyond the self must be inbuilt into any ethical perspective. It encapsulates the insight of the equality of all persons. Singer is quick to point out this does not imply that a particular ethical judgment must be universally applicable because circumstances differ and these make a difference. Any ethical point of view must go beyond one's likes and dislikes "to the universal law, the standpoint of the impartial spectator or ideal observer."[7]

Singer admits a practical ethical theory cannot be deduced from the notion of universality from which, however, several bare and formal ethical theories could be derived – and some of these could be inconsistent with each other. But if universality were to be loaded with a particular ethical theory, one could only deduce ethical views that were consistent with the theory one had already incorporated in the definition of universality. That aside, he believes the universality of ethics "does provide a persuasive, although not conclusive, reason for taking a broadly utilitarian position."[8]

For the purposes of this book I need not go beyond Singer's own brief account of his view of utilitarianism. It is a form of consequentialism according to which the morality of actions generally depends on their consequences. It is very persuasive and extremely influential in contemporary western culture and public life. It is hard to fault it as far as it goes. *Classical utilitarianism* broadly holds that whatever promotes the greatest utility or pleasure for the greatest number would be the morally right thing to do. Richard Hare succinctly sums up this position: "we should choose the action which maximises the welfare (i.e. maximally promotes the interests) of all *in sum*, or *in aggregate*."[9]

Some hold that certain types of action are so harmful to the community that they could never be justified. This is *rule utilitarianism*. Others contend that a certain type of act might generally be harmful to the community, but in particular cases it might be better to make an exception, e.g. torturing members of a terrorist organization to obtain information to prevent an attack on innocent civilians. This is *act utilitarianism*. In any case, utilitarianism goes beyond selfish individualism. Singer says utilitarianism

> requires me to weigh up all those interests and adopt the course of action most likely to maximise the interests of those affected. Thus at least at some level in my moral reasoning I must choose the course of action that has the best consequences, on balance, for all affected.[10]

He thinks this scarcely differs from classical utilitarianism if "pleasure" is interpreted broadly to include interests or desires and "pain" whatever is contrary to these. Yet Singer does not claim utilitarianism is the only ethical theory consistent with a typically universal ethical point of view. One based on justice or the sanctity of life would be universal but neither of these would be compatible with utilitarianism. He believes utilitarianism represents the minimum – the first step one must take to avoid being locked into a selfish and egoistic perspective.[11]

Singer, rightly in my view, argues against the Kantian conception of ethics of doing one's duty for duty's sake by staunchly defending the legit-

imacy of self-interest in ethics. He does not mean one should daily think
in terms of self-interest in deciding to do the ethically right thing. This
would not be realistic.[12] At the same time he does not believe there
is any factual evidence in human nature always linking ethics and self-
interest. There may be cases where a connection can be traced between
some character traits, self-actualization, and happiness, but this is far
from universally true. He believes human nature is too diverse for this
to be so and he illustrates his point by citing the example of a psy-
chopath.[13] He admits believers, who accept God and a divine purpose in
creation, may find meaning in life. But, he equally contends, atheists may
find a meaning in life in what evolution and natural selection have
randomly provided, i.e. beings who do have preferences. Because of this
"it may be possible for particular lives to be meaningful" even though
life as a whole may have no meaning, certainly not a "preordained
meaning."[14]

Singer comments that most people who seek happiness for its own
sake do not become happy, while others find it in pursuing other goals.
Though this cannot be empirically verified, it does match our common
experience of people who become happy and fulfilled by working for,
and achieving, their chosen goals.[15] He suggests living by the ethical point
of view is one way of transcending narrow selfish interests. He holds
those who do not go this far and simply live to further their own quality
of life are neither irrational nor in error, but his own preferred view is
clear. He implies that when we act ethically day by day, we further our
long-term interests of a happy and meaningful life, even if we do not
think of this at the time. For him happiness is the fruit of trying to achieve
chosen goals – goals one will not tire of, including living an ethical life.[16]
Indeed, happiness is not found by those who daily seek it from within,
but by those who live with an outward gaze for broader purposes than
their own self-interests.

There is no denying that we often have to judge ethically along the
lines of Singer's version of utilitarianism. The consequences of our
actions and how they impact on our own and others' interests certainly
have great ethical importance in decision-making. It would be generally
unethical to give more weight to one person's preferences of the same
order than another's, whether one acts in a private or public capacity. I
dare say most ethical decisions in healthcare would be utilitarian in
nature, and rightly so. Governments should follow utilitarian criteria to
administer public services for the common good. Hence it would be
unethical to locate a hospital where it would be electorally advantageous
for government rather than where it would best serve the interest of all

concerned. However, whether utilitarianism alone suffices as an ethical theory for persons remains to be seen.

1.2 Contemporary Concept of Person

My main interest is in philosophers whose concept of the human person has been employed in bioethics. I'll start with Singer, who when explaining his utilitarian views, speaks of himself, or anybody else for that matter, as a person. He uses the term person "in the sense of a rational and self-conscious being" and thereby excludes members of the species *Homo sapiens* who lack these characteristics.[17] His definition of person is crucial for interpreting his meaning of interests, understood broadly to include whatever people desire. Newborn babies have some interests, but because they cannot think or have desires, Singer holds they do not count as persons nor have the interests of persons: "Since no fetus is a person, no fetus has the same claim to life as a person."[18] For public policy, Singer suggests that a newborn's full legal right to life in some cases could begin a week or a month after birth.[19] He shares these views with other contemporary philosophers, especially his colleague Helga Kuhse. They were quite unambiguous when they wrote:

> We must recall, however, that when we kill a new-born infant there is no *person* whose life has begun. When I think of myself as the person I now am, I realise that I did not come into existence until sometime after my birth.[20]

Mary Anne Warren holds a similar view. For her the human fetus could not be a person because:

> it seems safe to say that it is not fully conscious, in the way that an infant of a few months is, and that it cannot reason, or communicate messages of indefinitely many sorts, does not engage in self-motivated activity, and has no self-awareness.[21]

Michael Tooley requires a person to be a "subject of nonmomentary interests," though he admits a theoretical possibility of a person existing once a relevant capacity, e.g. for thought, is acquired and not only later when this capacity is exercised.[22] Michael Lockwood does not believe that sentience suffices to count as a person:

> A person is a being that is conscious, in the sense of having the capacity
> for conscious thought and experiences, but not only that: it must have the
> capacity for reflective consciousness and self-consciousness . . . Mere sen-
> tience is not enough to qualify a being as a person.[23]

For these secular philosophers, babies could not be persons until they
had acquired the capacity to exercise some minimal rationally self-
conscious acts after birth. Singer thinks "some nonhuman animals are
persons."[24] He goes so far as to say

> The evidence for personhood is at present most conclusive for the great
> apes, but whales, dolphins, elephants, monkeys, dogs, pigs and other
> animals may eventually also be shown to be aware of their own existence
> over time and capable of reasoning.[25]

Consistent with his definition of a person, Singer concludes "the life of
a new born baby is of less value to it than the life of a pig, a dog, or a
chimpanzee is to the nonhuman animal."[26] If some animals were to be
deemed to be persons with a right to life, this would radically change
our western ethic and human-centered culture which gives preference to
humans over animals.

Lockwood introduces the concept of "human being" which comes
between that of person and "human organism," understood in the purely
biological sense of a complete living organism of the species *Homo
sapiens*.[27] He says:

> we need a term for whatever it is that you and I are essentially, what we
> can neither become nor cease to be, without ceasing to exist. I use the term
> *human being* to fill this slot.[28]

This implies a human being may become a person without ceasing to be
a human being. For him a fetus, as a nonpersonal human being, could
become a person. There is continuity of identity between a human being
and a person, but not between a living biological organism of the human
species and the human being and person. For Lockwood a week-old
human embryo is an organism that is biologically human but not a
human being nor a person.[29] A human being could not come into existence before the brain structures required for sustaining awareness of
identity were developed. Their continuity in time constitutes the under-
pinning for the ongoing identity of the human being:

When I came into existence is a matter of how far back the relevant neu-
rophysiological continuity can be traced. Presumably, then, my life began
somewhere between conception and birth.[30]

Walter Glannon holds a similar view:

> A person begins to exist when the fetal stage of the organism develops the
> structure and function of the brain necessary to generate and support con-
> sciousness and mental life. This is when the fetus becomes sentient, at
> around 23–24 weeks of gestation.[31]

This challenge to the traditional Christian view is not new. The
English philosopher John Locke (d. 1704) considered that to be a person
one must be able to exercise rational acts:

> We must consider what *person* stands for: – which I think is a thinking
> intelligent being, that has reason and reflection, and can consider itself as
> itself, the same thinking thing, in different times and places.[32]

What is new, is the wider diffusion of this concept of person in secular
academic circles and how it is used to undermine respect for the lives
of human individuals who do not qualify as persons by this restricted
definition of person. Singer's conclusions may be consistent with his
premises and be acceptable in many quarters, but that does not put them
beyond challenge. The claim that a newborn baby is not a person clashes
with the broadly accepted view of most people in the community and
this may be a sign some of his assumptions are faulty. The problem hinges
on the concept of person employed and which I will now address.

1.3 Traditional Concept of Person

Ethical theories presuppose at least an implicit philosophical concept of
the human person which underpins them and of which they are an
expression. An ethical theory has sense only for persons. A long tradition dating back to Boethius (d. 524) broadly defined a person philo-
sophically, not legally, as "an individual substance in a rational nature"
which may be simply put as *a living individual with a rational human
nature*.[33] In an ontological sense the person exists as the subject of human
existence even if they exist in virtue of their human nature which is also

rational. There are billions of human persons, in each of whom the same human nature is individualized. There is a multiplicity of races, cultures, ideologies, and individual differences, but all human persons are equal in dignity with the same kind of rational human nature, similar bodies, feelings and emotions. An understanding of the human person is not acquired *a priori*, but by the use of inductive philosophical reflection on persons whose common human nature is pluriform in its expressions.

I will first explore what it means to be a person using a subject-centered approach, followed by an objective approach based on human nature. These two non-mutually-exclusive approaches to our self-understanding as persons are complementary and represent the essential bipolarity of the human person. Many Christians differ significantly with Singer on the definition of a person and this in turn creates ethical differences as well.[34]

There are other philosophical approaches to understanding persons and human nature.[35] I dare not explain them all here. There are also other disciplines which study human persons but I do not intend to discuss them beyond mentioning that their findings complement a philosophical understanding of the human person and are both relevant to, and important for, ethics and ethical evaluations of many forms of human behavior. Psychology studies mental states, how people behave, and what may motivate them. It is to be noted that personality refers to the organized patterns of all an individual's characteristics and is not to be confused with the philosophical concept of person. Anthropology studies the origins, human and moral development and cultures of humankind. Sociology is similar but it concentrates on studies of the origin, development and functioning of human society and the basic laws of social relations.

Person: a subject-centered approach

I agree with Singer that great importance should be given to the interests of persons affected by our actions. This requires an understanding of persons from a subjective perspective. We readily recognize the fundamental distinction between *being* and *having*. One may own an object, but may not in turn be owned. Each of us is a living subject whose body cannot be reduced to an object of possession.[36] We experience the self in a variety of bodily activities such as walking, typing, and eating or in sensations like feeling warm in the sun. There are other more significant ways to experience ourselves. Think of how we become aware of ourselves through our feelings, emotions, pleasures, pains, growing up, friendships, sexual experiences, love, marriage and family life, community relationships, at work collaborating with others, sport and recreation, social and political life, and cultural activities. Through all our conscious sensations, activities, feelings, and encounters, the self is revealed as personal, male or female, and relational. These experiences originate from within the subject and so we recognize them as our own. A human person, then, does not exist in the abstract without a name, a gender, an age, a personality, family ties, a life influenced by a variety of experiences journeys and relationships, a nationality, a culture, a religious faith, or a system of values as well as a common human nature. Touch any of these factors and you touch the person.

By reflecting on our affirmations we further explore ourselves as subjects because we identify more with the inner core of the self when we use our power of intelligence to make statements. We have no choice but to bow to the truth when the evidence is clear, even if this means changing our minds. We powerfully identify with our inner self in serious conscientious judgements. Some truths about ourselves and a proposed course of action generate a moral imperative to do or omit it. We realize we cannot, without blame, act contrary to what we believe to be the truth of a moral imperative of conscience. This represents an awareness of ourselves as morally responsible agents within our subjectivity. Lack of respect for one's own or another's conscience is lack of respect for the person.

Our knowledge of what is attainable leads to the exercise of freedom whereby we have control of what we do and indeed of our lives. This sense of autonomy is highly valued by all. Love is one of the highest forms of the exercise of free choice: there can be no true love without genuine freedom, no matter how strong the sexual attraction may be. Free choice expresses our personal dignity most of all when we submit to the summons of conscience demanding that good be done to be true to ourselves as persons. Freedom is seen to be subordinate to the true good of oneself as a person. When we deliberately choose to do something, we own what we do and assume responsibility for it as a moral agent. Choosing wisely enables one to become more of a person. Guilt experienced after willful abuse of freedom makes us aware that the right use of freedom is a life-long challenge.

Our identity is inextricably interwoven with our interactions and personal relationships. In his seminal book *I and Thou*, Martin Buber, a German philosopher, stressed the importance of entering into mutually respectful personal relationships to experience and enrich our identity and personhood.[37] The development and experience of ourselves as persons is at its peak when we communicate and dialogue with others as equals, sharing love, secrets, hopes, desires, and misfortunes. In the absence of communication a relationship of love may become superficial, in spite of protestations to the contrary.[38] The experience of sincere and morally responsible relationships is unique to human persons and must be fostered for authentic growth in personalism, even if it is painful to trim back the culturally entrenched individualism of our times. We have a strong sense of belonging to families, groups, communities, and nations. Living in isolation from others impoverishes the person and risks reducing self-experience to sensations. One who loves, experiences liberation from whatever is base and degrading.[39]

Our desire for genuine and unending personal happiness, even after death, touches the core of our subjectivity. Good times and brief pleasurable experiences give no lasting satisfaction. The desire for happiness goes beyond sense pleasures and engages our intelligence and will: we cannot but want to be happy. This ever active seeking after happiness is typical of the dynamism of human persons. It drives all our endeavors and striving. As persons we realize we belong to a human community of equals and recognize others share our pursuit of happiness. We need to be affirmed, loved, supported and appreciated to attain happiness. We cannot be complete persons in isolation. We naturally desire to be in relationship with others. Failure to respond to others' needs for happiness is to fail ourselves.

Our basic awareness is of the self as a personal subject of conscious acts whether they are expressed primarily through the body or the mind. From our perspective, we are the center of our world. Each of us is aware of our unique personal identity, male or female, having the same identity develop with the passage of time. Though we perceive ourselves men or women, husbands or wives, doctors or nurses, employers or employees, we primarily see ourselves as persons. We are aware of our inherent value and intrinsic worth and that we should not be used as mere means by others. We recognize our dignity is founded in a human nature that includes reason and free will which enable us to pursue happiness by acting in a morally responsible way.

Ambiguity and limits are an integral part of ourselves. We strive after happiness yet often we experience frustration. We cannot explain why suffering and death are inevitable. Reflection on death makes us aware of our limits: modern medicine can delay death but it cannot take it away nor suppress our fears of it. The experience of sickness and disease brings home to us how fragile we are.

Person: human-nature approach

An objective approach using reflection on human nature is also needed to understand better the human person and to explain the foundation of a person's subjectivity, dignity, and capacity to be a moral agent. Interests, values, experiences and morally responsible acts are recognized as expressions of the person, made possible by the inherent capacities of human nature itself. Each person's awareness of themselves as a personal subject is compatible with many different abilities, activities, talents and traits. Rationally self-conscious acts are not merely acts of the brain, as though it was the organ for thinking as the eye is the organ for seeing. Indispensable though the brain is, it cannot think and is not itself conscious, but a person cannot think and be self-conscious without a functioning brain. The same person can be aware of being the conscious subject of both bodily and mental acts.

A person is a living human individual with a nature that enables them to perform bodily and mental acts. Jenny Teichman points out the obvious: "it would be ludicrous to be asked to give one's reasons for supposing that human beings are persons."[40] Again,

In ordinary life *person* and *human being* refer to the same things. For this reason the *ordinary* sense of the word *person* does not, indeed cannot, detach moral import from the concept of the human.[41]

The dual polarity of mind and body constitutes a body–mind or *psychosomatic* unity which is typical for members of the species *Homo sapiens*. We are one with our human nature: the human person and human nature though distinct cannot be wedged apart. Our common rational human nature underpins human solidarity and enables us to behave socially. Human nature, then, is the foundation and first principle of all our dynamism and activities of both body and mind. Because human nature is rational, i.e. enables us to have rationally self-conscious and free acts, every living human individual is a person.

Our power to understand and reason, to choose freely and to act morally together with the body and its organs, sensations, affections, feelings, and our sexuality are all part of our human nature and share in the dignity of the person. Their purposes and significance are to be interpreted from the perspective of the person and cannot be reduced to a purely psychological or biological level. We are subject to the determinism and laws of nature (e.g. the need of sleep and nutrition) that are beyond our control even though we often try to be their master through intelligent and responsible use of freedom. We can understand the inbuilt purpose of our vital organs, our sexuality and our biological, physiological, psychological, and social needs. They have to be carefully considered as we make our choices in the pursuit of happiness. Respect for the essential requirements and purposes of integral human nature is also respect for the person.

Secular philosophers do not generally believe in any reality that is non-material and do not accept a spiritual soul could be the foundation of a rational nature and the life principle of the human person. Consistently they do not believe that a fetus could be a person. It is true that human experience is the referral point for the significant and fruitful employment of all our concepts and objects of thought. However, simply because our ideas are originally derived from empirically observable situations and are most clearly employed in the world of our everyday experience there is no need to describe their employment as meaningless or false in cases where empirical criteria could not be available for their application. This would disregard the way we do successfully employ some meaningful concepts that go beyond our experience. We are able to think of abstract realities like virtue, God, or spirit and an unrestricted notion of reality that can refer to empirical and non-empirical beings alike. This kind of knowledge goes beyond matter alone.[42] The sort of total self-presence implied in rationally self-conscious acts, including free acts, cannot be explained simply in terms of quantified matter, material energy, or space–time relationships alone. Some underlying non-material power of understanding or intellect is required for typically human knowledge in addition to what is required sense knowledge. Traditionally this has been called a spiritual (immaterial) soul which animates the whole body. It may also be called the person's life principle.

The physical and biological laws of nature set limits to the use of our free choices. Though wishing alone cannot change natural forces in the world, by choosing to use our body we can freely exercise some power over the physical forces of nature and material energy. A free human action in the world introduces a variable in the sequence of natural causes. Our free actions show our limited dominion over nature, changing the direction of the sequence of natural causes and their consequences. Human freedom and knowledge require its subject to have an immaterial life principle which cannot be reduced to matter alone. This is another reason supporting the reality of the human soul.

Again on account of the unity of the human individual the soul must form one being with human nature and the body, thereby constituting a person with a rational human nature. The soul animates the body with all its activities without detracting from the causal influence of the body's vital systems, including the functions of chromosomes and genes in the formation and maintenance of the individual. Admittedly this is a mysterious aspect of a person's dual polarity within a single subject of existence.[43] It is better to admit some degree of mystery than to revert to the classical dualism of mind and body which flies in the face of our self-awareness and experience.

An immaterial soul could not derive from matter. It would have to be created, but not before the human individual begins. The soul's creation could occur when the individual is formed and thereby constitute a human person.[44] Naturally there could be no empirical evidence for the creation of the soul.[45] Lockwood himself and Tooley admit an immaterial soul could account for the underlying continuity of a human being's identity, but being unable to find any evidence for a soul, they favor a materialistic substratum – the functioning brain, as we have seen above.[46] For theists who admit a human person is animated by an immaterial life principle, there would be good reasons to hold that a human person begins as soon as the human individual is formed. I believe this is a reasonable assumption. These are the underlying reasons for the traditional concept of a human person with an inviolable moral status from the formation of the human individual, regardless of congenital abnormalities or subsequent disabilities.

On account of the possession of a human nature, the fetus and newborn baby is a person. As we have seen, some philosophers do not accept that it suffices to be a human individual or an individual member of the biological species *Homo sapiens* to count as a person.[47] They require minimal experience of oneself as a person with desires and interests to pursue. This restricted meaning of the term "person" needs to be critically examined in order to avoid confusion since the moral right to life of infants and fetuses is grounded in their status as natural persons. We usually talk and relate to persons who already are capable of exercising their rational powers and moral capacities but this should not mislead us into denying the status of a person to a human fetus and infant who have not yet sufficiently developed to be able to exercise rational self-conscious acts or enjoy personal relationships.[48] An organ has no power of sensation before it is first formed and ready for use. One cannot feel before one has a functioning sense organ of touch, one cannot see or hear before one has eyes or ears respectively. But this does not mean it is not possible for an individual to have a rational nature before rational acts can be performed.

It does not seem right to require the same conditions for the existence of a rational power as are required for sentience. The analogy does not apply, quite apart from the fact that reasoning is not performed by a bodily organ. It seems that before birth a human fetus already is a natural person, endowed with a rational nature because development and growth alone usher in the onset of the actual use of the natural capacity to perform rational and moral acts.[49] Time alone is needed for the requisite brain development to occur before these acts can be expressed. If I am right, the human infant actually is rational with the natural capacity to perform rational and moral acts in due time. Human nature enables fetuses and newborn babies to develop to the stage when these same individuals can exercise rationally self-conscious, free and moral acts. These changes brought about by growth and development into adulthood are real, but the developing *fetus* and *baby* does not become another individual. Fetuses and infants gradually realize their own inherent natural active potential to become more fully what they already are – persons with potential, not potential persons. They remain persons even if they subsequently develop congenital defects which may permanently inhibit the expression of rational acts. A newborn pup is unable to develop to the stage when it can exercise rationally self-conscious acts or to be a moral agent. Hence a dog is not a person.

1.4 Survival of Traditional Morality

I shall give an outline of my basic ethical outlook which is founded on the above account of the concept of a human person. Traditionally, ethics and morality practically had the same meaning. In contemporary usage, ethics more frequently is used for professional and public life, while morality is used more for one's personal life. In this chapter I shall freely use both terms interchangeably since the traditional meaning of morality is broader and can also include professional ethics.

Persons, truth, and moral necessity

Ethics is concerned with the behavior of persons and not of animals. Something definite and unambiguous is understood when we say an

action is moral or immoral. An analysis of our moral differences in evaluating some kinds of actions shows we believe truth is important for
morality. An action is immoral because it is contrary to the good of
person(s) and so gives rise to a moral obligation to avoid it. This obligation or moral necessity is derived from our understanding of the person
and directs us to choose to perform or omit an action. Moral necessity
is unconditioned or absolute because it cannot be set aside, regardless of
the circumstances, the inconvenience or consequences. A genuine moral
duty is universal since it holds for all persons, situations and cultures.
Rape and perjury are immoral everywhere. This is so because morality
is essentially related to the core of our personhood where human dignity
and solidarity originate. From an ethical perspective all persons are equal
and should be treated as such without discrimination.

The ethical evaluation of acts can be expressed in propositions which
may be true or false. For this to be done we need to know that the
traditional sources of morality for any action include its object which is
freely willed or chosen, the agent's intention or motive, and other relevant
circumstances. The *object* of a human action is what is deliberately willed
in a moral, not a purely physical, sense. One who deliberately pulls the
trigger of a loaded pistol pointed at another's head cannot reasonably say
they had simply squeezed the trigger: the moral object chosen would
clearly be to kill the person. An agent's chosen moral object could also
have a distinct intention, i.e. an end or purpose sought. One who robs a
bank to pay medical bills chooses to rob, but the intention is to pay bills.
These matters are presupposed in moral discourse about objects.

The moral imperative exists, but what makes an action so good that
it must be done, or evil and should be avoided? The meaning of *good* is
pivotal for ethics. The *good is that which all seek* – an end or a purpose.[50]
Its meaning is not derived from another notion because *good* is a basic
or primary notion but it is still relative to the concept of person. Whatever is a true *good* for the person is a *good of the person*; *evil* is opposed
to the true *good of the person, i.e. not good.* From the perspective of the
acting person, the *object* of a good human action is the good that is deliberately and freely chosen and which specifies the act's morality. The
object refers to the action's subject matter, its proximate end and its
objective purpose, i.e. what the action is naturally suited to bring about.
In the words of Pope John Paul II:

> The object of the act of willing is in fact a freely chosen kind of behav-
> iour. To the extent that it is in conformity with the order of reason, it is
> the cause of the goodness of the will; . . . An act is therefore good if its

object is in conformity with the good of the person with respect for the
goods morally relevant for him.[51]

This implies one should sacrifice one's life rather than deny one's religious faith or act against one's conscience.[52]

The first formal moral principle, which grounds other moral norms
is: *good should be done and evil avoided*.[53] It does not mean every good
action must be done: only actions whose object is good should be chosen
and those whose object is bad should not be chosen. Inbuilt into the very
notion of bad or evil there is a negative relationship to what is good for
person(s). In a derived sense *good* may also refer to what is good or
harmful for animals or plants. It is not good to harm unnecessarily
animals or the environment.

The object of an action is not good if it is opposed to the good of
person(s) or prevents the satisfaction of their basic needs be they biological, psychological, relational, social, or environmental. Some goods
may be teleological, i.e. chosen goals. But I believe chosen goals should
not negate the important inherent teleologies or purposes of the person's
nature. We are subject to certain biological, psychological, social, and
environmental purposes that we disregard at our own peril. John Paul II
puts this succinctly:

> Christian ethics . . . does not refuse to consider the inner "teleology" of
> acting, inasmuch as it is directed to promoting the true good of the person;
> but it recognises that it is really pursued only when the essential elements
> of human nature are respected.[54]

Hence we deeply resent being told lies because our minds are designed
for the truth, apart from other harms lies may cause. Hence natural, well-
ordered, and purposeful dynamism is a part of the meaning of what is
good for person(s).

The recognition that an action conflicts with the good of person(s)
generates an unconditioned demand to choose to avoid it. Moral necessity cannot be reduced to logical, physical, or psychological necessity. It
seems to arise because it is absurd to approve choosing an action that is
opposed to the good of person(s). Ironically we do at times choose to
dress up evil as good. Milton exemplifies this in *Paradise Lost* when he
has Satan utter this futile wish: "Evil be thou my Good." Being true to
ourselves is not an extrinsic imposition on our autonomy. Far from
enslaving us, morality helps to liberate ourselves from every form of
inhuman servitude.

Theists can take the foundations of morality further if they believe God created the world and the first human persons. It can reasonably be assumed the Creator had a divine plan for persons and the essential features of their common human nature. This would also apply in the hypothesis of evolution since the potency of what could evolve would have been inborn from the original creation. Whether a human individual originates as the result of evolution, the fusion of sperm and egg, or from an early human embryo, the same creative ensoulment within the emerging individual would have been necessary to constitute a person. A divine plan for the essential features of persons' human nature with some inborn dynamisms and purposes would be reasonably expected of a wise and provident Creator. It is not surprising theists hold that the good of the person(s) ultimately depends on God's provident creative plan. This does not mean only theists can hold an ethical theory. Richard Holloway rightly asks

> even if a religious connection to a good ethic is established, is it always necessary to accept the religion in order to have the ethic?[55]

Inadequacy of utilitarianism

It is necessary to have a criterion to determine what is ethically good or bad, right or wrong. *Utilitarianism* is an important and widely used criterion of morality, but I do not believe it is the primary or basic criterion of morality. One should subordinate some of one's interests for the benefit of others if one is to live ethically. The primary criterion of morality is related to the dignity and true good of the person(s) before any calculations are made about the beneficial effects an act may have for others. A person's ethical obligation to others is based on the duty to be true to oneself as a moral agent. One should not act against one's conscience for the sake of friends. It is also true that a person's rational and social nature requires due attention be given to the interests of others. The need to live ethically and moral truth arise from a person's rational nature and subjectivity wherein awareness of one's absolute value dawns. Hence moral truth is to be considered before the balancing of one's own and others' interests.

It may be asked how are a person's interests to be evaluated when others' interests are not at risk or relevant? Is there no criterion for personal, private morality? This would be anomalous since ethical obligations originate in persons. Interests do not exist in a vacuum. How can interests alone be the source and criterion of their own ethical value? Could interests be of ethical significance when their subject is discounted as the foundation of value? Surely the human individual as the subject of interests is the source of the ethical value of interests. This, however, does not imply that persons have no duties in relation to the needs and interests of animals to enjoy life and to be spared unnecessary pain.

For Singer newborn infants first enter the moral equation because they are sentient, not because they are persons. Utilitarians are open to this criticism on account of their failure to appreciate rational human nature as the foundation of a person's subjectivity, objective dignity, absolute value, moral responsibility, and interests. This in turn is due to its under-lying empirical criterion of significance which rules out *a priori* any pos-sibility of accepting an immaterial soul as a human person's life principle. If rationality is only explained in material terms, it could not be present before it could be empirically verified in much the same way as any other material property. But one who accepts the human individual is animated by an immaterial rational life principle would have no difficulty in explaining how a fetus and newborn baby could have a rational nature long before the onset of the age of reason, i.e. prior to the experience of minimally rational self-conscious acts. In other words, it is philosophi-cally plausible to accept that any living individual with a rational human nature is a person.

Criterion of morality

Feelings, emotions, and intuitions are often reliable indicators of the morality of particular actions. This is not surprising when we think that our senses, feelings, emotions, and intuitions are an integral part of ratio-nal human nature and of the person. As body and soul form one being, so too our sense knowledge is one with our intellectual knowledge. In the early stages of the development of our knowledge, conceptualization, the use of reason and judgments of moral evaluation do not yet occur. Human knowledge starts at the level of sense and feelings where appre-ciation of values begins. Feelings usually signal our first positive or neg-ative response to a suggested action. By way of sense knowledge and feelings it first dawns on reason intuitively that some actions are good and authentically human while others are not.

The philosopher Alfred Ayer first popularized the importance of emo-tional attitudes of approval or disapproval of acts with their morality in what became known as the *emotivist theory of ethics*.[56] However, we realize that our emotive attitudes for or against some kinds of actions are the consequence of our prior rational recognition by reason of their moral status. Our feelings, attitudes, and intuitions cannot solve complex or difficult moral dilemmas. There is a residue of meaning for some immoral actions that cannot be reduced to our emotive attitudes which lack a critical capacity. We need to look further afield than feelings for a rational and critical power of evaluation for an adequate criterion of morality.

Feelings may be right, but they cannot justify any moral evaluations or statements of moral truth. We need to be on guard against our own and others' prejudices. Apart from an adequate concept of the human person, we need the goodwill to want to be sincere in our quest for moral truth. Many moral truths are not sufficiently obvious to be discovered without goodwill, sincerity, and the hard work of reasoning things through. Our concepts of person and morality are relative to culture, but they should never be totally subordinated to the prevailing culture. Think of the moral development in relation to the evil of slavery, the legitimate rights of women in the last couple of centuries, and the right to privacy in recent decades.

In general, reason alone can perform the complex task of analysis, comparison, and evaluation required to ethically judge the object of actions with respect to the nature and true good of person(s). Although people use reason in their search for moral truth, they cannot all be right if their moral conclusions differ. This is why *right reason* has been traditionally adopted as the criterion of objective morality.[57] This implies reason has to be employed in a rational way to determine what is right in concrete cases. This is *practical reason* in action. In all this the concept of the human person is the *referral point* for the moral evaluation of the object of human acts in relation to the good of person(s) affected. While some goods depend on free choice, e.g. one's career, others do not, e.g. duties of justice to all, the care of the sick, the observance of professional ethics.

In the light of a person's dignity, essential nature, integral human experience, and relationships to other persons, animals, and the environment, right reason is able to discern that the objects of some acts conflict with the true good of person(s) and hence judges them to be immoral. It judges a deliberately chosen action in itself is immoral if the nature or kind of action, humanly understood, is inherently opposed to the good of person(s), regardless of additional factors *extrinsic* to the action itself such as customs or motives. For this reason such acts in Catholic moral theology are often called *intrinsically evil* or immoral. John Paul II rightly stated;

> without in the least denying the influence on morality exercised by cir-
> cumstances and equally by intentions, the Church teaches that "there are
> acts which *per se* and in themselves, independently of circumstances, are
> always seriously wrong by reason of their object."[58]

Motives and other circumstances may vary, but the variations would be morally irrelevant to the truth that rape is always morally wrong. The deliberate bombing of civilian populations, terrorism, torture, female genital mutilation and adultery are examples of intrinsically evil actions.

In the light of our self-understanding reason is able to discern true goods as distinct from whatever merely appeals to our senses or our friends. Reason can rationally criticize our attitudes and even our incli-nation to go along with members of a group to which we belong. In applying a traditional moral norm to concrete cases it is necessary to use practical reason to interpret it in the light of its presuppositions – his-torical, cultural, social, scientific, economic, and factual – in order to find the moral truth.[59] Sometimes it may not be possible to have at hand a sufficiently accurate definition of the moral objects of some actions for a certain judgment to be made in difficult and complex issues. Time may be needed for further elucidation. This allows moral freedom to follow one or other sound probable moral opinion, i.e., one supported by solid reasons.

There is no need to put all good or bad actions in the same basket. There is a grading or a *hierarchy* of goods to be preserved and evils to be avoided. There are always serious and less serious evils to consider in our moral judgments and this is not without its importance for the edu-cation and mental health of individuals and of the community. On account of our social nature and our duty to promote the well-being of others, we are, to some extent, subordinated to the common good without implying we may be reduced to mere means to achieve it. Every person is endowed with an inviolable dignity and value that transcend the social order and state authorities. We are never morally bound to violate our informed conscience, even to obey state law.

Ethical judgments on different kinds of action are reached by way of impartial philosophical inductive reasoning. Relevant information is to be considered in the light of our concept of the human person, their inte-gral good and relevant higher ethical principles. Practical reason judges which is the right ethical norm in the circumstances and whether the object of a particular human action is inconsistent with it.[60] In a trial all the jurors hear the same evidence. They may initially differ in their assessment of the evidence before they fulfill their duty of sincerely searching for a verdict beyond reasonable doubt. The same duty requires us to dialogue and search sincerely for the truth in the theory and practice of ethics. It is the absolute value of persons that gives the unconditioned character to our judgments on what is required for the true good for persons in moral imperatives.

More on object, intention, and circumstances

In the Catholic tradition the agent's intention is important for the moral evaluation of actions. Aquinas gives the reason, saying "the end gives moral character to an action" because "the interior act of the will and the external action, considered morally, are the one act."[61] The physical harm involved in amputating a person's leg may also be called *premoral* or *ontic* evil. The same surgical procedure could be bad, i.e. mutilation, or good, if its intended object is lifesaving to remove a leg infected with gangrene. From a human viewpoint we are dealing with *one moral action* precisely because the premoral evil of amputating a leg can be objectively integrated into an action willed for the greater good for the patient, i.e. with proportionate justifying reasons of benefit over harm.[62] It is morally permissible to use the force required to defend oneself against an unjust aggressor even if the death of the assailant is foreseen, but not willed, as a side-effect.[63]

In the above example, one could not say that "amputating a leg" is an action whose object is bad without taking for granted its purpose is mutilation:

the relevant aspects of *intention* and *circumstance* obviously have to be understood as included in whatever intrinsically harmful action is under consideration. This would be presupposed too, so that it would only become moral evil once it was actualised into a human action by direct conscious intent. The abstract *act in itself* could only have potential moral significance as pre-moral evil unless it were presupposed to be viewed in relation to intention and *circumstances*.[64]

In the second example the foreseen death of the assailant is the result of an act of legitimate self-defense. Could not this "killing" also be interpreted as somehow *intended* and the agent responsible for it? Aquinas would probably admit that the one who kills licitly in self-defense is responsible for the death, but not in a moral sense. It would not entail *moral culpability*.

The above ambiguities persuaded some influential moral theologians to propose a new moral methodology, known as *proportionalism* from the late 1960s.[65] Richard McCormick sums it up as follows:

> Common to all so-called proportionalists, however, is the insistence that causing certain disvalues (nonmoral, pre-moral evils such as sterilisation, deception in speech, wounding and violence) in our conduct does not by that very fact make the action morally wrong, as certain traditional formulations supposed. The action becomes morally wrong when, all things considered, there is not a proportional reason in the act justifying the disvalue . . . They are saying that an action cannot be judged morally wrong simply by looking at the material happening, or at its object in a very narrow and restricted sense.[66]

Proportionalists may have influenced Catholic teaching on direct abortion where, as we shall see in chapter 5, mention is made of the reason for its immoral object. I myself, however, do have serious reservations with proportionalism as a general moral theory. Aquinas spoke highly of intention's role in morality, but he does not neglect the importance of the *object* in moral theory and action.[67] Indeed, when asked to say why an intention is good we have recourse to the intended object and its relationship to the integral good of person. For Aquinas there is a certain primacy of the *object* in morality, as the following citations show:

> The goodness of the will depends properly on the object.[68]

> The primary goodness of a moral act is derived from its suitable object.[69]

> Every action derives its species from its object.[70]

> The specific difference in acts is according to objects, as stated above [Q 18, a 5]. Therefore good and evil in the acts of the will is derived properly from the objects.[71]

While Aquinas permitted the foreseen, but unintended, killing of an assailant in self-defense, he ruled out adultery as a morally permissible way of saving one's life because "it has no necessary link to the preservation of one's own life as sometimes the killing of a man may have."[72] Adultery cannot be integrated into one lifesaving action. Considered abstractly, the disvalue of marital infidelity should not be compared with the desired benefit of saving a life but with its negative impact on the good and inviolable value of the acting person. This is why the action would be morally evil:

> Where we find an action by its objective nature pitted against the absolute value of person, the direct intending of the same action objectively could never be morally good because it would acquire its own independent negative moral existence and so be unable to be morally one with any other good intention, no matter how good. The same applies to directly intending to kill an innocent person (means) to save twenty innocent persons' lives (end).[73]

Morality and natural law

Due to the influence of rational human nature on the shaping of traditional morality, it has been called natural law morality. Effectively it is practical reason discerning human goods in the light of the person with a rational human nature.[74] We pay dearly if we act against human nature in the misguided pursuit of happiness, e.g. abuse of drugs. As John Paul II said:

> natural inclinations take on moral relevance only in so far as they refer to the human person and his authentic fulfilment, a fulfilment that can take place always and only in human nature.[75]

For morality, the human person's nature is not to be reduced to purely biological and natural inclinations without regard to the dignity and good of the person in the unity of the body and its rational life principle.[76] The focus of the natural law, then, is the good of the person, as said by John Paul II:

> the ordered whole complex of "goods for the person" ["bonorum pro persona"] which serve the "good of the person": the good which is the person's perfection. These are the goods safeguarded by divine laws and which contain the whole natural law.[77]

The presence of defects in biological functions does not mean they are natural. It is a challenge to discern what is natural, good, and truly human and what is defective and pathological. What is artificial might not be natural: that does not matter so long as it is not contrary to the true good of persons.

We ever interpret afresh what is truly good for persons on the basis of our deepening understanding of persons in the world. There is subjective development in human self-understanding and of its implications for moral responsibilities. Think of the moral development in relation to the evil of slavery, the legitimate rights of women in the last couple of centuries, and the right to privacy in recent decades. Particular formulations of moral norms of the natural law cannot be beyond refinement. The formulation of the natural law is never perfect.[78] There will always be scope for improvement in our understanding of its contents.[79] This argues for development in our understanding and refining of formulations of the moral norms of the natural law and for fidelity to its true purpose and the moral requirements of persons living in community.[80]

In a sense we can also speak of some *objective* development of human nature which is not entirely static, but somewhat dynamic and without detriment to the substantial identity of human nature over the millennia. Development occurs particularly in the economic, family, social, and political organization of human life. It is obvious that such developments will affect not only the content of particular moral norms (say, usury, the minimum standard of education, universal suffrage, citizens' responsibilities to the state, etc.) but the whole concept of person, especially from that of individual person to that of persons as responsible members of society. This does not imply moral relativism nor a denial of objective morality. A constancy of direction in the development of the natural moral law can be discerned, even if this is not apparent to all.[81]

Moral pluralism

Granted the fundamental differences between secular and traditional concepts of the human person and authentic human goods, we can expect moral pluralism in society for some time. We argue to convince one another of the truth of our moral beliefs. If we really thought that there were no moral truths there would be no point in arguing or debating. Discussions on controversial moral issues in the community can help resolve some moral differences, or at least pinpoint exactly the source of divergence. It is important to attempt to resolve moral differences to enable the truth to emerge, to free people from pseudo-obligations and to prevent unnecessary divisions in the community. Honest and open dialogue in the community by competent ethicists on controversial issues may facilitate a convergence towards objective moral truths.

Unless the necessary clarifications are made, the forthright statement of objective moral truths risks being counterproductive and falling flat on the ears of others who do not share their premises. Dogmatic statements on moral principles without any clarifications or justifications do little to foster intellectual debate and the search for ethical truth. Though objective moral truths do not depend on popular acceptance for their truth, it is helpful to create the conditions most calculated to facilitate their recognition and acceptance. Clearly dialogue between proponents of diverse moral views promotes mutual respect and is desirable.

2

Life, Health, Ethics, and the Bible

Christians believe the Bible contains the word of God written under the influence of divine inspiration. The Jews believe the same but only for the Hebrew Bible, usually called the Old, and at times the First, Testament by Christians. Though the Bible is primarily destined for believers in God's revelation, many of its teachings are appreciated by people who are neither Christians nor believers in God because its message of authentic humanity has a ring of truth for them. The Bible offers an account of the dignity of the human person and of the meaning of human existence in the light of God's enduring providence and love for all humanity. It would be interesting to explore how Christian beliefs affect the attitudes and decisions of healthcare professionals and the ill in relation to sickness, disease, and death.

2.1 Biblical Interpretation and Bioethics

The Bible has a contribution to make in the quest for a solution to many difficult contemporary bioethical problems. It is necessary, however, to be careful to interpret biblical texts correctly in the light of the unique character of the Bible as the word of God, the living Christian tradition, and sound modern biblical scholarship. This is the task of biblical hermeneutics. The significance of the theological message found *in the text* written for the community of believers *in front of the text*, be it Israel or the Christian Church, cannot be properly understood without reference to the world behind the text.[1]

The full meaning of any biblical text depends on the world of its author, i.e. its nationality, history, culture, community bonds, and local circumstances. This is the world *behind the text*. Biblical texts tell us something about the world in which they were written as though they were "windows through which one can gaze to see what lies on the other side of the window."[2] That being said, it is important to respect the world *in the text* – the literary and theological structure of the entire document in which a passage is found. The meaning of a particular text cannot be isolated from its complete context. Every text forms part of a whole and only in the light of the whole should it be interpreted. Its meaning should not be distorted to fit into the mind-set or ideology of the reader. The world *in front of the text* refers to the reader who encounters the text and responds by interpreting it in their own world and culture.[3] A similar dynamic applies to a community when reading and responding to biblical texts.

It is instructive to consider Paul's words to the Romans:

> For this reason God gave them up to dishonourable passions. Their women exchanged natural relations for unnatural, and their men likewise gave up natural relations with women and were consumed with passion for one another, men committing shameless acts with men and receiving in their own persons the due penalty for their error (Rom. 1:26–7).

It would, however, be entirely wrong to conclude that AIDS was a divine punishment for homosexual activity. This would clearly misinterpret this last verse just quoted. AIDS is caused by HIV infection alone and not by any particular kind of behavior. To interpret this text in this way is to forget that Paul was principally teaching the need to have a right relationship with God by referring to certain forms of sexual behavior which were indicative of loss of contact with God who establishes right order.[4]

These fundamental points of sound hermeneutics need to be kept in mind to reduce the risk of a fundamentalist use of a particular text. A biblical text may no more be used uncritically to resolve theoretical or practical difficulties in biology or medicine than in astronomy. Whenever an attempt is made to address a modern problem in the light of the biblical tradition all three *worlds* of the Bible have to be balanced if the ancient text is not to be abused and provide a disservice to the contemporary world and to religion itself.

2.2 Life, Health, Sickness, and Death: Old Testament

Gift of life

The written word of God gives believers a noble view of human life and
of personal dignity. The Genesis story of creation is an apparently simple,
but in reality complex, account of the beauty and goodness of all that
God made – the heavens, the waters, the earth, the sun, moon, stars, and
all things, living and nonliving alike, in the world. In its present form,
the result of a careful blending of the older (the so-called Jahwist and
Elohist traditions) and the more recent (the so called Priestly tradition),
the story reaches its high point in the creation of the first humans, Adam
and Eve, who are equal partners endowed with an identical personal
dignity:

> Let us make humankind in our image, after our likeness; . . . So God
> created humankind in his own image, in the image of God he created it;
> male and female he created them (Gen. 1:26–7).[5]

Israel is repeatedly reminded that God is the author of all subsequent
human life: "Before I formed you in the womb I knew you" (Jer. 1:5).
(See also Job 10:8–11). A serene optimism pervades the original account
of the creation: "And God saw everything that he had made, and behold,
it was very good" (Gen. 1:31).

God is the giver of life to men and women, who are called to reflect
God's creative and provident goodness. They belong to God in a special
way and have no dominion over human life: "You shall not kill" (Exod.
20:13). They are, however, given responsible stewardship over living
creatures, and are to name them (see Gen. 1:28). They are not to fear
the sun or moon which other nations worshipped as idols since these
impersonal false gods are creatures of, and subject to, the one God, the
Creator of humanity.

In the biblical tradition pregnancy and motherhood are esteemed since
they enable women in a special way to collaborate with the Creator in
communicating the gift of life to newly created human beings who are
destined to enjoy the status of their parents. In simple terms, the Genesis
story illustrates that men and women share the same nature and are equal
in personal dignity and social relations. The union of a man and a
woman in marriage takes precedence over parental relationships and

leads to a further community of man, woman and the child of their union:

> Then the Lord God said, "It is not good that man should be alone; I will make him a helper fit for him." . . . a man leaves his father and his mother and cleaves to his wife, and they become one flesh (Gen. 2:18; 24).[6]

They were subject to God's authority, and were commanded not to eat the fruit "of the tree of the knowledge of good and evil" (Gen. 2:17). Yielding to temptation they disobeyed God, were punished and lost God's special favour resulting in the suffering and death, but they were not left without hope of salvation (Gen. 3:1–24).

The Bible sees human life as essentially one even though individuals have their personal characteristics and belong to different families, communities, social strata and nations.[7] The individual and communitarian dimension of human life is presented as essential from the beginning of Israel. The Old Testament does not accept any materialistic or purely naturalistic view of the human being as though man or woman could be reduced to physiology alone. Neither Greek nor Cartesian dualism form part of the Biblical perspective of human life. Israel's understanding of the human person is more one of an animated body than an incarnate spirit.[8] The concrete existence of a human being is a unity of flesh and blood, heart, soul and experiences in a single organism: "You shall love the Lord your God with all your heart, and with all your soul and with all your might" (Deut. 6:5).

One may be poor, infirm or lowly but the value of human life depends on its Creator. Life is presented as a treasured divine blessing, a supreme earthly good. Life and happiness are almost synonymous:

> Health and soundness are better than all gold, and a robust body than countless riches. There is no wealth better than health of body, and there is no gladness above joy of heart (Sir. 30:15–16).

A long life is the reward promised to those who lead a good life: "Honour your father and your mother, that your days may be long in the land which the Lord God gives you" (Exod. 20:12). Earthly life, though good in itself, is portrayed as surpassed by the love of God: "Because thy steadfast love is better than life, my lips will praise thee" (Ps. 63:3). Male and female human sexuality is likewise viewed as a special gift and blessing, a sharing in God's prerogative to create human life: "And God blessed them, and God said to them, 'Be fruitful and multiply, and fill the earth'" (Gen. 1:28).

Sickness and health

Sickness, disease, suffering and military defeats are presented in the Bible as a result of sins which have been with humanity from its origins when Adam and Eve disobeyed God and lost his favor. God promised salvation but Israel's history was seldom without hardships which were likewise related to the sins of individuals or the nation. This can be seen especially in the historical books of the Bible.[9] The constant spiritualizing of sickness and disease meant its incidence was related to God who either punished the wicked or healed the repentant who sought forgiveness (see Exod. 7:15).

> For Israel there was one supreme healer to whom the sick looked for recovery:
>
> If you will diligently hearken to the voice of the Lord, your God, . . . I will put none of the diseases upon you which I put upon the Egyptians; for I am the Lord, your healer (Exod. 15:26).

This consciousness of God as the supreme healer was strong in Israel and so recourse to magic for healing was foreign to the Hebrew mentality and repudiated as contrary to their covenanted relationship with God. His healing gifts were given to priests who soon assumed responsibility for the health of the community. Midwives and prophets had a share in this responsibility. The status of physicians as a separate class was not high in early Israel.[10] It gradually improved over the centuries from the years of the monarchy to Jeremiah's day when a simple balm was sought as a remedy (Jer. 8:22), to when the book of Sirach praises the physician and his role:

> Honour the physician with the honour due to him, according to your need of him, for the Lord created him; for healing comes from the Most High and he shall receive a gift from the king (Sir. 38).

Infant mortality in Israel would most likely have been as high as it was in neighboring countries – with as few as three births out of ten reaching adulthood in Egypt.[11]

Granted the limited scope for developing therapies the Mosaic Code was geared to prevent disease, and it was quite effective, granted the knowledge at hand and which was taught by the priests.[12] The law of the Sabbath (Exod. 31:13–17), apart from its principal purpose of honoring and worshipping God by requiring rest from work, also made weekly provision for physical well-being and functional efficiency, both individual and social. The laws on clean and unclean foods cannot be reduced to mere prescriptions against magic, fetishism or cult worship in Egypt. They promoted health and vigor by only permitting the eating of meat from vegetarian animals. The ban on eating pork preserved the people from ingesting parasites and tapeworms frequently found in pigs. The law of circumcision for male infants was extremely significant for the religious observance of the covenant. Until recently, it was also deemed desirable for hygienic reasons. The laws governing sexual relations protected fecundity as well as physical and mental health by banning marriage between close blood relations. They also protected society as a whole from being subordinated to the interests of a few prominent families. The laws on cleanliness, in spite of water shortage, lessened the spread of contact diseases. The laws on sanitation, even for soldiers in the field, were hygienic and contributed to preventing the spread of air-borne and fly-borne plagues and diseases. Isolation was required of those infected with contagious diseases like leprosy until their recovery was verified by priests. The Bible shows there is a serious responsibility on the part of individuals and of society to preserve and protect the health of all in the community.

Death

Death is presented in the Book of Genesis and the Christian tradition as a punishment for sin: "You are dust and to dust you shall return" (Gen. 3:19).[13] Again,

> God created man for incorruption, and made him in the image of his own eternity but through the devil's envy death entered the world and those who belong to his party experience it (Wis. 2:23–4).

Premature death also is often presented as a punishment for sin (see Prov. 10:27) and "The wicked shall depart to Sheol, all the nations that forget God" (Ps. 9:17). "Sheol" was popularly conceived as an inert pit of dust, darkness, and of no return for the dead, bereft of personhood.[14]

Notwithstanding the tragic origin of death for humanity, death normally occurs as a result of old age and is accepted as the will of God: "What man can live and never see death? Who can deliver his soul from the power of Sheol?" (Ps. 89:48). In ancient Israel the people were satisfied to make provision for their own family and nation by having children. They accepted the reality of death serenely without much thought for any life after death. Indeed, death came to be considered relief from a life of suffering and pain: "Death is better than a miserable life, and eternal rest than chronic sickness" (Sir. 30:17). These thoughts were expressed shortly before the after-life began to loom large in the tradition of Israel. It made its first appearance in the Bible from the second century BC with more frequent references to it in the New Testament.

2.3 Life and Healing: New Testament

In the New Testament times physicians were already a well-established profession for the care of life and health. They are given a respectable mention in the Gospels (Matt. 9:12; Luke 4:23). There is an ancient tradition linking the Evangelist Luke with "the beloved physician" of Col. 4:14.[15] The early Christian communities were aware that there is more to life than its earthly aspects.

The first Christians naturally inherited the centrality of life from its roots in the traditional culture of Israel. God is often spoken of as the living God (Matt. 16:16) with life and immortality in himself (John 5:26). He is represented as the Lord of life and death: "But God said to him, Fool! This night your soul is required of you; and the things you have prepared, whose will they be?" (Luke 12:21). The acceptance of the unity of the human being continues into the New Testament. Flesh and blood are considered one with the human being: "Blessed are you Simon Bar-Jona! For flesh and blood has not revealed this to you but my Father who is in heaven" (Matt. 16:17).

True life

The mystery of Jesus brings a fundamental new dimension to the reality of human life for his followers – the reality of true life: "I am the way, the truth and the life" (John 14:6). Paul, writing to Timothy, speaks of Christ "who abolished death and brought life and immortality to light through the gospel" (2 Tim. 1:10). Jesus' self-gift to the Father through his sufferings and death revealed both his own and the Father's love of humanity whereby people may acquire the gift of true life through faith, not through any personal moral striving of their own. The new life represents the fullness of earthly life: it is the life of faith, grace and divine love in human hearts and is also called the new creation: "Therefore, if anyone is in Christ, he is a new creation" (2 Cor. 5:17).

The new life enables one to live like Christ and to love God and neighbor, even now, without being held back by human weaknesses:

> Truly, truly, I say to you, he who hears my word and believes him who sent me, has eternal life; he does not come into judgement, but has passed from death to life (John 5:24).

This new life brings about a growing awareness of the worth of the gift of life in Christ and its implications for living in conformity with the life of Christ.[16] Whoever has the new life believes and follows Christ without counting the cost, keeps the commandments, and lives out the beatitudes, thereby showing one already is part of God's Kingdom and becoming more Christ-like. The inner kernel of the gospel, found in the person, actions, and preaching of Jesus, transcends all historical, social, and cultural frameworks. It is the fundamental norm for all who wish to imitate Jesus' way of living and loving:

> You shall love the Lord your God with all your heart, and with all your soul, and with all your mind. This is the great and first commandment. And a second is like it, You shall love your neighbour as yourself. On these two commandments depend all the law and the prophets (Matt. 22:37–40).

To live and behave in this way, believers in Jesus Christ are called "to mature manhood, to the measure of the stature of the fullness of Christ" (Eph. 4:13).

This new life transforms our normal human understanding of the experience of trials, difficulties, sickness, sufferings, and death. These are the weft and warp of the mystery of human existence. Jesus, who is fully human and like us in everything but sin (see Heb. 4:15), took on our human predicament and so experienced typical human anguish. When he was dying he cried out: "My God, My God, why hast thou forsaken me" (Matt. 27:46). Fundamental to Christian belief, however, is that, within three days, all was changed by the power of God in the triumph and glory of Jesus' resurrection. Jesus warned his disciples that discipleship had its crosses on earth (see Luke 9:23). Christians believe that as Jesus triumphed over his trials with glory through his resurrection, so also will they if they are faithful in the new life in Christ and steadfast in hope.

Healing miracles of Jesus

There is ample evidence in the New Testament that during his public
ministry Jesus had a reputation of showing sympathy for the sick and
the infirm by working miracles to heal them without blaming them for
their sickness:

> And he went about all Galilee . . . healing every disease and every infirmity
> among the people (Matt. 4:23).[17]

He did not impute any personal fault in relation to any particular infir-
mity. When his disciples asked whether the man born blind had sinned
or his parents, Jesus replied: "It was not that this man sinned, or his
parents, but that the works of God might be made manifest in him"
(John 9:3). His compassion did not allow him to refuse to cure the ill
who came to him. He did not simply let them bear their pains with
patience.[18] For Jesus, disease is an evil which should be destroyed since
it is the result and sign of the power of Satan and of the presence of sin
in the world. If we accept the variation in the translation of Isaiah 53:4,
then Jesus as the Suffering Servant took on humanity's physical pains
on the cross so that human restoration included the physical as well as
spiritual: "Surely he has borne our sicknesses [griefs] and carried our
diseases [sorrows]."

Jesus approached the sick person as a unity of mind and body. He did
not simply cure a disease but healed the whole person with the gift of
faith and new life. Jesus' dialogue with the Samaritan woman at Jacob's
well is a case in point. Although largely the result of a long story-telling
tradition and the skill of the Johannine author, it is a masterpiece of
nondirective therapeutic counseling where the woman is led gradually to
receive the gift of true faith (John 4:7–26). The Sermon on the Mount is
a recipe for a peaceful, healthy and happy life for all who believe in
Christ (Matt. chs. 5–7).

More importantly, these miracles were part of Jesus' mission to inau-
gurate on earth the Kingdom of God which was opposed not only to sin
and the power of the devil, but also physical evils like sickness and
disease.[19] Unless his miracles are understood as signs of the Kingdom of
God the point of Jesus' healing miracles is missed and increases the risk
of us becoming engrossed in questions of fact, historical or medical or
otherwise. Healing for Jesus and his disciples had a theological meaning
of demonstrating the power of God to destroy the evils which afflict

people. Jesus acknowledged the power of Satan over the bent woman whom he cured and so emphasized that disease is an evil and as such is not part of the divine order:

> And ought not this daughter, a daughter of Abraham whom Satan bound for eighteen years, be loosed from this bond on the sabbath day? (Luke 13:16).

Jesus was not in competition with physicians in their professional work. He did not address the medical or scientific aspects of disease but what sick people, even today, are concerned about, namely, its human meaning.[20] People now ask *why* they get sick, or *why* does God allow it or *how* could God be good if He allows children to be born with genetic abnormalities. Jesus did not seek out all the sick and diseased in Israel to heal them. This was not his mission. What he did was to show God's power at work over evil as a sign that in God's own time He will complete His plan of salvation by eliminating all evil for those who choose to enter His Kingdom. Jesus' purpose was to increase the gift of faith and new life in the sick he cured, and indeed in all his disciples, to enable them to welcome the Kingdom of God.

The community of believers has continued Jesus' healing ministry through the centuries. Health professionals continue this ministry by opposing evil with all their intellectual, scientific, and medical talents. As Moloney says:

> In the end, however, the task is to point beyond the good things of this life to the Lord of all life, made known to us through the life and teaching, death and resurrection of Jesus of Nazareth.[21]

2.4 Life after Death in the Bible

In the early days of Israel this earthly life was the only one considered and valued since no mention was made of an after-life, as we have already seen. But by the early second century BC the thought of a life after death began to appear, especially in the context of the fighting, sufferings, and martyrdom endured for the faith of Israel. Israel first thought of the after-life in terms of the resurrection of the body since their only knowledge of life was that of a living body.[22] As a result of Greek influence reference to souls began to appear. At times the bodily aspects are more prominent (see 2 Macc. 14:46) and at other times mention is made of the soul without excluding the whole person:

> For God created man for incorruption and made him in the image of his own eternity . . . But the souls of the righteous are in the hands of God, and no torment will ever touch them (Wis. 2:23–3:1).

The belief was firmly echoed that the God of Israel would take good care of, and reward, those who were faithful to him: "And many of those who sleep in the dust of the earth shall awake, some to everlasting life, and some to shame and everlasting contempt" (Dan. 12:1).

Jesus' sufferings and human misery were real indeed. He felt abandoned and was afraid of his impending death but, without loss of faith, accepted the will of his Father:

> Abba, Father, all things are possible to thee; remove this cup from me; yet not what I will, but what thou wilt (Mark 14:36).

All was changed by Jesus' resurrection which is the foundation of Christians' belief in their own resurrection (Rom. 6:5).

Afflictions, sufferings, weaknesses, disease, and sickness, real and terrifying as they may be, will be overcome by sharing in the promised resurrection. For believers in Christ, these are not ultimate evils since with the grace of God, it is possible to attain the eternal bliss for which we were destined by creation.[23] St. Peter reminds Christians that what God did for Jesus He will eventually do for us, i.e. change suffering into glory (I Pet. 4:13).

This belief in the resurrection and an after-life continued throughout the New Testament times and the Christian tradition. The life, sufferings, death, and resurrection of Jesus were crucial for the salvation of the whole of humanity. In the Christian perspective true life after death is more important than life on earth precisely because what happened to Jesus after his death is promised for all people of good will. The martyrs knew what their gain would be by their fearless fidelity to Christ. It is immoral to kill others and ourselves, but it not immoral to wish to die to be with Christ in glory. St. Paul wrote:

> I am caught in this dilemma: I want to be gone and be with Christ, which would be very much the better, but for me to stay alive in this body is a more urgent need for your sake (Phil. 1:23–4).

In short, the new life in Christ is now lived through faith and grace, but after death it continues in glory, including the eventual resurrection of the body. Important though this earthly life is, it is surpassed in importance by the true life in Christ. In fact, one with an excessive concern for this life could risk losing true life and with it a blessed eternal life (Mark 8:35–6).

2.5 Relevance of the Bible for Health Ethics

The fundamental theme that the Bible offers for our purposes is the dignity of human persons created male and female in the image of God and called to enter the Kingdom of God. Reading and reflecting on the biblical literature of the Old and New Testaments forms a basic mentality of reverence for the life of every human being without distinction as to the stage of one's development, age or condition of health. The Bible does not offer a solution for any concrete bioethical problem, but it does provide an optimistic view of the meaning of human life, despite the continuing presence of evils, hardships, illnesses, and death. The Bible provides an encouraging and noble frame of reference for the meaning of the human person, human life, sickness, death, and ethics in the light of which healthcare professionals, case by case, should resolve their daily bioethical and medical dilemmas.

Belief in an eternal life of happiness and the eventual resurrection of the body sustains the hope that the evils of suffering, sickness, disease, and death will eventually be overcome. Christian healthcare professionals will be aware of the relativity of sickness, suffering, and death as they attend to their tasks of treating sick people and their diseases with compassionate care. The Christian faith makes it easier to avoid futile treatments which result in the prolongation of the dying process of some newborns, the sick, and the aged.

The biblical perspective on human life and healthcare is not only relevant to believers. Indeed one cannot understand the western literature without an appreciation of how its perceptions and thought patterns have been influenced by the language of the Bible. In this way the Bible is the basis for many authentically human features of western literature, culture, and the values enshrined in common law and in legislation.[24] One need not be a believer in God or Christ to appreciate the noble humanism, meaning of human existence, value of human life and healthcare as these things are portrayed in the Bible. This perspective is shared by many in our society who are not believers because of its appeal and relevance to our contemporary world. This view is shared by Richard Holloway who, referring to Christian morality asked

> Can the ethic not stand on its own as something that is likely to commend itself to people who want to try to live well and believe in the importance of morality for healthy human communities?[25]

The ethos of hospitals founded and run by people with religious convictions is universally esteemed and appreciated for its inherent worth by believers and nonbelievers alike.

3

Ethical Principles for Healthcare

The basic ethical principle for medical interventions is respect for human dignity and the true good of persons affected, with due regard to other relevant goods, beginning from human life itself. Secondary principles are needed to interpret more precisely what constitutes human goods, but they should not be interpreted to the point of negating the supreme ethical principle of always promoting the true good of person(s). However, the ethical aspects of healthcare from conception to birth onwards are made in the light of one's concept of the human person and basic ethical principles, be they religious or secular. Judaism and the Christian tradition draw guidance from their biblically derived beliefs as we have seen. Other Great Religions also rely on their sacred texts. Secular ethicists likewise rely on a range of ethical premises, e.g. the famous *Georgetown principles* of respect for autonomy, nonmaleficence, beneficence, and justice.[1]

3.1 Christian Vision of Human Dignity

Before dealing with healthcare ethics I shall summarize the impact of Christian beliefs on human dignity since these beliefs may impact on decisions made by patients and clinicians alike. In chapter 2 we have reviewed the divinely inspired insights the Bible offers, which confirm much of what reason can discover concerning the sublime personal dignity of men and women, the worth of the divine gift of life and our need to live morally. The Bible goes a lot further by explicitly affirming the presence of a personal and provident Creator God who is interested in the lives and destiny of all.

Christians believe the dignity of human persons is based on the exalted call to communion with God.[2] Through baptism human persons are given the grace of Christ to share in a sublime destiny and become the adopted children of God. Christ became a member of the human family to show the way for his disciples. The Second Vatican Council is explicit about Christ: "as a man he . . . took a complete human nature just as it is found in us unfortunates, but one that was without sin" (see Heb. 4:15, 9:28).[3] God's design was for Christ to assume the human condition, endure their trials, and experience the human predicament whereby he could "sympathise with our weaknesses" (Heb. 4:15). The life, deeds, and teachings of Jesus portrayed in the gospels represent authentic human living.

Being a Christian neither imposes nor detracts anything from our humanity. Precisely because Jesus is truly man as well as truly God a Christian may say with Terence, "*Homo sum: humani nil a me alienum puto*" ("I am a human being: I reckon nothing human is foreign to me").[4] Jesus is no outsider, but one of us and of human stock, in solidarity with all humanity. Indeed in the words of Vatican II once more: "Whoever follows Christ the perfect Human Being, becomes himself or herself more a human being."[5]

The Christian faith offers hope for believers and their loved ones for the future and strength in the midst of present anxieties, fears, and sufferings. They believe afflictions, sickness, and death, real as they may be, will be overcome by the resurrection, guaranteed by Christ who triumphed over death for humanity.[6] This is why death and suffering, though tragic, are not absolute evils for Christians. As Catholic teaching states:

> The Christian faith teaches that bodily death, from which man would have been immune had he not sinned, will be overcome when that wholeness which he lost through his own fault will be given once again to him by the almighty and merciful Saviour.[7]

3.2 Respect for Human Life

Theological perspective

Respect for human life in western culture is founded on God's commandment – "You shall not kill" (Ex. 20:13). Life gives people an opportunity to assume moral responsibility for definitively influencing their destiny by the exercise of free choice. Believers hold that their moral value as persons depends on how they live, not on continuing to live at all costs. Professor Moloney rightly comments:

> the theological commitment of Christianity to a life which extends beyond the limitations of this life is seldom heard in contemporary health care discussions.[8]

In the light of God's creative design and absolute dominion over human life and persons' responsibility for it, there is an ethical duty to respect human life. The Bible portrays human life as sacred from conception. Put negatively from a biblical perspective, it is immoral to directly intend to terminate, or needlessly risk, God's gift of human life. Recently Pope John Paul II confirmed this Christian tradition when he declared that "the direct and voluntary killing of an innocent human being is always gravely immoral."[9]

Philosophical perspective

Empiricist philosophers like Singer and Tooley base their arguments for the right to human life on the desires and interests of the persons concerned. There could be no intrinsic right to life, for such philosophers, unless the subject concerned has a desire to live, which in its turn, requires the capacity to have the concept of oneself existing over time.[10] It would be immoral to kill one who desires to live, but it leaves little protection of the rights and lives of abnormal or simply unwanted fetuses and newborns. As mentioned in chapter 1, due to the restricted concept of person employed by these philosophers newborns have no intrinsic right to life.[11]

On the other hand, as discussed in chapter 1, the traditional definition of a person as a living individual with a rational human nature suffices to establish an objective right to life. The foundation for the exercise of rational acts is present, or believed to be present on reasonable grounds, from the beginning of the human individual in virtue of the immaterial life principle which is one with the human body. Admittedly here we are dealing with a theoretical doubt which could generate a practical doubt. One should not act when one's conscience has a practical doubt, otherwise one would be willing to embrace the immoral option. If the doubt cannot be solved directly, it should be resolved indirectly.

One way of doing this is to follow the morally safer course but there is no universal duty to do so. However, one is bound to follow the morally safer course where there is a certain prior obligation to be satisfied. One may doubt whether an early embryo is an individual and a person but, according to a long Christian and Catholic tradition, it is certain that human life from conception should be respected even if one doubts it is already personal. Hence direct destruction of embryonic life would be always unethical.[12]

Absolute respect for human life until death also applies to human beings in a permanent unconscious state. Nobody has direct dominion over the lives of human individuals regardless of their stage of life or condition of health. The State may not take, or legalize the taking of, the life of any innocent human being. Nobody has the right to make life and death decisions by directly interfering with the natural course of events to cause death deliberately or by refusing to respond to the call of duty to provide the medical treatment reasonably required to sustain life. Human life ought to be legally as well as morally inviolable from deliberate direct assault.

3.3 Duty of Reasonable Care of Health and Life

Health, understood as the state of physical, mental, and social well-being, is an important human good. Awareness of the health of body and mind is a characteristic of our times. It may be superfluous to insist, but it is necessary to say, that there is a duty to take reasonable care of our health. This is so because health is an inherent good of the person, a condition for the normal functioning of the whole person, psychologically, mentally, and socially. It is wrong to neglect our health and impair our ability to attend to our responsibilities.

The Christian belief in an eternal life of beatitude does make an impact on interpreting the duty of reasonable care. It has been axiomatic that everything possible and reasonable in the circumstances should be done to cure patients and to save lives. In the days prior to high-technology this was a good rule of thumb. Catholic teaching gives sound guidance on whether there is a duty to undergo all possible treatments:

> In the past, moralists replied that one is never obliged to use "extraordinary" means. This reply, which as a principle still holds good, is perhaps less clear today, by reason of the imprecision of the term and the rapid

progress made in the treatment of sickness. Thus some people prefer to speak of "proportionate" and "disproportionate" means. In any case it will be possible to make a correct judgement as to the means by studying the type of treatment to be used, its degree of complexity or risk, its cost and the possibilities of using it, and comparing these elements with the result that can be expected, taking into account the state of the sick person and his or her physical and moral resources. . . .

It is also permissible to make do with the normal means that medicine can offer. Therefore one cannot impose on anyone the obligation to have recourse to a technique which is already in use but which carries a risk or is burdensome. Such a refusal is not the equivalent of suicide: on the contrary, it should be considered . . . a desire not to impose excessive expense on the family or the community.[13]

Treatment that would be considered routine in a well equipped urban hospital might be beyond the means of one in rural areas. It is not ethically necessary to use every means to sustain the lives of the terminally ill or of all extremely premature babies. It is up to healthcare professionals in dialogue with their patients and/or families to interpret the duty of reasonable care in each clinical situation.

The duty of care for health and life is not unlimited. This implies that healthcare professionals and the State are not bound to go to unreasonable lengths to provide every possible treatment, regardless of other considerations, so long as basic comfort and normal nursing care, including artificial nutrition and hydration according to need, are provided. The prospects for the patient's improvement from treatment, its likely eventual burdens, the family's circumstances, and other pressing demands made on medical resources enter into the complex notion of *the duty of reasonable treatment and care in the circumstances*.[14] Moloney suggests we give due importance to New Testament sources of Christian beliefs on the relative importance of life on earth:

Could it not sometimes be said of a certain fanaticism to protect and prolong life at all costs that the Old Testament understanding of God's blessings being available only to "this life" still predominates?[15]

Clinicians need to be prudent and in general give the benefit of any reasonable doubt to treatment rather than nontreatment. There is, however, no need to give or continue treatment if the sum total of its burdens is out of proportion to the benefits for the patient, i.e. if it is not good for the person. It is a matter of knowing when to change to palliative care where patient comfort, not active treatment, serves the integral good of the person. Pope John Paul II in his Encyclical Letter *Evangelium Vitae* summed this up well:

> when death is clearly imminent and inevitable, one can in conscience "refuse forms of treatment that would only secure a precarious and burdensome prolongation of life, so long as the normal care due to the sick person in similar cases is not interrupted." Certainly there is a moral obligation to care for oneself and to allow oneself to be cared for, but this duty must take account of concrete circumstances. It needs to be determined whether the means of treatment available are objectively proportionate to the prospects for improvement.[16]

Failure to respect the natural dying process is failure to respect the good and dignity of the dying person.

3.4 Doing Good and its Side Effects

Moral dilemmas may arise when we realize that harm may result as an unwanted side effect of the good we do. Doctors have more than their share of moral dilemmas of this sort. I shall offer a solution without becoming involved in debates concerning the principle of double effect.[17] As we have seen in chapter 1, the Christian tradition has distinguished morally between *directly willing* an immoral action, and permitting or tolerating foreseen harm as a side effect of a chosen morally good action. One may perform a morally good action from which a good and harmful effect may possibly follow provided the foreseen harmful effect is not chosen or directly willed and the benefits are proportionately greater than the harmful effects. There is a moral duty to avoid choosing to cause harm resulting from an action unless the directly willed good could not reasonably be otherwise obtained and there are proportionate justifying reasons of benefit over harm to permit the unwanted harmful side effect.[18] One's moral integrity is not necessarily damaged by *permitting foreseen* harm in such cases, but it is always eroded by directly choosing an action whose object is immoral or by *permitting* harm without proportionate justifying reasons.[19] I have only given a brief account of a complex issue.[20]

It may be not always be possible to cure the primary disease and restore health, but there is always a duty to treat symptoms and to do all that is possible and reasonable to lessen pain and suffering. Drugs may be given for the relief of pain, even though it is possible life may be somewhat shortened as a side effect. This should not be confused with deliberately choosing to cause a painless death, even if death soon follows in both cases.[21] It is also morally permissible to withdraw burdensome treatment from the sick and the terminally ill to lessen pain, even if it is foreseen that the lives of patients may be somewhat shortened, provided normal nursing care, including nutrition and hydration, are continued and the chosen purpose is the effective relief of pain.[22] Consequentialists, however, who do not give great importance to the moral object of an action would not admit the validity of the moral distinction between acts and omissions in such cases when the outcome, sooner or later, is the same, i.e. death: the doctor would be deemed to be morally responsible for the death in both cases.[23] A proportionalist justification is rightly used in cases of foreseen, but unwanted, side effects of a good act. But surely in a moral, if not a legal, sense, the withdrawal of burdensome treatment does not entail an intention to kill even if as a result death is foreseen.

Again this same moral reasoning may also apply to doing a good action which may involve material cooperation or collusion in an unethical action done by another as a result of one's good deed. Obviously one may not *formally* cooperate by sharing in the immoral intent of another. The morality of *material* cooperation depends on how closely one's cooperation assists another in doing an immoral action and how great a risk one takes by failing to comply and cooperate. For proportionately grave reasons one may perform an action that is good in itself, even though it may *materially* assist another to perform an unethical action. In cases of material cooperation in the bad actions of others one should do what is reasonably possible to achieve the good sought and to minimize any likely harmful side effects.

3.5 Responsibilities of Healthcare Professionals

Primacy of the human person

Prior to being a doctor or a patient, one is a person. Paul Tournier, after practicing as a physician and psychologist for many years, turned to philosophy to express his valuable insights on the meaning of the human person gained during his professional life. He points out that we usually live and move in a world of persons or of things, but not both. He stresses that treatment is not only for an organ or part of the body, but for the whole person. Patients have to be encountered in an atmosphere where they feel welcome and accepted as persons, regardless of their social status. Medicine is not to be practiced in a world of things, but of persons, fellowship and sympathy. Healthcare professionals need to foster a sense of the person in their own lives if they are to show it in their professional lives.[24]

Clinicians' responsibilities

Clinicians are trained to assess the balance of benefits and harms before advising patients on treatment options. The ethical exercise of this professional role should be respected. Speaking of lay people the Church teaches:

> let them realise that their pastors will not always be so expert as to have a ready [the Latin text adds *concretam*, concrete] answer to every problem (even every grave problem) that arises; this is not the role of the clergy; it is rather up to the laymen to shoulder their responsibilities under the guidance of Christian wisdom and with eager attention to the teaching authority of the Church.[25]

Medicine, however, is not unlimited in its capacity to cure and save lives. Clinicians should not regard the existence of some incurable diseases or the inevitability of their patients succumbing to death as indicators of failure. Clinicians are human, not divine. A time comes when healthcare professionals may, or should, cease strict medical treatment in favor of initiating palliative care in the best interests of their patients. For believers in life after death, it may be easier to realize that the withholding or withdrawing of unwarranted medical treatment is ethical in cases of incurable and/or terminal diseases.

Need of informed consent for treatment

Doctors may have expert medical knowledge, but patients have to freely make decisions after receiving the relevant advice from healthcare professionals. Tournier emphasized an individual's right to self-determination with respect to their own body and life as well as their bodily and psychological integrity.[26] Doctors should inform competent patients in plain language of their treatment options, the likelihood of recovery and any foreseeable risks. Before making decisions on treatment options, patients need to consider all the relevant information, e.g. their marriage and family responsibilities and their capacity to bear the burdens of one or other treatment. An informed and competent patient has a right to decide in a morally responsible way when medical treatment, as distinct from palliative care, is unwarranted, or when its continuation is too burdensome and may be withdrawn. In this way patients share in making decisions and assume responsibility for them. Medical treatment is to serve patients without relentlessly subordinating them to the technological imperative.

Doctors, community, and the law

Medical practice is subject not only to ethical demands but also to the law, through which the standards and values important to the community are determined and legally enforced. Doctors must obey the law, not least for the reputation of the medical profession. The law rightly forbids doctors performing acts that constitute a direct assault on human life and holds them legally liable for damage caused to patients as a result of medical malpractice or negligence. For its part, the community should allow doctors the necessary freedom to follow their own professional judgment in assessing risks and benefits in clinical practice. Doctors should not be blamed if a cure cannot be provided for every disease. This is part of the human predicament. Medicine is not an exact science. Errors may be made in good faith without any suggestion of incompetence or negligence. At times it is impossible to know what the best treatment is. There may be several reasonable treatment options. What is important is that the agreed treatment given be reasonable in the circumstances.

We live in a litigious age where some people believe others, or society, should compensate them for their misfortunes or poor state of health. Creating a climate where doctors are fearful of being sued for malpractice without reasonable grounds, does not help in making the best medical decisions for patients, and ultimately, does not promote the common good of the community. Doctors do not need to be distracted from exercising their professional judgment to the best of their ability by forcing them to diagnose and treat patients with an eye to avoiding bothersome litigation. It is unfortunate that many excellent doctors are declining opportunities to pursue specialist careers in obstetrics and gynecology out of fear of potentially unreasonable litigation for children's birth defects. The practice of defensive medicine is not in the public interest and may lead to patients being needlessly admitted to intensive care units.[27]

3.6 Christian and Secular Ethicists in a Democracy

The basic moral values of western culture that are derived from traditional Judeo-Christian beliefs are seen to have an intrinsic worth, irrespective of a religious faith in their divine origin. Believers and secular thinkers alike share many of these values because they realize they are good and are necessary for living together in community. Respect for the dignity of all persons, human life, justice, truth, marriage as an institution, and the family are accepted in every civilized society. Secular scholars, for example, emphasize the importance of autonomy and the need for informed consent of competent patients for medical treatment. These values are also recognized as important and accepted by Christians. There are, however, disagreements on many other major ethical and bioethical issues. This creates dilemmas for the legislature in a democratic state when it comes to framing laws for controversial issues from conception to birth, e.g. the regulation of human reproductive technology, destructive embryo research, human cloning, abortion or euthanasia for severely defective newborns. It is important that supporters of different views on such issues be given a chance to put their case without the need of recourse to violence.

At times it is said that people should not impose their religious ethical views on others by means of legislation. This is true as far as it goes. But this does not imply that ethical values held by religious people are purely religious values that can only be derived from a religious source like the Bible or that such values are relevant to believers alone. Authentic human values based on a religious faith may still be appreciated for their inherent worth by reasonable people without religious faith, in much the same way that authentic human values espoused by secular ethicists retain their value for believers. Many moral values found in the Bible can also be established by the use of reason, even if not all agree. These values may be legitimately advocated by reason and democratic means to influence public policy in much the same way as secular thinkers promote what they believe to be important for legislation. When Christian and secular ethicists make proposals on health ethics they should try to convince law-makers by the reasonableness, truth, and eminently human character of their ethical stand for the common good, and not simply state their religious or ideological beliefs.

John Stuart Mill was right in saying a democratic state should not legislate to restrict the freedom of its citizens or prevent them from following their conscientious convictions except to protect the rights of individuals or to prevent harm to the common good.[28] One may believe extracorporeal conception is unethical but still hold that it is not in the public interest to restrict citizens' autonomy by banning it. But the direct killing of severely defective newborns would be quite another matter. Law-makers should not relax laws which protect innocent human life from any form of deliberate killing. The UK House of Lords rightly stated that this prohibition "is the cornerstone of law and of social relationships."[29]

In the political sphere, Christians legitimately differ amongst themselves as well as with secular thinkers. Law-makers, however, should always vote on ethical issues according to their own informed conscience, after giving serious consideration to the views of all in their quest for the truth and the right legislative policy to adopt for the good of all. It is important that the legislature be guided by rational arguments, not simply emotional invective. What the majority approves becomes law in a democratic state as many an opposition party knows only too well. The same dynamic applies when the legislature debates issues of health ethics. Both Christian and secular thinkers should argue their case as best they can, but accept the outcome when the relevant legislation is passed, whilst retaining the right to use moral means to achieve their goals.

Part II

Ethical
Issues

4

The Human Embryo

Having considered the status of the human fetus as a person I will now consider when a human embryo begins. Examples will then be given of the destruction of human embryos in a variety of nontherapeutic procedures. I will then discuss the reasons why moral respect is due to the early human embryo and why others disagree, followed by a moral evaluation of the use of human embryos in research and clinical practice.

4.1 Beginning of the Embryo

For centuries it sufficed to speak of respecting human life from conception. From *in vitro fertilization* (IVF) we know that a human zygote or embryo is formed in a process that lasts 20 to 22 hours after penetration of the egg by a sperm. Because this is the start of fertilization and of a continuous coordinated process of human development, some hold that this marks the beginning of the zygote, when the contents of the sperm's head enter the egg's cytoplasm as their membranes fuse. I think the zygote could not exist before fertilization is completed.[1]

The evidence seems to support the view that human life begins in the new cell that results from the fusion of sperm and egg when both haploid sets of chromosomes mingle and are yoked together at syngamy to form the diploid nucleus of a new progenitor cell. From this stage onwards maternal and paternal genes work together as a single informational unit, the genetic code, for the formation of the entire human individual. While sperm entry is the start of fertilization, its completion is syngamy, resulting in the formation of a new progenitor cell, the zygote. It is at syngamy that the embryo's genome is actually constituted:

The genetic constitution of the organism is . . . restored by the intermingling of maternal and paternal chromosomes, which is the essence of fertilization.[2]

The fusion of sperm and egg at syngamy, then, coincides with the formation of the zygote.[3] The Church teaches that "the zygote is the cell produced by the fusion of two gametes."[4]

The zygote and a single cell from the four-cell, and possibly the eight-cell, embryo are *totipotent* because they have the actual potency to form the entire blastocyst, placenta, and offspring in a continuous, coordinated biological process, given a favorable uterine environment. This implies a cell removed from a four-cell embryo would be an embryo.[5] A human embryo, then, may be defined as *a totipotent single-cell, group of contiguous cells, or a multicellular organism which has the inherent actual potential to continue species specific, i.e. typical, human development, given a suitable environment.* A totipotent cell or group of contiguous cells is an embryo because of what it is and its actual potential, not because of what it may in time become. An embryo cannot exist before typical human development begins. It does not mean that an embryo affected by a lethal abnormality such as trisomy 18 is neither totipotent nor an embryo. But the product of an unsuccessful attempt at fertilization that is inherently incapable of forming a developing zygote is not an embryo. Freezing an embryo suspends metabolic activity and development.[6] Cryopreserved embryos are not dead but dormant, living in suspended animation. They retain their actual potential for human development which resumes after thawing.

In a weaker sense, *totipotency* has also been used to refer to the capacity of the progeny of one or more cells to contribute to all types of cells in a chimeric offspring following their aggregation with an animal embryo. Totipotent cells in this weaker sense are not embryos, but are derived from a blastocyst. They are usually called pluripotent embryonic stem (ES) cells. During research with mouse ES cells after implantation, they have been unable to form an entire blastocyst, fetus, and offspring unless they are aggregated with trophoblast cells.[7]

4.2 Research and Clinical Use of Embryos

Before making an ethical assessment of the use of human embryos in research and clinical practice I will explain what is involved with some examples of nontherapeutic destructive research. It is important to note that much of this research is done with the long-term goal of widening the applications of preventative medicine as well as developing new therapies. While as much research as possible ought to be done with animal models, it is deemed necessary to use human embryos in research to avoid unpredictable species-specific side effects. Researchers make this point by recalling that the teratogenic effects of thalidomide on the development of human fetuses were very significant, but not so for other mammals.[8]

Infertility treatment

Embryo research can be used to discover some of **the causes of infertility**.[9] Male infertility may result from too few sperm. Motility of sperm is also needed to enable fertilization to occur since sperm must pass through the cervical mucus, the egg's zona pellucida and then bind successfully to the egg's membrane. Postcoital testing of semen is unable to test these capacities of men's sperm without trying to fertilize human eggs. The information obtained could correlate sperm abnormalities with embryonic defects which may cause infertility by embryo losses *in vivo*.

Research involving the use of early human embryos can help improve **IVF success rates.** It is unrealistic to expect IVF to have 100 percent success when the scientific estimation of the natural rate of early embryo losses from the blastocyst stage to completed implantation is about 22 percent.[10] Only 29 percent of eggs used in IVF that complete fertilization within the normal time of 20 hours are chromosomally abnormal compared to 87 percent of those that take more than 20 hours. These defects would account for the loss of many early embryos due to failed implantation or an inability to develop to term.[11] Only 51 percent of 293 IVF zygotes develop to the blastocyst stage.[12] Hence IVF clinicians do not usually transfer abnormal embryos. Research then is needed to see why so many IVF embryos do not survive by failing to divide or to implant. It is also known that only 25 percent of early IVF embryos have normal chromosome numbers in every cell.[13] Success rates would rise if only embryos found to be chromosomally normal were transferred. Research is also needed to see if fertility drugs used for superovulation have deleterious effects on eggs, embryos, or the woman's hormonal environment. Following what occurs naturally in the case of identical twins, it has been suggested that splitting embryos might improve IVF success rates by doubling the number of embryos that can be implanted. This has had success in mammals and its effectiveness could be tested for human embryos.[14]

Some early human embryos are cryopreserved to await a normal cycle free of the effects of superovulants to prevent any possible damage to the embryos after transfer to the uterus. From 25–40 percent of embryos do not survive the thaw process.[15] Research on embryos is sought to improve both cryopreservation techniques and the culture medium to prevent these losses, e.g., cleavage failure and developmental arrest prior to transfer to the uterus. There is, however, a need for long-term follow-up studies of cryopreservation of embryos.[16] As we shall see in chapter 6, human eggs and ovarian tissue may be cryopreserved for later use in IVF. This could involve research on embryos.

Medical research

Human embryo research could be used to improve and verify the **efficiency of the hormonal contraceptive pill**.[17] If the process of fertilization is blocked at any stage, conception is effectively prevented. Drugs could be used to impede fertilization. Alternatively research could be conducted to produce an antisperm vaccine which would prevent sperm binding to the egg's zona pellucida or to the membrane surrounding the egg itself. The contraceptive effectiveness of these methods could be tested in human IVF trials and this would involve discarding eventual embryos formed and tested before these pills would be used clinically.

Proto-oncogenes are normal genes which are expressed in cell multiplication in the early embryo and which may be modified in the fully developed individual to bring about uncontrolled cell growth which forms malignant cancers. Researchers would like to study the role of these genes in early human embryos and how the developing embryo controls these genes as part of the wider research to understand the causes of cancer. This information could be used to find a way to prevent or arrest cancer in humans.[18]

The insertion of genes into a fertilized egg or an early human embryo is not done because the changes caused by this kind of germ line therapy may be harmful for the individual and they would be inherited by future offspring. If a gene is found that gives resistance to HIV infection without risk of harm or of passing it on to future offspring, such genetic engineering could, after safety is assured, open the door to preventive medicine by **gene therapy for human embryos**. Scientists are working on how to insert a gene with therapeutic potential into a mouse embryo whereby it becomes part of every cell of the body, except its germ cells since they do not want any modifications to be inherited by future generations. This could be achieved by giving the mouse DNA-based sequences that are designed to respond to a *trigger drug* to "knock-out" added therapeutic genes in the germ cells. It is hoped these developments can be utilized in the future for the correction of genetic defects in humans.[19]

Spare IVF blastocysts perish if the inner cell mass (ICM) is removed from them to give rise to ES cells.[20] ES cells can then be treated for culture and placed on a feeder cell layer where they flatten out and multiply without differentiating. They can grow in culture for months with undifferentiated proliferation. They have stable developmental potential to form all three embryonic germ layers after prolonged culture. There is no evidence that an ES cell or a clump of ES cells is organized or functions as an embryo. The source embryo and the ICM cease to exist when the ES cells flatten out in culture and begin to multiply without organization. If an embryo is disaggregated and loses its actual potential for typical development it ceases to exist even though some ES cells live on in culture and multiply.[21] ES cells, then, are not totipotent nor embryos themselves.[22]

ES cells could be used to learn more about normal and abnormal early human development. They could also be differentiated to form blood, cardiac muscle, and nerve cells for use in transplant therapy.[23] Human ES cells grown in culture have been induced to differentiate along the neuronal pathway and these "differentiated cells expressed specific markers of mature neurons."[24] Human ES cells have also recently been manipulated to produce blood cells.[25] In preliminary work cultured human neuronal cells derived from ES cells have been transplanted to stroke patients.[26]

Research is continuing to identify the controlling mechanisms for specific lineage differentiation and growth in order to use cloning technology and ES cells to produce stem cells for use in transplants.[27] There would, however, be a risk that these cells may be rejected if they are not compatible with a patient's tissue. This could be overcome if a couple of hundred spare IVF embryos were to be used to produce many different ES cell lines. These could supply a close histocompatible match for almost any patient in need of a transplant for, e.g. thalassaemia, degenerative diseases, or injuries. A few hours after a patient is tested, a matching type would be available. Again research would be needed to perfect these therapies.

Alternatives to using ES cells

Following success in animal models, adult human liver cells have been
derived from bone marrow stem cells.[28] Human stem cells can also easily
be obtained from umbilical cord blood. After animal trials, the first
autologous transplant of human adult stem cells into an artery near the
heart has repaired infarcted myocardial scar with some success.[29] A
patient's body cells may also be able to be dedifferentiated by the controlled use of reprogramming factors from a human egg's cytoplasm to
form directly pluripotent stem cells for therapeutic purposes without first
forming cloned embryos. Such cells, being genetically identical to the
patient's cells, would not be liable to rejection.[30] A cow's skin cells have
been reprogrammed to become multipotent stem cells which were then
transformed into cardiac cells: this will no doubt soon be done in the
human.[31] Human stem cells in culture could, in time, also be modified
so that they would not be recognized as "foreign" and so become universal donor cells free of immune rejection problems.[32] The potential for
applications of this work for human medicine is enormous.

Cloning human embryos

Cloning may be defined as "the genetic duplication of DNA, genes, chromosomes, nuclei, cells, embryos or individual organisms" or simply as
"the production of a cell or organism with the same nuclear genome as
another cell or organism."[33] After 276 attempts, Dolly the sheep was
cloned in Scotland by fusing the nucleus of a ewe's udder cell with
another sheep's enucleated egg and born on July 5, 1996. This raised the
possibility of human cloning.[34] The nucleus of a somatic cell in an adult
mammal contains practically the whole genome of the individual, but
only a few genes are expressed to produce specific proteins, say muscle,
gut or eye tissue. After a somatic cell is inserted into an enucleated egg
it is dedifferentiated or reprogrammed by the egg's cytoplasmic contents.
Once the egg is activated a totipotent cloned embryo is usually formed.
US researchers from Advanced Cell Technology, Worcester, using the
Dolly technique, performed a world-first somatic nuclear transfer from
human adult cumulus cells to 17 enucleated human eggs. Only three of
the cloned human embryos developed up to the six-cell stage and no
attempt was made to implant them. It is not known if they were chromosomally normal.[35] After implantation the cloned embryo could
develop into a fetus and a baby who would be practically genetically

identical to the somatic nucleus donor. This is termed "reproductive cloning." As happened to Dolly the reprogramming of a cloned human fetus would probably not be perfect and this could cause many lethal embryonic or fetal abnormalities. Media reports in early January 2002 suggest this may be true, as Dolly has developed arthritis prematurely. Research shows that there is instability in cloned mouse ES cells and offspring.[36]

One day it may be possible to use an adult patient's somatic cell to clone a human embryo from which pluripotent ES cells could be obtained, grown in culture and used to produce stem cells to treat the patient's defective bone marrow, cardiac muscle, or degenerated nerve tissue, e.g. Huntington's or Parkinson's diseases. This would be "therapeutic cloning" for autologous transplantation; the cells would not be rejected because they would be genetically identical to the patient's cells.[37] Work has already been done with mouse ES cells.[38]

Preimplantation genetic diagnosis (PGD)

The first genes of the early human embryo's genome are activated between the four- and eight-cell stage.[39] While an embryo's genomic DNA can be tested earlier, the expression of an embryo's genome could not be tested before the eight-cell stage when proteins produced by the embryo's own genes can be identified. It is possible to test early IVF embryos for genetic diseases before implanting normal embryos and discarding defective ones. Both fertile and infertile couples with inheritable diseases, or carriers of them, and women known to be at an increased risk of giving birth to offspring with congenital genetic abnormalities may be interested in PGD. This is done by using polymerase chain reaction (PCR) which amplifies many thousands of times a tiny part of a gene or protein.[40] This allows diagnostic DNA analysis for genetic abnormalities to be made from a cell or two excised by *embryo biopsy* from an eight-cell embryo. Embryos can be tested for sex-linked disorders, single-gene defects like cystic fibrosis, Duchenne muscular dystrophy, and haemophilia, or chromosomal disorders.[41] Depending on the type of test, it may take up to three days to get a result. Embryos found free of defects are transferred to the uterus and the rest are allowed to succumb or made available for research.

There is no significant difference in the survival rate of eight-cell human embryos after a single-cell biopsy.[42] The risk of abnormal development would be less if trophoblast cells were biopsied at the blastocyst stage.[43] Since the first birth after PGD in 1990, blastocyst biopsy of up to 10 cells is now practiced and by 1997 over 160 children world-wide had been born following PGD for chromosomal and single-gene disorders. PGD could also be extended for multifactorial diseases and for social reasons such as gender selection and behavioral traits or even for an increased risk of a genetic predisposition for breast cancer.[44] Eight genes can be explored at the same time and possibly many more in the future.[45] One problem is that only about 40 percent of IVF embryos develop to the blastocyst stage.[46] The difficulty of PGD for fertile couples is that it requires IVF, an invasive procedure which few fertile women would choose, even though it has a 23 percent implantation rate per blastocyst.[47] At present a PGD cycle costs US$6,000 to $10,500 and is reliable but not always 100 percent accurate.[48] In a widely reported case a couple with a child, Molly, affected by "Fanconi's anaemia," an inherited disease, agreed to have implanted two of their 15 IVF embryos found by PGD to be free of the disease and also perfect tissue match donors for Molly. After a child, "Adam," was born, his healthy cord blood stem cells were successfully transplanted to Molly whose bone marrow was soon 100 percent derived from Adam.[49]

The sex of IVF embryos can also be determined by single-cell biopsy whereby male embryos at 50 percent risk of an X-linked disorder would not be implanted.[50] The use of fluorescent *in situ* hybridization (FISH) using DNA probes is a great advance and is the preferred method for the sexing of embryos and detecting chromosomally abnormal embryos.[51] It may soon be possible in clinical practice to treat an embryo or fetus with a genetic disease as early as 28 days after fertilization by the insertion of healthy genes or genetically modified stem cells from healthy blastocysts or donors.[52] But at present there is no guarantee that defects might not be inadvertently introduced into these embryos.

4.3 Respect Due to the Embryo

First I will give biblical and theological reasons for respecting the life of the human embryo, followed by reasons given for the human embryo being a person from conception. Then I will argue that the human embryo deserves respect as a potential person. Finally I shall give utilitarian and other reasons for respecting human embryos.

Biblical and theological reasons

Believers in the Bible find ample grounds for showing moral respect for human life from conception. The biblical evidence we have already seen in chapter 2 strongly supports the belief that human life and its formation are in the hands of God, the Creator. Women and men share in God's plan of transmitting life. The Bible does not address the issue of human fetuses and individuals as persons because all human life belongs to God in a special way, who alone has dominion over human life and the individual's formative process. From early Christian times human life has been regarded as sacred and morally inviolable from the start, even when it was assumed the soul was not created for several weeks after conception.[53] The Christian tradition never denied that infringements of this moral law were serious. An expression of this living tradition is the solemn statement made by the Second Vatican Council, regardless of when the spiritual soul is created to constitute a human person: "Life once conceived must be protected with the utmost care . . ."[54] I believe this theological insight for protecting human life rightly expresses a profound perception of the value of all human life. It also has appeal for some who do not believe in God.

The embryo as a person

Another argument for the moral respect due to human life from conception is to show that the zygote already is, or probably is, a human individual and person. The zygote is a *totipotent* cell whose newly constituted genome, interacting with the maternal environment, in a continuous process directs cell multiplication, purposeful unidirectional development and differentiation of tissues required for the growth of the one and same living individual. The genetic identity of the adult individual is practically the same as that of the embryo, who possesses the actual potential to develop and grow into an adult, given a suitable uterine environment. The zygote and the resulting adult are the same living being. The zygote organizes itself into an embryo, fetus, infant, child, and adult without ceasing to be the one and same living *ontological individual*.[55] In this view, extraembryonic tissues, membranes and the placenta are temporary, but constituent, organs of the embryo and fetus which become redundant after birth and are discarded. This argues for the zygote being an actual, not a potential, human individual. Once the human individual is formed at fertilization a duty of absolute moral respect arises. There would also be good reasons to hold that the immaterial soul or life principle is created within the zygote to complete the formation of a person, but there could be no empirical evidence for this.[56]

Michael Tooley admits it is easy to see why some people hold a fertilized egg is a person if they believe an immaterial soul is within the embryo since it would then have "the *capacity* for self-consciousness and rational thought."[57] Massimo Reichlin says that the active potentiality of the zygote to develop into a fetus, a child and adult argues for the presence of an individual with a human nature from conception. He regards the zygote as an actual human individual with developmental potential, not a potential human individual.[58] As for when twinning occurs, the individual formed in the zygote could continue when the second one begins. This would resemble a plant retaining its identity when a slip is cut off and planted in the soil to give rise to a new plant.[59]

I agree with Reichlin's general line of reasoning but differ as to what stage a definitive ongoing embryo is formed with the active potency to develop into a human adult without a change of ontological individuality or identity. I am not alone in finding the argument that the zygote is an ongoing human individual unconvincing.[60] But I admit it is plausible both on account of its intrinsic merit and by reason of the number of eminent scientists and philosophers who support it.[61] So long as there are good reasons to believe the zygote is already a human individual and a person, prudence requires that any reasonable doubt should be ethically resolved in favor of treating the zygote as a person. The same principle of prudent caution is applied for new drugs: they should not be approved for general use before it is certain they are safe. This does not mean the search for the truth should cease, provided it is conducted with a sincere sense of objectivity and moral responsibility.

The Church does not formally teach that the human individual and person begin with sperm entry into the egg.[62] Pope John Paul II, however, in his 1995 Encyclical Letter *Evangelium Vitae* leaves no doubt that from conception the embryo is to be treated as a person:

in fact "from the time that the ovum is fertilized, a life is begun which is neither that of the father nor of the mother; it is rather the life of a new human living being [*novi viventis humani*] with his own growth. It would never be made human if it were not human already. This has always been clear, and ... modern genetic science offers clear confirmation. It has demonstrated that from the first instant there is established the structure or genetic programme of what this living being will be: a man [*hominem*], and indeed this individual man [*hunc hominem individuum*], with his characteristic aspects already well determined. Right from fertilization the adventure of a human life begins, and each of its capacities requires time – a rather lengthy time – to find its place and to be in a position to act." Even if the presence of a spiritual soul cannot be ascertained by empirical data, the results themselves of scientific research on the human embryo provide "a valuable indication for discerning by the use of reason, a personal presence at the moment of the first appearance of a human life: how could a living human creature [*vivens creatura humana*] not also [*etiam*] be a human person?"

Furthermore, what is at stake is so important that, from the standpoint of moral obligation, the mere probability that a person is involved would suffice to justify an absolutely clear prohibition of any intervention aimed at killing a human embryo. Precisely for this reason, over and above all scientific debates and those philosophical affirmations to which the Magisterium has not expressly committed itself, the Church has always taught and continues to teach that the result of human procreation, from the first moment of its existence, must be guaranteed that unconditional respect which is morally due to a human being in his or her totality and unity as body and spirit: "*The human creature [creatura humana] is to be respected and treated as a person from conception.*"[63]

The early embryo as a potential person

A third argument for respecting the early human embryo is based on its potential to become a human individual and a person. This is a view that I also support. It has been said that "a consensus seems to have emerged on both sides of the Atlantic, opting for the term 'potential person' when referring to the early embryo."[64] The fact that the genetic identity of the human individual is formed in the zygote does not mean the human individual is already formed. During development at the two-cell stage both contiguous cells appear to be distinct cells, i.e. ontological individuals with the same genetic identities. Each begins with its own life-cycle and has its own nutrients for sustaining its life and energy needs. The zona pellucida encases the cells and is composed of nonliving glycoproteins in noncellular form. The first two cells, even if they interact, seem to be distinct cells, entities or ontological individuals and not a single organized two-cell ontological individual. The same applies to the four-cell embryo. According to this view the human individual appears to be formed after the zygote stage even though the zygote has a natural actual potency for cell multiplication and differentiation to form one or more human individuals.

At the eight-cell stage cells are not committed to one developmental pathway. They multiply and differentiate as they gradually undergo restriction of developmental potential. Cells destined to form extraembryonic tissues differentiate first as the blastocyst is formed. I now admit this is a rudimentary embryonic organism. It is only about the primitive streak stage that specific cells are destined to form the entire definitive embryo and fetus. When single cells from four-cell white, black, and brown sheep embryos are aggregated in an empty zona pellucida and placed in a recipient ewe, a white, black, and brown chimeric sheep can be formed. Such a sheep does not begin at fertilization. If cells of *genetically dissimilar* embryos can be aggregated to form a chimeric sheep, this suggests that *genetically similar* embryonic human cells could *normally* do the same. This implies purposeful development occurs *between* cells, but not *within* an ongoing multicellular ontological individual from the two-cell stage. The development of the early embryo depends on a cascade of events involving the inside and outside position of cells, each one of which has the complete genotype. There is no fixed predetermined plan for every cell and its progeny. The totipotency of the early embryo does not imply that a human individual is formed before a definitive human individual(s) is formed with heterogeneous parts which support its life and ongoing development.

The formation of the primitive streak marks the formation of a multicellular human individual with a craniocaudal body axis and bilateral symmetry. The cells that do not become part of the newly formed human individual continue as extraembryonic membranes and the placenta, an auxiliary organ for the embryo and fetus. There is no conceptual problem for the cells of the three germ layers being integrated to become a new organized human living ontological individual which continues as the same entity or individual throughout all subsequent stages of development and growth. It seems a human individual and person could not begin before cells of the rudimentary embryonic organism form a distinct ongoing living body at the primitive streak stage, animated by a divinely created immaterial life principle.[65]

The *totipotency* of one of the first four cells to give rise to the blastocyst, placenta and the human individual gradually gives way to the *totipotency* of groups of cells, e.g. half of an 8- or 16-cell embryo. The potential for identical twinning by a separated *totipotent* group of cells is lost at the late blastocyst when a single primitive streak is formed. This is because differentiation has progressed to the point of being restricted to forming only one ontological individual. With the formation of a single primitive streak the embryo is *totipotent* with the actual potential to continue development as the one and the same human individual. Instead of viewing development in the first two weeks after fertilization as *development of* the human individual, it seems preferable to interpret the process as cell multiplication and differentiation *to form* a human individual and the placenta. Hence it seems it would be more accurate to speak of "proembryo" than "pre-embryo," although the use of these terms does not alter the respect due to the early embryo.[66]

Development does not follow a blueprint contained in the zygote as though its genotype represents a miniature preformed human individual. The zygote's cell progeny do not contain specific instructions for one or another tissue, organ, or limb, even though the specification of embryonic axes have been found to begin before cleavage in normal mouse development and it is now known that at the two-cell stage most of the cell progeny of the first cell to divide will preferentially contribute to the ICM from which the fetus arises.[67] Each cell contains the full complement of genes whose selective activation is influenced by its location, previous history, cell-to-cell contacts, as well as cytoplasmic, electric, and biochemical signals. There is scope for chance encounters and factors to determine which cells will form different parts of the human individual.[68]

As Lewis Wolpert put it:

ultimately, it is cell behaviour that provides the link between genes and pattern and form. There are thus no genes for "arm" or "leg" as such, but specific genes which become active during their formation. The complexity of development is due to the cascade of effects, both within and between cells, when the synthesis of particular proteins is changed.[69]

Neither the presence of the genetic program of an individual from the zygote stage nor the fact that the first cell to divide at the two-cell stage usually contributes its cell progeny to the ICM demonstrates that a human individual is already formed. I think it is necessary to show that the first two or four cells are actually organized as an ongoing body or single entity, and not just distinct cells, before it can be claimed with certainty that a human individual is already formed. Purposeful interactions between cells to form an individual does not necessarily imply the human individual is already formed. The evidence, then, does not seem to justify asserting beyond doubt that the human individual is actually formed at the zygote stage. The zygote is not yet an actual

ontological human individual, but it has the natural actual developmental potential, given a favorable environment, to become an ontological human individual. It is to be noted not even adults can realize their
life potential without nutrition and fluids and the right temperature and
environment.[70]

Buckle analyses the various meanings of potential, and concludes that
the fertilized egg is not the same entity as the embryo formed some 14
days after fertilization. He believes the fertilized egg's potential lacks a
basis for the moral respect due to an actual human individual.[71] Warren
admits the potential of the early embryo warrants respect but says that
"the rights of any actual person invariably outweigh those of any potential person, whenever the two conflict."[72] Finally Resnik agrees that
zygotes, as potential persons, deserve special moral concern and ought
to be treated more as children than commodities or property.[73]

The argument for respecting human zygotes as potential persons based
on their natural actual and proximate potency to become human individuals in the Creator's plan, in my view, suffices to justify a duty of
absolute respect for embryos and their formative process from the beginning of the zygote.[74] The moral necessity to show respect for embryonic
human life is a profoundly human insight and reflects the respect due to
life normally resulting from a couple's mutual self-giving and our shared
humanity, apart from religious considerations. There is no justification
for the reductionism that sees embryonic human life, naturally or artificially conceived, as no more than genetic products, devoid of significance
and value. From a theistic perspective, the formative process and the fruit
of human generation has a claim to unconditioned moral respect, especially if it may also be a person. On the other hand the passive potency
of a sperm or an egg to become a human embryo does not warrant
attributing moral respect to them before they fuse to form or become a
zygote.

Other reasons

Many are convinced that the early embryo could not be a human individual nor a person and give little credence to the potentiality argument,
especially secular humanists and those who do not accept the metaphysical premises on which the traditional concept of the human individual and person are based. Because the development of the human
being from embryo to fetus, newborn to older child, is a continuous
process Singer thinks the development of the moral status of the human

being is likewise continuous. He suggests an infant might be accorded the same right to life as other persons some 28 days after birth.[75] He says: "the grounds for not killing persons do not apply to newborn infants."[76] Consistently, as we have discussed in chapter 1, those who do not believe the early human embryo is a person because it has no interests or desire to live, do not grant it the rights of a person.[77]

If embryos are not deemed to be persons who can be harmed, on a utilitarian calculus of benefits and harms, most of the examples of destructive human embryo experimentation or research mentioned above would be ethically permissible. Utilitarian criteria do not provide any direct ethical grounds for protecting human embryos whose only intrinsic title to respect would be their capacity to experience pleasure or pain. As Kuhse and Singer put it:

> We believe the minimal characteristic needed to give the embryo a claim to consideration is sentience, or the capacity to feel pleasure or pain. Until that point is reached, the embryo does not have any interests and, like other nonsentient organisms (a human egg, for example), cannot be harmed – in a morally relevant sense – by anything we do.[78]

The human embryo, however, would *indirectly* warrant moral worth and respect if it was wanted by its parents and they wished to prevent any harm to the developing embryo and future person it will become.

Baroness Warnock, on the other hand, believes the human embryo deserves some special moral consideration simply because it is human, even though it would have no rights because it is not deemed to be a person. Warnock agrees that human embryos warrant moral respect, but not the absolute respect due to persons. She favors research on human embryos for serious reasons, provided they are not implanted, since there would be a great risk of damage to children yet to be born. She also believes the community should not ignore the moral sentiments of those who feel outraged at the lack of respect for human embryos by subjecting them to destructive research. As we have seen in chapter 1, feelings are not divorced from our intellectual intuitions of what conflicts with our self-understanding as human persons. The views of people with such strong feelings should have some influence on a utilitarian calculus when balancing the benefits and harms for the respect due to human embryos.[79] To avoid the real dangers of the "slippery slope" she agrees with the pragmatic compromise of limiting human embryo research to 14 days, when she holds distinct embryos and individuals are formed.[80]

4.4 Ethical Evaluation of the Use of Embryos in Research and Clinical Practice

The gaining of scientific knowledge and expertise for infertility treatment is not problematic, but a high sense of moral responsibility is needed for its acquisition and use.[81] A crucial ethical problem arises from the *creation of spare embryos* which may be discarded or subjected to **unethical destructive research for scientific and medical research**. As we have seen, moral respect for human embryos should take precedence over utilitarian and pragmatic considerations. The routine cryopreservation of embryos is also unethical because of its arrest of their development and its high risk to their lives. Whatever the knowledge or other benefits gained destructive embryo research is immoral: this is the response of those who hold that human life and its formative process is morally inviolable. Others favor beneficial research on embryos because human embryos are not believed to be persons.[82]

I believe it is ethically imperative that human dignity and integrity be rigorously safeguarded for present and future generations by banning destructive embryonic research or risky manipulation of human embryos. Human dignity gives value to the human genome and each person's unique genotype: these need to be protected from harm. The *Universal Declaration on the Human Genome and Human Rights* puts it this way:

> The human genome underlies the fundamental unity of all members of the human family, as well as the recognition of their inherent dignity and diversity. In a symbolic sense, it is the heritage of humanity.[83]

Cloning by fission of an early human embryo occurs naturally and creates identical twins with the same father and mother. Splitting an IVF embryo might increase a couple's prospects of having a baby, but it is unethical since it destroys the original embryo if two new embryos are formed or it lessens the prospects of survival if the original embryo continues and a new one is formed. The deliberate creation of identical twins by embryo splitting is undue manipulation of, and exercise of dominion over, the origin of such twins.

There are reasonable grounds to believe that a human embryo cloned by **somatic nuclear transfer** to an enucleated egg would be totipotent, with the natural actual potential, once implanted, to develop into a fetus, infant, and child. It would be contrary to human dignity and ethically unacceptable to asexually create human embryos by any cloning technique. Bob Williamson says that cloning a human being would be contrary to a person's sense of autonomy.[84] Furthermore, in the light of the embryonic losses in cloning Dolly, it would be unsafe to clone human embryos and it should be forbidden since it risks causing serious fetal defects.[85] Safety risks aside, reproductive cloning seems to be clearly unethical since this atypical and unnatural mode of reproduction would undermine the child's sense of personal and family identity and dignity. The cloned child would be engineered deliberately to be practically an identical copy of another person and, unlike the case of normal adoption, would also be deprived of a natural father, a genetic mother and their blood relatives. The child's genetic parents would be the parents of the donor of the nucleus – not to mention the unreal expectations that would be made of the growing cloned child. Again the *Universal Declaration on the Human Genome* says:

> Practices which are contrary to human dignity, such as reproductive cloning of human beings, shall not be permitted.[86]

It is certainly contrary to our sense of worth as persons to engineer animal/human hybrids. It would be offensive to insert substantial parts of the human genome into an animal egg, potentially resulting in a pig–human hybrid. Likewise the recent cloning of a hybrid human embryo from the nucleus of a human body cell and an enucleated pig egg is unethical.[87]

Although I disagree, Udo Schüklenk and Richard Ashcroft see no harm and many benefits in reproductive cloning and in therapeutic cloning of human embryos.[88] Among others, Julian Savulescu argues that

> it is not only reasonable to produce embryos as a source of multipotent stem cells, but that it would be morally required to produce embryos and early fetuses as a source of tissue for transplantation.[89]

Tooley dismisses objections against cloning human embryos ("mindless human organisms") to serve as organ banks claiming they are the same arguments invoked against abortion. He also believes cloning human persons is in principle morally acceptable.[90] Neither John Harris nor David McCarthy find cloning human beings unethical.[91] Researchers and academics approve of research on human ES cells derived from blastocysts and grown in culture for therapeutic purposes.[92] However, they overlook the risk of serious harm from the therapeutic use of cloned ES cells since these could also be affected by faulty reprogramming.

In the light of the moral status of any human embryo I believe that the destructive use of cloned human embryos, even for therapeutic purposes, would be as unethical as destructive research on normal IVF human embryos, even if its beneficial consequences have to be forgone. Pope John Paul II in an address to transplant specialists warned that

> attempts at human cloning with a view to obtaining organs for transplants . . . insofar as they involve the manipulation and destruction of human embryos, are not morally acceptable, even when their proposed goal is good in itself. Science itself points to other forms of *therapeutic intervention* which would not involve cloning or the use of embryonic cells, but rather would make use of stem cells taken from adults. This is the direction that research must follow if it wishes to respect the dignity of each and every human being, even at the embryonic stage.[93]

Researchers who use ES cells would normally be acting in collusion, or tacit agreement, with the destruction of the embryos from which the ES cells are obtained. The research creates a market for ES cells: the link with the destruction of embryos would be undeniable.[94] President Bush said on August 9, 2001 that he would give federal funding for research on

> existing stem-cell lines, where the life and death decision has already been made. . . . without crossing a fundamental moral line by providing taxpayer funding that would sanction or encourage further destruction of human embryos that have at least the potential for life.[95]

While the President did not materially collaborate in the destruction of human embryos, one wonders if it will be possible to deny funds for new ES cell lines in the future.

As we have seen above, there is also a need to continue research on the promising therapeutic and preventative medical potential of **adult stem cells** to avoid using IVF or cloned human embryos.[96] In the light of recent research, the use of cloned embryos and ES cells derived from them for therapeutic purposes would be very risky since they are likely to be affected by abnormalities. Empirical evidence will be needed to see if the success of therapies using adult stem cells is comparable to the success of any other cure. If this is shown to be the case, there would be no need to destroy embryos to obtains ES cells. However, the use of pluripotent stem cells created directly by reprogramming somatic cells would not seem to be unethical but its safety would need to be verified by research in animal models before clinical trials begin. Such cells, being genetically identical to the patient's cells, would not be liable to be rejected. Public funds should be provided for research on umbilical cord, placenta and adult stem cells to develop therapies. President Bush did well to promise $250 million for such research.[97]

The **use of PGD** is linked to the discarding of affected embryos. Many believe that PGD is ethically acceptable.[98] Some hold that in justice there is an ethical duty to prevent defective embryos becoming persons since they would have to endure so much suffering caused by severe diseases or disabilities that their lives would not be worth living. They hold pro-life advocates need to justify their stand in view of the suffering that they indirectly cause in practice.[99] Others believe the decision is a matter for parental autonomy.[100] These positions are consistent with the ethical view that embryos are not persons nor human subjects with an absolute right to life.

For those who hold human life should be safeguarded from conception and that embryos should be treated as persons, PGD followed by selective termination of embryos detected with a genetic defect, or even a genetic predisposition for late onset cancer, is unethical even if this would result in fewer subsequent abortions and less suffering for disabled offspring and their carers.[101] With embryos often being discarded, David King is right when he says that PGD is inherently eugenic: couples may be under social pressure to have PGD, whose purpose is to reduce the number of births with genetic defects.[102] The deliberate discarding of human embryos at any stage is unethical: bad actions may not be done to prevent suffering. Human embryos should not be subjected to unjust discrimination as if only embryos free of genetic defects are worthy to be born alive.

In **embryonic gene therapy** the effects of random, and even of cautious, insertion of genes into a zygote's nucleus or into an early embryo are extremely unpredictable and could cause mutations, cancers or the repression of other sensitive genes.[103] The changes would be inherited by future generations and this would be unethical manipulation of human life and exercise of dominion over the origin of human individuals. Unlike somatic gene therapy, germ line therapy may be seriously harmful to future offspring.

But if its safety can be guaranteed, the insertion of healthy genes or non-embryonic pluripotent stem cells in embryos or early fetuses to cure disease need not in principle be unethical if harm is not caused. Pope John Paul II stated:

> One must uphold as licit procedures carried out on the human embryo which respect the life and integrity of the embryo and do not involve disproportionate risks for it, but rather are directed to its healing, the improvement of its condition of health or its individual survival.[104]

As research capitalizes on the new genetic information **embryonic therapy** could one day be an ethical reality that may save the lives of some defective embryos and fetuses.

In the light of the new developments mentioned earlier, an ethical case could be made for the therapeutic insertion of a gene into an early embryo provided this would not harm the offspring and future generations, if, say, the genes could be "turned off" in the germ cells.[105] It would be naive and unethical to use irreversible germ line therapy for a diseased embryo today when in 20–30 years' time better preventive gene therapies may be available for the next generation.[106] Trials with animal models would be necessary to gain an assurance that the risks of clinical trials for present and future generations would be truly proportionate. At present it is premature to move into clinical practice. Marc Lappé and John Harris, however, make a good point when they cautiously support germ line therapy once it is certain the offspring will be healthy.[107] If human dignity is to be upheld, respect for embryos and the well-being of offspring need to be born in mind as the therapeutic role of medicine grows with the knowledge gained from the human genome project and advances in detecting defects in embryos increase.

5

The Pregnant Woman and her Fetus

5.1 Support for Pregnant Women

Pregnant women and their partners are usually committed to maintaining a healthy lifestyle. Pregnant women are often supported by their partners once they understand what they endure during pregnancy and recognize their own fears and needs as fathers. The expertise of obstetricians and midwives ensures the outcome of most pregnancies in developed countries is without complications. Women in the lower socioeconomic bracket usually receive prenatal care but they would have less chance of access to prenatal care givers of their choice.[1]

Once women know they are pregnant, their future offspring are important for them, but more so after they feel their first movements which reinforce the bonding between them. From this stage mothers are keen to protect them. Restrictions on lifestyle are usually accepted to enhance prospects for the birth of a healthy child. Pregnant women have a right to all relevant information and to be involved in decisions relating to delivery, especially caesarean sections. There is evidence that this is not always the case and that women are dissatisfied with this neglect.[2] The anxiety of a pregnant woman is not allayed until she learns the good news that her baby is healthy.

Women who need the greatest emotional support and comfort are those who have recently had a stillbirth or a late miscarriage. Each woman who has experienced a pregnancy loss has unique physical and emotional needs. Depending on how early the loss occurs, parents should be encouraged to hold, cradle, and weep over their deceased child. It is good for the family to experience mourning openly, to name their child and discuss their attitude to a religious service for their child with their relations and friends. Even when not required by law, mothers who wish to have a burial service for their fetus have a right to require it. Eventual autopsy results for a stillbirth should be given to the family sensitively. Genetic counseling, by assessing the risk of abnormality in future pregnancies, could assist in making a decision on whether, and when, to plan another pregnancy and thereby offset any undue influence of feelings of grief or guilt.[3]

Instances of ambiguous attitudes of older children on the mother's return home after a stillbirth should not be taken personally because the negativity displayed is merely a sign of the experience of their own shock and grief at the loss of a baby sibling. At times children may show signs of unsupported dependency, quite oblivious of their mother's loss and deep personal grief. The mother and the father may require support and counseling from a professional to cope with feelings of misplaced guilt, fear, anger, and sadness.

5.2 Embryonic and Fetal Mortality and Morbidity

Before dealing with the ethical dilemmas of decisions involving the loss of human fetuses, it is necessary to learn the scientific facts concerning the incidence and causes of fetal losses before considering our ethical responsibilities to prevent them. Research by Allen Wilcox and colleagues has shown that of 221 healthy women trying to conceive in 707 menstrual cycles, 198 (28 percent) achieved a "biochemical pregnancy" as indicated by a highly sensitive and specific assay for elevated levels of a pregnancy hormone – human chorionic gonadotrophin (HCG) – in urine specimens before the first missed menstrual period.[4] The HCG is produced by the trophoblastic cells of blastocysts a week after fertilization when the process of implantation begins. Of these 198 women 43 (22 percent) lost their embryos before pregnancy could be clinically recognized. Only 155 women out of the original 221 (70 percent) had a clinically recognized pregnancy during the 9 months of the study. Subsequently 19 of the 155 clinically recognized pregnancies miscarried at the mean gestational age of 11 weeks, i.e. 12 percent. The total loss of biochemically detected pregnancies from the blastocyst stage was 62 (43 + 19) out of 198 i.e. 31 percent.[5] The 12 percent loss after implantation is close to the generally quoted 15 percent loss by spontaneous abortion for all recognized pregnancies.[6] Of the 221 women in the trial, 23 (10 percent) failed to achieve a biochemical pregnancy. Of the women who had an early loss of pregnancy 95 percent conceived again and had a clinically recognized pregnancy. Most women (124) became pregnant during the first three cycles with a 25 percent probability of achieving a clinically recognized pregnancy per cycle.[7] There is evidence that the risk of early pregnancy loss increases when implantation occurs 9 or more days after ovulation.[8]

Wilcox admitted his methods could not detect losses of early embryos before the blastocyst stage and offered no reasons to explain why in up to two-thirds of cycles no biochemical pregnancies were detected.[9] Peter Braude and his fellow researchers suggest that the reasons may include anovulation, failed fertilization or preimplantation losses before HCG is produced.[10] Failure of fertilization could be due to genetic faults in the formation of sperm or egg during meiosis, the postovulatory ageing of ova before fertilization, or other causes of infertility in the sperm or egg.[11] Michelle Plachot agrees with Braude and cites evidence to suggest that genetic faults in egg or sperm account for about 40 percent of preimplantation embryos affected by a chromosome anomaly in normal and IVF embryos.[12] The above suggestions are in agreement with the findings of Mark Sauer and his colleagues who found that of 41 ova recovered by uterine lavage from fertile women, 10 were undivided, 20 did not go beyond the 2–18 cell stage, one not beyond the morula stage, and only 10 (25 percent) developed to the blastocyst stage.[13] John Biggers estimates that 50 percent of embryos naturally conceived are lost by the time pregnancy is recognizable.[14]

Inspection of spontaneous embryonic and fetal abortions provides evidence that most of them are afflicted by congenital abnormalities. The incidence of gross chromosomal anomalies in spontaneously aborted fetuses in the first trimester ranges from 62–80 percent, but falls to about 25 percent in the second trimester. These may be caused by chromosomal or environmental factors (e.g. drugs), or a combination of both. About 5.4 percent of all clinically recognized pregnancies are affected by a chromosome abnormality and this would account for 32–42 percent of all spontaneous embryonic and fetal deaths.[15] Other causes include the effect of increasing maternal age on ova, vitamin deficiencies, cardiac disease, infection, viruses, e.g. rubella, stress, hypoxia and fetal growth retardation, poor placental circulation etc. Environmental factors associated with increased risk of fetal death include teratogenic substances which cause death directly or cause a malformation when fetal organs are being formed.[16]

About 2 percent of pregnancies are ectopic, i.e. they develop outside the uterus, and 97 percent occur in pathological fallopian tubes. They are the main cause of maternal deaths in the first trimester and account for 9–13 percent of pregnancy-related deaths.[17] Expectant management of subacute ectopic pregnancies results in their resolution without surgery in up to 80 percent of cases by spontaneous tubal abortions or by resorption, resulting in a 30–50 percent probability of not being able to conceive naturally.[18]

Australian research with 585 participating couples has shown that men working in some trades increased the odds of miscarriage in their partners by 1.75 times while there was no difference between women who worked and women who undertook home duties. But for women under 35 years and working at home the risk of a miscarriage was 1.91 times higher.[19] X-rays of the abdomen and back of women were associated with 1.89 times increased risk of miscarriage, and it was 4.28 times higher if their male partners had the X-ray due to its effect on sperm formation. Women who are exposed to glues at home had a 1.87 times increased risk of miscarriage while their male partners increased the risk of miscarriage by an odds ratio of 2.36 by exposure to glues, 3.19 to oil paints, and 2.27 to oven cleaners. Exposure to multiple factors further increases the risk of miscarriage.[20] The rate of miscarriage rises from 3.7 percent for couples without exposure to a single risk factor to 75 percent for couples exposed to six or seven factors. The odds ratio of miscarriage was also found to increase with age over 35 years, 2.46 for women and 2.33 for their male partners.[21]

Evidence of the harm caused by pregnant women who smoke is coming to light. Miscarriages are increased by up to 27 percent and the risk of underweight babies at birth is higher. Their daughters also have a similar increased risk of miscarrying and their sons are likely to be affected by undescended testes. Passive smoking also contributes to these problems, including cot deaths. Children brought up in homes where smoking occurs have a lower birth weight, are shorter, have smaller airways in their lungs, suffer more from asthma and respiratory infections and other symptoms, are fivefold more prone to be affected by allergies and are exposed to a greater risk of glue ear. The abuse of addictive drugs and the excessive consumption of alcohol or caffeine also harms the outcome of pregnancies, their offspring, and may increase the miscarriage rate.[22] Finally recent research shows that unwanted emotional stress caused by serious life events (e.g. death of a child) during the first trimester of pregnancy may cause congenital fetal defects, especially those of the cranial neural crest.[23] Clearly, education in schools on risky behavior to avoid is imperative. It is generally agreed a pregnant woman "is morally obliged to avoid inflicting prenatal injury" on her fetus provided this does not require her to sacrifice other important interests.[24]

5.3 Induced Abortion

Incidence

It is estimated that globally 150,000 abortions are performed each day, equivalent to over 54 million abortions per year.[25] The reported number of legal abortions in the United States was 586,760 in 1972, 1,297,606 in 1980, 1,429,577 in 1990, and 1,267,415 in 1994. The Supreme Court decisions on legal abortion in *Roe v. Wade* and *Doe v. Bolton* in 1973 explain this increase but abortions may have been under-reported before 1973 because they were illegal.[26] The estimated number of legal abortions in Australia in 1990 was 79,019.[27] The legal abortion proportion per 100 known pregnancies was 9 for the Netherlands (1986), 18.4 for England and Wales (1987), 23 for Australia (1990), 29 for the United States (1985), and 54.9 for the former USSR (1987).[28]

Reasons

Whatever the reason, abortion is never an easy decision. In developed countries abortions usually occur because of unwanted pregnancies. In the majority of cases the reasons are economic, social, career related, reluctance to be a single mother, a desire to keep the family at its present size, or an inability to cope with another child for personal, health, lifestyle, or domestic reasons. It is sometimes sought after rape, incest, severe psychological trauma, or to save the mother's life.[29] Jacques Suaudeau links failed contraception to abortion because procreation is not wanted.[30] Some young women have abortions because they find they are unable to cope with continuing a pregnancy. Some single women without family and social support find a solution to their problems by recourse to abortion. Some do not want to tell their parents they are pregnant or to risk letting pregnancy and the responsibilities of motherhood prevent them completing their secondary and/or tertiary education. Many women choose to have an abortion if prenatal diagnosis shows that their fetus is affected by some serious congenital abnormality. Others prefer abortion to giving their child up for adoption. Pressure also comes from their partners who do not want to assume the responsibilities of being fathers or of supporting their children. Mothers, however, find it difficult to decide to have an abortion once bonding is intensified by seeing ultrasound images of their fetuses, especially if their friends shared in their joy.

Surgical and medical methods

Currently in the UK during the first trimester the vacuum aspiration method is used in about 99 percent of abortions under local or general anesthetic. It is safe for the mother and lasts less than 10 minutes, and up to 98 percent may be performed as day procedures. The risk of complications is low – only one-tenth of the risk of continuing the pregnancy and giving birth. Medical induction of abortion in pregnancies up to 9 weeks' gestation may be obtained by administering orally mifepristone 600 mg, formerly known as RU 486, followed 48 hours later by oral or vaginal prostaglandins. Complete abortion occurs in 95 percent of cases with 85 percent occurring within 4 hours of treatment, and incomplete abortion in 4 percent. There is a failure rate of 1 percent. Nausea, vomiting, and diarrhea occur in 30 percent of cases.[31] Surgical evacuation is avoided, except for the 5 percent of patients with incomplete or failed abortion. Doses of mifepristone as low as 200 mg also suffice for effective abortion.[32]

During the second trimester two techniques are most frequently used. The first is surgical, cervical dilation with uterine curettage and evacuation, which is usually used in the USA. Major complications occur in only 0.4–1.7 percent of cases. The second technique is medically induced abortion using a locally administered prostaglandin. This is the preferred method in the UK. Its complications include vomiting and/or diarrhea, bleeding in 1.7 percent of cases, and incomplete abortion in up to 30 percent of cases. Its action brings on strong and sustained contractions of the uterus which usually cause fetuses to die of oxygen deprivation prior to birth. This lessens stress for the mother and staff. Some maternal deaths have been linked with intra-amniotic administration of prostaglandins.[33] A combination of mifepristone and prostaglandin is also effective as a simple non-invasive method for abortion up to 20 weeks gestation.[34] Finally, third trimester abortions do occasionally occur when lethal or untreatable abnormalities are detected late in pregnancy in viable fetuses.[35]

Postcoital methods

Some postcoital methods usually prevent pregnancy by inhibiting implantation and can be used by women who do not wish to become pregnant after unprotected sexual intercourse or when a barrier method unexpectedly fails. Mifepristone is also a postcoital drug which is very effective in preventing pregnancy because it inhibits implantation of embryos. It is marketed for abortion in France, Sweden, United Kingdom, China, Austria, Belgium, Finland, Greece, Israel, and Spain.[36] Recent research show that doses of 10–50 mg of mifepristone are effective.[37]

The insertion of a copper tipped intra-uterine device (IUD) within a week of sexual intercourse is known to prevent pregnancy. Medicated and copper treated IUDs inhibit the process of the embryo's implantation in the lining of the uterus and may also prevent, or interfere with, the process of fertilization.[38] Copper ions released from these IUDs into the fluids of the uterine cavity and the fallopian tubes may kill sperm and/or egg and thereby prevent fertilization.[39]

Some emergency contraceptive pills (ECPs), also known as "morning after pills," can prevent pregnancy by inhibiting or delaying ovulation or by rendering the lining of the uterus inhospitable for implantation of an embryo. An example of this is the Yuzpe regimen of oestrogen-progestogen pills which are prescribed by a doctor to be taken within 72 hours of unprotected intercourse and repeated 12 hours later.[40] They may also inhibit transport of sperm or ova.[41] It is most effective in preventing pregnancy when commenced about 12 hours after unprotected intercourse.[42] A survey of 10 clinical trials of the Yuzpe regimen found it 75 percent effective in reducing the number of actual pregnancies compared to the expected number.[43] This means 25 percent of expected pregnancies did occur. Another recent example of ECPs is the high dose progestogen, levonorgestrel, which is 89 percent effective.[44]

A study involving women of proven fertility showed pregnancy rates for sexual intercourse near the time of ovulation ranged from 50 percent within 3 days of ovulation to 66.7 percent (6 pregnancies from 9 cycles) on the day of ovulation to 20.5 percent 2 days after ovulation. These results were based on self-observation of mucus symptoms, not objective criteria of ovulation. The pregnancy rate for 309 cycles over 8 fertile days was 18 percent but for 197 cycles over 7 days it was 23 percent.[45] In the general population the conception rate of unprotected intercourse per cycle is generally put at 25 percent, at 60–70 percent for six months, at 80–90 percent for 12 months, and 90–5 percent for 24 months.[46] Research which involved 221 women who planned to become pregnant showed that in 625 menstrual cycles for which dates for ovulation could be estimated, 192 (31 percent) conceptions occurred during the 6-day period ending on the estimated day of ovulation. Evidence of conception was based on an elevated level of hCG produced by a blastocyst. If intercourse occurred every other day during these 6 days, the conception rate was estimated to be 33 percent, but it was 15 percent if intercourse randomly occurred only once.[47] It needs to be remembered that the timing of the fertile period can be very unpredictable, even for women whose cycles are regular.[48]

Within 5 minutes of sexual intercourse the first batch of sperm reach the fallopian tubes where conception normally occurs.[49] Although the median life of sperm in a woman's genital tract is 1 to 3 days after intercourse, sperm are able to live in a woman's cervical crypts for up to 6 days and still be able to fertilize an egg. But an egg is only capable of being fertilized for about 12 hours, and at most 24 hours, after ovulation. Most eggs are fertilized by sperm derived from intercourse one or more days before ovulation. It is not surprising, then, to find that an important review article concluded it is likely the Yuzpe regimen mainly works by suppressing ovulation.[50] In fact, research shows the Yuzpe regimen prevents ovulation in 21–7 percent of cases when taken one or more days before the expected ovulation day, whereas progestogen-only ECPs inhibit ovulation in 33 percent of cases when given 3–4 days before ovulation, and possibly even longer.[51]

Contraceptives – abortifacient?

It is ethically necessary to distinguish contraceptive methods which prevent pregnancy by impeding implantation of an embryo from the use of pills which suppress ovulation and/or methods which prevent conception. Progestogen only pills, *mini pills*, prevent conception by inhibiting ovulation in about half of the cycles, and in the others by thickening the cervical mucus to block sperm penetration or by thinning the endometrial lining of the uterus, which may impede an embryo from implanting. They also reduce the number, and action, of the cilia (hairlike outgrowths) in the fallopian tube which may slow the transport of the ovum and thereby affect fertilization and possibly sperm capacitation and presumably account for an increase in the rate of ectopic pregnancies above normal.[52] The pregnancy rate per year for perfect users is

0.5 percent but for typical users it is estimated to be about 5 percent.[53] It is not known the extent to which the progestogen-only pills prevent implantation.[54]

The primary mode of action of the combined estrogen-progestogen oral contraceptive pill is the inhibition of ovulation and the thickening of the mucus which makes it impenetrable for sperm and so impedes transport to the fallopian tubes; it also changes the morphology of the endometrium whereby it may be unreceptive to the implantation of an embryo, but this is not its primary mode of action.[55] Since combined pills suppress ovulation more effectively than mini pills, it is no surprise that their *method* failure pregnancy rate is 0.1–1 percent and for typical users the failure rate is 3–6.2 percent.[56]

There is evidence that in women using progestogen-only pills the ectopic pregnancy rate is about 6 percent, and 0 percent for women using the combined pill.[57] As noted earlier, the incidence of ectopic pregnancy in the general population is about 2 percent. This is supported by further evidence that the use of both types of pills at the time of conception were associated with more effective prevention of intrauterine pregnancy than ectopic pregnancy.[58] This supports the view that both pills have a slight undetermined risk of preventing intrauterine pregnancy by impeding implantation.[59] Without providing any scientific evidence of the precise incidence of the prevention of implantation, an important study concluded

> These data suggest that the morphological changes in the endometrium of OC users have functional significance and provide evidence that reduced endometrial receptivity does indeed contribute to the contraceptive efficacy of OCs.[60]

John Wilks has shown how oral contraceptives could prevent implantation but does not give any rate of its incidence.[61]

Norplant is an effective progestogen contraceptive implant. It mainly prevents ovulation, thickens the cervical mucus which acts as a barrier to sperm to prevent conception and also thins the lining of the endometrium. After a month long trial of 32 sexually active women using Norplant, there was no evidence of blastocysts producing hCG when a sensitive and specific assay was used that can detect hCG as early as 7 days after ovulation. This shows no blastocysts were formed. It was suggested that hostility to sperm penetration of the mucus and impaired maturation of oocytes prevented fertilization when ovulation did occur. It was admitted hCG could not be detected before 5 days in the

Norplant group and in the 20 noncontracepting control women of proven fertility who were trying to conceive. It was concluded that early or menstrual abortion was not a part of Norplant's mechanism of action.[62] A later study noted that Norplant induced an abnormal hormonal milieu which could render fertilization more difficult and that subclinical abortion among Norplant users was very exceptional. It was concluded that subclinical abortion does not contribute to Norplant's efficacy.[63]

The possibility that both pills discussed may prevent implantation does not imply this occurs. In addition to the direct evidence for Norplant, there is indirect evidence these pills do rarely have an early abortifacient action as a side-effect.[64] However, bearing in mind the high natural losses of early human embryos, scientific grounds are lacking to say that the efficacy of all three contraceptive methods discussed above actually depends on an abortifacient effect. As in the Norplant trial, more accurate results could be obtained by taking relevant hCG readings of three large groups of women, each of which uses one of these contraceptive methods.

5.4 Long-term Sequelae of Abortion

A single abortion appears to have little or no significant sequelae or effects on a woman's menstrual or gynaecological morbidity or on subsequent preterm delivery in teenage pregnancies. In a survey of 690 women who had an abortion in the last 4–7 years, the sterility rate increased from 2 percent in the control group to 3.6 percent. Prostaglandin-induced abortion does not seem to affect cervical competence during future pregnancies, but termination during the second trimester performed by mechanical dilatation of the cervix could result in some long-term damage.[65]

It is difficult to obtain an accurate account of the emotional consequences of induced abortions that are not influenced by the positive and negative attitudes of the authors of studies in relation to abortion itself. The later the termination in the second trimester, the greater the negative psychological sequelae are for the woman. Women who have an induced abortion for social reasons, experience more guilt than those who have a spontaneous abortion. There is evidence that women whose pregnancies are terminated medically experience more guilt than those whose pregnancies are terminated surgically. But women having repeat abortions have a preference for medical abortion, probably on account of its less invasive nature. The experience of guilt and loss of self-esteem by both parents for not having formed a healthy child are compounded by the deliberate decision to terminate a previously wanted pregnancy.[66] Again women who terminate pregnancies following detection of fetal defects experience poorer psychological outcomes and acute grief – up to 20 percent even two years later, not to mention depression and guilt.[67]

Coerced abortion, prior emotional problems, and youth are risk factors for developing adverse psychological sequelae. Postabortion trauma may be provoked by a pregnancy-related event such as friends having babies or political debates on abortion. It may also be increased by a lack of adequate prior information on the adverse sequelae likely to be experienced in subsequent years coupled with the lack of support from family and friends.[68] There is evidence of deliberate infliction of self-harm by those who had a termination or who were refused an abortion. In some cases the degree of psychological harm experienced by women who have an abortion supports the case for continuing, rather than terminating, pregnancy.[69]

Brief periods of distress are commonly experienced after an abortion, but this is not a psychiatric disorder. Many women suffer significant postabortion trauma and seek professional help, but this alone gives no indication of the percentage of women who regret that they had an abortion. Inability to cope with an unwanted pregnancy is central to the problem. The adverse sequelae occurring in women after an abortion are long-term in about 10 percent of cases. At times these sequelae seem to be the flow-on of symptoms present prior to abortion, e.g. emotional instability or history of psychiatric illness. The risk of harm after an abortion is greater among younger women, those with poor social support and those from sociocultural groups which are opposed to abortion. There is also evidence of enduring adverse psychological sequelae in both the mothers and children when abortion is denied.[70] In a Finnish study it was found that the suicide rate after an induced abortion was three times greater than the general suicide rate for women aged 15–49 years. It was concluded that there may be common risk factors for both suicide and induced abortion or that induced abortion may have a harmful effect on mental health.[71]

It seems clear that professional counseling is required to advise women of the likely short- and long-term implications of having an abortion so that their decisions may be truly informed and free. The full implications of abortion for a woman may not become apparent until she has experienced a pregnancy to term. Many questions remain unanswered. Better research conducted on the psychological effects experienced by a broad cross-section of women who have had an abortion would be helpful. Women who experience postabortion depression, grief, and guilt do not return to abortion clinics for counseling, but seek it elsewhere. The need to safeguard informed and free consent prior to abortion seems to require that preabortion counseling should be offered by agencies other than the providers of abortion.

5.5 Fetus with Anencephaly

As we shall see in chapter 7, it is now possible to detect many lethal fetal abnormalities with certainty by about 16 weeks gestation. Examples of untreatable lethal anomalies are some chromosomal defects and anencephaly, a neural tube disease, on which I will focus since most newborns with anencephaly die within 12 hours of birth. The normal elevation of the neural tube folds is impeded, leading on about day 24 after ovulation to the proximate cause of anencephaly, i.e. a failure of closure of the anterior end of the neural groove which develops into the brain. The posterior end closes on day 28 after fertilization, by which time all neural tube defects are determined. The anterior opening in the tube allows the protrusion of the developing and differentiated brain where exposure to amniotic fluid causes its degeneration and collapse by 8 weeks post ovulation. It is thought that the failure of the cranial vault formation is, for the most part, secondary to the initial brain malformation.[72]

The permanent absence of the cerebral hemispheres means that the fetus with anencephaly will never exercise rational and free acts. The brain stem, however, continues to function. It connects with the upper part of the spinal cord and controls automatic functions like respiration and heart beat. The fetus sometimes presents with other nonneural malformations of the heart, lungs, pituitary or adrenal glands. It is one of the most frequently found conditions that is incompatible with sustained life, both before and after birth.[73] It has been estimated that the incidence of neural tube defects drops dramatically from 2.5 percent of embryos on day 26 to 0.06 percent at term and that most of these are lost by the end of the eighth week. An interplay of environmental and genetic factors is believed to be important for causing anencephaly. It occurs more in Ireland and the UK than anywhere else.[74]

The remote underlying causes of anencephaly are not known for certain. Multivitamins and folic acid must be involved since an increase in their intake prior to the time of conception decreases the incidence of neural tube and other birth defects considerably. The diet of women contemplating pregnancy should include leafy green vegetables since they are rich in folate; or folic acid supplements available from pharmacies should be taken.[75] The original cause of anencephaly may be traced back to a defect involving multiple biochemical metabolic abnormalities, including folic acid, in the third week after fertilization.[76] It seems that there is a genetic predisposition, but not a genetic determination, for anencephaly. Up to 95 percent of these infants are born to families with no previous history of neural tube defects.[77]

In 1975, before prenatal diagnosis was widespread, Australian statistics show that of 131 *fetal deaths* with anencephaly, it is known when 115 died in relation to labor. Of these, 34 died a few weeks before labor had commenced and 81 died during labor. The final weeks of pregnancy, then, are life-threatening for fetuses with anencephaly.[78] In the same year there were 49 newborns with anencephaly of whom 34 died under 12 hours, including 17 who died within an hour of birth, and the remaining 15 died in the following week.[79] This means of 180 anencephalic perinatal deaths, 73 percent (131) were fetal and 27 percent (49) were neonatal. Far more fetuses with anencephaly die before birth than after. These facts are important for a complete ethical evaluation.

It can be calculated from Australian statistics for *neonatal deaths* from anencephaly and similar lethal anomalies for the years 1988–95 that of 139 live-born infants, 119 (86 percent) died within a day (63 of whom died within an hour of birth), 13 (9 percent) died a day later, and the remaining 7 (5 percent) died before day 6.[80] Australia's live birth rate for anencephaly dropped from 5.1 per 10,000 births in 1985 to 1.7 in 1994. This drop would be explained by the rise in prenatal diagnosis and the rise in the number of reported induced abortions for anencephaly from 3 in 1985 to 84 in 1994.[81]

Labor and delivery of fetuses with anencephaly at term is excessively difficult because brow presentation and shoulder dystocia is likely to cause the baby to be stuck in the birth canal, and cause extreme trauma to the mother as well as a high risk of pre-eclampsia, hypertension, hemorrhage, and subsequent difficulties in pregnancy or delivery. A caesarean section is usually required on account of unacceptably high risks in labor for the mother. This would usually result in the death of the baby because of a lack of a cranial vault to protect the baby's brain from sudden exposure to atmospheric pressure and tearing as the head is lifted out. Both kinds of delivery would be exceptionally painful for infants with anencephaly. They may need tubal feeding or a drip in some circumstances to satisfy their nutritional requirements. They may begin to suck from 32 weeks but lack the ability to do so in a sustained and coordinated way up to term. Some nourishment may be taken from the breast or a bottle for the short period of life at their disposal.

Not even a normal fetus can live outside the uterus at 16 weeks' gestational age beyond a few minutes. The cause of death for a normal infant delivered from 16 to 20 weeks would be an incapacity to inflate the lungs due to lung immaturity. Prior to the use of the neonatal intensive care unit (NICU) in England and Wales during 1946–50, all babies weighing <1000 g at birth died. This was equivalent to about 28 weeks' gestation or less.[82] Only 9 percent of infants born alive between 24 and 28 weeks in a large tertiary care center from 1966–1970 survived at a time when intensive care did not include much beyond parenteral infusions of glucose and electrolytes.[83] Before the days of NICU, by 29 weeks 30 percent of all newborns were capable of long-term survival, by 30 weeks over 50 percent survived, by 32 weeks over 60 percent survived, by 33 weeks at least 66 percent survived, and by 34 weeks over 80 percent survived.[84]

The application of a prostaglandin gel to soften the cervix, followed by appropriately regulated doses of oxytocin and the rupturing of the membranes, would generally enable the live birth of an infant with a lethal abnormality after 33 weeks. Death would almost certainly be caused by the infant's lethal defect, not prematurity. Since most infants begin to develop a coordinated ability to suck from 34 weeks there is normally a partial need for tube feeding up to this stage.

5.6 Ethical Evaluation of Issues During Pregnancy

Reasons in favor of abortion

Many women do not believe abortion is immoral, especially before they have become mothers themselves. To many abortion is a matter for each pregnant woman to decide, provided she understands what is involved. It is seen by some to be a matter of a woman's autonomy to control her own body and fertility in relation to letting a pregnancy go to term unless she wants her baby. Abortion is perceived by some as an issue of women's reproductive rights and no longer a remedy for rape or a matter of saving the mother's life. Abortion is now seen by many to be a matter of women's health, to be decided by women alone, not by society's lawmakers, religious leaders, or doctors. Others who recognize women's rights believe fetuses acquire rights once they become patients after viability, from which stage a woman's right to abortion may be restricted.[85]

Granted the enormous impact these attitudes have had in western culture, it is easy to appreciate why women with unwanted pregnancies see few moral problems in having recourse to safe induced abortion. Research shows that of 30 primigravid women who wanted their pregnancies to go to term, most did not recognize their fetuses as persons early in the pregnancy and only referred to their fetus as their baby in the third trimester. In fact up to 8–12 weeks' gestation, 70 percent did not believe the fetus was a real person. By 18–22 weeks' gestation, after fetal movements had been felt, perceptions changed, and 63 percent said their fetus was a real person. By 36 weeks 92 percent believed the fetus was a person.[86]

I have already discussed in chapter 1 the view of philosophers who hold that a person could not be formed before the capacity for exercising minimal rational self-conscious acts is acquired. I also dealt with the ethical implications of this view in chapters 3 and 4, namely that a fetus would have no intrinsic value before sentience and no personal rights before birth. Christopher Belshaw argues along these lines in the context of the abortion debate.[87] For those who do not hold the fetus is a person, utilitarian criteria are used to justify abortion for health, personal, social, or economic reasons, provided a painless method is used. In this, they agree with Aristotle who permitted abortion for population control, but insisted it be done before a fetus was capable of sensation or of feeling pain.[88] Richard Hare believes abortion is prima facie and in general wrong because it stops a person coming into existence but that countervailing reasons could morally permit it.[89] Laura Purdy accepts women have duties, but not absolute moral duties, to care for their fetuses: "women's rights might sometimes trump considerations about fetal welfare."[90]

Mary Anne Warren argues for the right to abortion on the grounds it would be unreal to expect women to avoid sexual relations with men when pregnancy is not wanted, in view of the unreliability of contraceptives or the lack of access to them for some women.[91] She also discusses whether the "personlikeness" of the fetus should be a sufficient basis to warrant moral respect be shown to the fetus. She dismisses this because the fetus lacks self-awareness and the capacity to reason or communicate in a variety of ways. Because the fetus is less "personlike" than a mature mammal or the average fish, she concludes that the fetus would not "have any more right to life than, let us say, a newborn guppy."[92] And certainly, she says, this limited right to life is not greater than a woman's right to abortion.

A case in defense of abortion is made by Judith Jarvis Thomson who, for the sake of argument, is prepared to grant that the fetus is a person.[93] She argues that a kidnapped woman would not be obliged to remain connected to a famous unconscious violinist with damaged kidneys who depended for survival on support from her kidneys for 9 months. She says a woman has rights over her own body in virtue of her autonomy as a person. She admits both are innocent and have a right to life. However, she argues that the woman would have no moral duty, if she had a choice, to remain kidnapped in hospital to save the famous violinist's life, heroic and generous though such a gesture would be. The violinist would have no right to the lifesaving use of the woman's body, even if only one hour were needed. She applies the same argument to the fetus in the uterus as a result of rape. The fetus would not have a right to remain in the woman's uterus until birth and the woman would have no moral duty to carry the pregnancy to term. She admits a woman may have a duty out of decency to allow the fetus to remain in her uterus for a very short time to save its life, but this would not imply a strict right of the fetus to remain in the uterus. The general argument may be extended to the rights of a woman over her body in the case of a "mistaken pregnancy" so that she would not be morally obliged to carry a pregnancy for nine months.

Thompson, in this case, made a judgment on the act in itself, regardless of the consequences. Utilitarians would probably disagree and argue that the overall benefit in the case of the famous violinist, would tip the utilitarian scales in favor of the duty of the woman to remain connected to the violinist for 9 months to save their life. On the contrary, the utilitarian balance would probably not tip in favor of a fetus conceived as a result of rape.

Subsequently, Thompson developed her thinking and says her denial of a right to life for the fertilized egg or fetus is based on "the idea that having rights presupposes having interests."[94] She admits, however, that she has "no conclusive reason for denying that fertilized eggs have a right to life."[95] But she denies that the doctrine for the right to life from conception can be known to be true by reason and asserts, "There is nothing unreasonable or irrational in believing that the doctrine is false" or "entirely without support."[96] She then argues her case that abortion should not be illegal "on a ground that neither reason nor the rest of morality requires women to accept . . . the reason for the constraint has to be one that the constrained are unreasonable in rejecting."[97] As I said in chapter 1, this view is consistent for one who does not believe in an immaterial soul.

Reasons opposed to direct abortion

One needs the courage of King David and the wisdom of Solomon to embark on the moral evaluation of abortion. It is not a matter of judging the motives of a woman who has an abortion, but of giving an account of the morality of *direct* abortion based on respect for human life from conception.[98] Pope John Paul II taught *direct abortion*, namely,

> abortion willed as an end or as a means, always constitutes a grave moral disorder since it is the deliberate killing of an innocent human being.[99]

The immorality of abortion is the same whether it is achieved by surgical or pharmacological means.

What underpins this teaching is the personal status of the fetus and embryo which has already been discussed in earlier chapters. The philosophical basis for according the fetus the status of a person is found in the rational nature of the human fetus whose life principle is an immaterial soul which actuates the body, including the dynamism of the genetic code which directs organized growth and development at the empirical level. Human life is a basic good and a condition for the experience of values, including freedom, autonomy, and being a moral agent. A fetus is a subject of intrinsic worth and personal value before acquiring an ability to express rationally self-conscious acts. This stand is supported by a philosophical belief in God as Creator of an immaterial life principle as well as respect for fetal development.[100] It is anomalous that the value of the life of a fetus should depend on the choice of the mother and/or father. The fetus is defenseless and totally dependent on the mother for support and survival. Janet Podell, a former pro-choice feminist, changed her mind after having her first child:

> It was impossible to ignore the plain fact that this baby was the same living being who had been kicking me in the ribs for months. His life was clearly an uninterruptible continuum that had begun long before I could feel him move . . .[101]

Abortion deprives a real person, not merely a potential person, of life and of the opportunity to develop to the age of reason when free and morally responsible acts can be made.[102] One should always treat illness and alleviate the suffering of a pregnant woman but not by *direct* abortion, which is a breach of the duty of care owed to the fetus by the mother and doctors. It would be unethical to alleviate the trauma of a woman made pregnant by rape to choose induced or *direct* abortion as a means. In cases of an unwanted pregnancy it would be unethical, out of misguided compassion, to approve *direct* abortion or to materially cooperate at close hand to procure it. A pregnant woman's right over her body does not include a right to deliberately terminate the life of a fetus. In cases of third trimester and late term abortions, the fetus is viable and capable of extrauterine life independently of the mother when given neonatal intensive care. This fact usually makes late term abortions morally repugnant even for those who are not opposed to early abortions.[103]

The taking of *postcoital* drugs with the purpose of preventing an embryo implanting in the uterus is the equivalent of a *direct* abortion. Hence these drugs are called abortifacients.[104] The primary purpose of the *contraceptive methods* considered above is the suppression of ovulation and/or the prevention of fertilization. These methods do not depend on an abortifacient effect to prevent pregnancy, even though rarely this may occur. Their use for contraceptive purposes would not be unethical from a pro-life perspective even if there is a very slight risk of preventing implantation as an unwanted side effect. Drug companies, even if not obliged by law, should include accurate information on the modes of action of contraceptive products in the customer information leaflet so that women may choose methods that do not involve any significant risk to possible early embryos.

The duty of reasonable care of a pregnant woman to her previable fetus does not preclude the performance of a medically necessary procedure whose object or immediate purpose is to save the pregnant woman from a life-threatening condition if it could not be delayed until the fetus was potentially viable outside the uterus. This would not be a *direct* abortion since the death of the fetus would be an unwanted and justified side effect.[105] An example would be the necessary and lifesaving removal of a pregnant woman's malignant cancerous uterus with its previable fetus. In a case of ectopic pregnancy in the fallopian tube, it would be ethical to remove the pathological section enclosing a previable fetus or simply the chorionic villi and fetus, leaving the tube still functional, provided there is no *direct* harmful assault on the fetus.[106] When there is heavy bleeding caused by the placenta prematurely separating from the uterus it would not appeear to be a *direct* abortion nor unethical to induce early labor to complete an irreversible miscarriage of a previable fetus to save the life of the mother instead of losing both mother and fetus. Likewise, in a rare case of severe very early onset pre-eclampsia/eclampsia, delivery of the placenta and previable fetus by induction of labor or caesarean section would not seem to be *direct* abortion if this was the only way to save the mother from imminent death due to multiple organ failure caused by a pathological placenta with abnormal trophoblastic invasion of the maternal arteries, including fetal DNA.[107]

In this book I have restricted my treatment of abortion to its ethical aspects. The termination of a pregnancy is a tragedy for both the pregnant women and her fetus. Abortion is not a good thing, but for many it is seen as a necessary evil. Most doctors would prefer to use their expertise and skills to save and not terminate life. It is difficult for an appreciation of the intrinsic value of human life at all stages to thrive in a pro-choice society. Humanity risks losing its moorings if a pregnancy is deemed a simple mistake to be erased at will.

Treatment of women who have been raped

Women who have been raped are often immobilized by shock and need professional counseling to cope with the trauma caused by the assault. They need to be able to turn to a significant, trusted, and understanding person who will help them access immediate medical care from a doctor with the appropriate skills, including forensic training. Professional care minimizes the effect that the assault has on victims' lives. Follow-up counseling would also be needed for the women, their families, and supportive friends.

Victims of rape need encouragement to report the crime to police and to freely consent to provide samples for DNA testing as forensic evidence of the attack so that rapists can be brought to justice.[108] An assessment needs to be made of their degree of psychological trauma, which is often severe, and they need to be given appropriate psychiatric or psychological therapy. An ethical response to rape cannot ignore the prolonged trauma experienced by these women, especially if pregnancy results. It is hard for people who have not been subjected to sexual assault and pregnancy resulting from it to grasp the indignity suffered and the degree of personal pain inflicted and possibly life long brokenness yet to be endured.

Sexual offenses are crimes and should be denounced as such. The presence of sperm in the woman's reproductive tract represents an extension of the injustice of the original sexual assault if conception is possible. Since we are dealing with an act of violence it is ethically permissible to prevent conception after rape. The same applies if rape occurs within a marriage relationship because sexual intercourse without consent is not a marital act. However, from the perspective of the sanctity of human life, it would be unethical to deliberately prevent the implantation of an embryo which results from rape. It needs to be admitted, however, that some rape victims in their confusion and distress, may, in good faith, believe they are morally justified to prevent an embryo from implanting or to have an early abortion.

In rape cases, it would seldom be known with certainty whether ovulation had already occurred or was due to occur on the day of rape, because the assault might have happened on any day of the woman's cycle. However, after a blood test she could be advised if the rape took place during her fertile period and whether it was possible for conception to have occurred on one of her seven fertile days, including the day after ovulation. For most of the cycle, then, ECPs would have no effect: they would not inhibit ovulation nor implantation.

In the light of the estimates given earlier, and assuming rape was the only instance of unprotected intercourse occurring randomly during a woman's fertile period and the correct doses of EPCs (Yuzpe regimen) were taken, the actual number of pregnancies for 100 raped women would drop from the expected number of 15 to *four*. This would be due to the regimen's 75 percent success rate, i.e. a 25 percent failure rate of *four* pregnancies – not an effective abortifacient at all. This means 11 expected pregnancies would have been prevented. It is unlikely that all of the failed pregnancies would be due to the prevention of implantation since it is known that EPCs suppress ovulation in 25 percent of cases if taken one or more days before the expected day of ovulation. Add to this that conception might be prevented by impeding sperm transport. Conservatively, one could assume that the risk to the life of an embryo would be about 8 percent or less. Indeed in the light of today's knowledge of EPCs' mode of action, it has been suggested their pregnancy failures

> may be more likely if ovulation and fertilization have already taken place at the time of treatment and, thus, prevention of implantation may not be one of the primary modes of action.[109]

It would seem to be ethically permissible to administer ECPs as soon as possible within 72 hours of rape to prevent conception if, after inquiry, there were no reasonable grounds to believe an embryo had been already conceived. In this case a risk of loss of an embryo due to the medication would not be more than about 8 percent, not disproportionate or significant after rape.[110] By the same token it would be ethical for an accidentally injured pregnant woman to have necessary, but not lifesaving, surgery, if it were to pose a similar risk to the life of her fetus. But an ECP could not ethically be taken if a test showed conception had, or most likely had, occurred. On ethical as well as medical grounds ECPs should not be used for family planning. But fear of their abuse does not negate their right use after rape. I agree with the US Catholic Bishops who said that a woman who has been raped may defend herself from conception from it and approved the following:

> If, after appropriate testing, there is no evidence that conception has occurred already, she may be treated with medications that would prevent ovulation, sperm capacitation or fertilization.[111]

Early delivery of a fetus with anencephaly

Nature of the ethical problem

Fetuses with anencephaly warrant special attention because of the serious ethical problems that their condition poses for pro-life parents and doctors. While some mothers are willing to allow these pregnancies to go to term, others find it too distressing once they know that their babies will inevitably die of their lethal abnormality soon after birth. The question arises whether the duty of reasonable care requires a pregnant woman whose fetus is affected by anencephaly to let her pregnancy go to term, or whether it is ethically permissible to induce early delivery once the diagnosis has been made. An ethical answer to this problem cannot ignore the above-mentioned facts relating to delivery of premature normal and abnormal fetuses.

Granted the lack of scientific evidence mentioned above for a genetically determined cause of anencephaly and in the light of the evidence of the proximate origin of anencephaly at 24–6 days after fertilization, this fetus should be accorded the status of a person from conception. It is difficult to deny that the infant with anencephaly who has a heart beat and can breathe spontaneously is a human individual. The individual's brain formation began but is incomplete, resulting in an individual with a poorly functioning brain-stem and malformed, degenerated hemispheres. The fetus and infant with anencephaly is a human individual

with a rational nature on account of a divinely created immaterial soul
or life principle and who, due to a malformed cortex and brain damage,
will never to able to express rational activities. We are not dealing with
an individual who is "brainless," "brain-absent," or "brain-dead." In
the light of what has been said in chapter 4, no convincing philosophical argument has been presented to warrant denying the status of a
human individual and person to the fetus and infant with anencephaly.[112]

What an anencephalic pregnancy can cause to the fetal-maternal relationship is relevant in ethical decision-making. As we have seen, labor
and the delivery of these fetuses are difficult at term. Shoulder dystocia
can cause the baby to become stuck in the birth canal, resulting in
extreme trauma and a high risk of hemorrhage in the mother. A caesarean section is sometimes needed for the mother's health. Due to the
absence of the cranial vault, birth at term is often painful for the baby.
Moral principles, however, require that a living human individual, no
matter how deformed, be treated respectfully as a person until the
contrary is proven beyond reasonable doubt.[113] As we have seen, in
Australia in 1975 over two-thirds of fetuses with anencephaly died
before birth, and of these about 30 percent died a few weeks before labor
had commenced and about 70 percent during labor.

Case in favor of delivery from 16 weeks

Fetuses with anencephaly will never be capable of long-term survival.
They will never be able to actualize their potential to exercise rational
and personal acts: their typically *human* development is complete. Maintaining such a pregnancy, it is said, merely "preserves limited physiologic
growth."[114] On this basis an ethical case is made for early delivery once
the diagnosis of anencephaly is confirmed with certainty from 16 weeks.
It is argued that to relieve her distress the mother would be justified to
withdraw her life-support of pregnancy by early induction and thereby
allow her defective fetus to die of its inherent fatal condition soon after
delivery. This early delivery need not be deemed a lethal act or *direct*
abortion provided the fetus is not deliberately killed. The guiding
analogy employed is that there is no ethical duty to provide treatment
that is extraordinary, disproportionate, excessively burdensome, or even
futile to sustain human life.

It is thought by those who support this opinion that it is different
from *direct* abortion of a fetus whose death is caused by removal from
the uterus because the fetus is too premature to survive outside the supportive environment of the uterus.[115] Long-term survival of an infant

with anencephaly outside the uterus is impossible on account of a defect that is incompatible with extrauterine life. Whether a fetus with anencephaly is delivered at 16, 24 or 40 weeks, death follows soon after birth. The extra weeks of uterine life would not be of any benefit to the fetus and would cause additional distress to the mother. This is not saying that the fetus has no value. It is saying that the prolonging of uterine life of a fetus with anencephaly would be of no value to the fetus. It seems too much for a mother to await the painful experience of labor at term, followed by the death of her child caused by a lethal pathology, not early delivery. It has also been suggested that early delivery could be equated with spontaneous abortion, the correcting of an error of nature, since most miscarried fetuses are grossly deformed.[116]

Case against delivery from 16 weeks

There is some appeal in the above line of reasoning and one could easily understand that some mothers in good faith would have recourse to early delivery at this stage. However, the reasons given are not convincing. Although pregnancy can be burdensome, it is a natural supportive environment for the fetus and cannot really be compared to an extraordinary artificial life-support system as though it were *medical treatment* to cure disease or some pathology. A lethally deformed fetus is still a living human individual and a person towards whom a duty of reasonable care is owed.

Granted we are dealing with fetuses with lethal anomalies, it would be futile to unduly prolong the dying process by employing NICU facilities after early delivery. The delivery of a normal fetus from 16–28 weeks' gestation would *per se* be a *lethal act* since at that stage not even a healthy fetus could survive without NICU. Knowing that a fetus is afflicted with anencephaly does not ethically justify Feinberg's position of terminating the life of a severely malformed fetus whose prospects for life after birth would be hopeless.[117] Justice and the duty of reasonable care rule out the deliberate termination of a pregnancy if the fetus would soon die of prematurity.

It is not convincing to argue that early delivery in these cases would be the ethical equivalent of imitating nature's way of eliminating grossly deformed fetuses. The primary purpose of pregnancy is not to lose fetuses, but to enable a fetus to develop and grow to the stage of maturity required for survival without the life-support provided by the uterus. A 100 percent probability of some aged and seriously sick people dying naturally within a short space of time is no excuse for imitating nature to accelerate their encounter with death by euthanasia. The deliberate nontherapeutic early induction of a fetus with anencephaly, or even of a healthy fetus, before any normal fetus would be mature enough to survive outside the uterus without NICU would be ethically indistinguishable from *direct* abortion. The fetus would die of prematurity as a direct result of early induction, not anencephaly.

Criteria for early delivery of a fetus with anencephaly

Each case needs to be assessed for the good of both mother and fetus when making judgments that are both clinically and ethically correct in the light of the earlier discussion of the medical facts and the statistics on the natural death rates of fetuses with anencephaly before and during normal labor. There are limits to the duty of care owed by a pregnant woman to a fetus with a certain diagnosis of anencephaly. It is enough to bear in mind what has been said above regarding the hazards to the mother during labor at term if a fetus with anencephaly presents with a low brow and shoulder and the risk of a caesarean delivery. It seems unreasonable to require a pregnant woman to carry a pregnancy to term beyond the limits of the duty of reasonable care against her reasonable request, only to await the death of her child soon after birth. Births of normal fetuses are induced up to two weeks early for the health of the mother or for reasons of social convenience without any detriment to the health of the newborn infant.

It seems the moral respect due to a fetus with anencephaly who has no prospects of long-term survival could be ethically reconciled with a compassionate desire to alleviate her distress and minimize potential health risks for the mother. This could be done by inducing labor at a stage when a healthy fetus would have a reasonable chance of survival with fewer health risks for the mother. Bearing in mind that clinical assessments vary for each individual case, induction from 33 completed weeks would seem reasonable since normal infants have a two out of three chance of survival from 33 weeks without treatment in NICU. The mother could have the consolation of nursing her baby until natural death occurs due to the infant's inherent lethal condition. This stage was deemed to be the threshold of viability prior to NICU. Henry Davis summed up the moral consensus of the 1950s as follows:

> Expulsion of the fetus between the seventh and the ninth month is premature birth or acceleration of birth, not abortion.[118]

In such cases the risk of death from immaturity would be absorbed by the greater risk of death caused by anencephaly itself soon after birth. In effect, the early induction of labor from about 33 completed weeks would almost certainly not expose infants with anencephaly to any new risk of death beyond that of their lethal defect, granted it would not be appropriate to place them in a NICU. By this stage the mother's duty of reasonable care for her fetus would have been satisfied. The withdrawal of pregnancy support by early induction would not be *direct* abortion since the normal fetus would also have reasonable prospects of long-term survival at this stage.[119] Maternal distress is relieved by early induction of a fetus for whom continuing pregnancy would not be morally obligatory and who would die of a lethal defect, not prematurity.[120] It goes without saying that comfort and nursing care, including nutrition and hydration according to need and appropriate to the condition of the newborn, should always be provided. Even in the case of a late term induction of a fetus with a lethal defect, the cause of death would be the lethal defect, not induction.

Infertility
and Artificial
Reproductive
Technology

Ethical debates have not ceased on *in vitro* fertilization (IVF) since the birth of Louise Brown, the first IVF baby, was born on July 25, 1978 in the UK. In Australia in 1996 there were 3,164 births after artificial reproductive technology (ART), accounting for 1.2 percent of all births.[1] Before entering into a discussion and evaluation of the ethical issues arising from the treatment of infertility, it is necessary to understand what is meant by infertility, its treatment options, their success rates, and the burdens experienced by couples undergoing treatment.[2]

6.1 Infertility

Incidence and causes

It is important to distinguish infertility from sterility. A person who is unable to generate any offspring is sterile, e.g. a woman who has no ovarian follicles or a man who does not produce any sperm. Sterility occurs in 3–5 percent of couples.[3] Infertility, on the other hand, is an inability to conceive for one to two years by a couple who are having acts of unprotected sexual intercourse during the woman's fertile days.[4] From 10–15 percent of married couples are infertile.[5] The incidence of infertility increases with age, particularly of the female partner. Three national US surveys found that 7 percent of couples whose female partners were aged 20–4 years were infertile, 9 percent for those aged 25–9, 15 percent for those aged 30–4 years, 22 percent for those aged 35–9, and 29 percent for those aged 40–4 years.[6] Infertility statistics include cases of tubal ligation and vasectomy. While the normal monthly fertility rate ranges from 15 to 20 percent, subfertile couples where the woman is less than 30 years of age may have a monthly fertility rate of 4–5 percent for up to 3 years.[7]

The causes of a couple's infertility may be in one or both partners. A woman may fail to ovulate due to a hormonal disorder or because of polycystic ovary syndrome. Occasionally a superfertile partner can make up for what is lacking in a subfertile partner. The causes of infertility among couples who presented for infertility treatment in Australia and New Zealand in 1997 were tubal 12 percent, male factor 33 percent, endometriosis 6 percent, other causes 9 percent, multiple causes 27 percent, and unexplained 13 percent.[8] But the rates for tubal and male factors for 1979–95 were 34 percent and 19 percent respectively. The increase in male infertility in 1997 explains the drop in the percentage for tubal causes.[9] In the UK single and multiple causes of female infertility in all treatment cycles were tubal disease 36 percent, endometriosis 8 percent, unexplained 45 percent, and other 19 percent.[10] Stress is also a seasonal factor that adversely affects female fertility.[11] Although one cause of infertility may be dominant, often more than one factor may affect a couple's fertility.

In the USA it has been suggested that female infertility is caused by failure to produce fertile eggs in 10–15 percent of cases and by pelvic factors like endometriosis, infection, or tubal blockage in 30–40 percent of cases. Education could prevent, or at least minimize, female infertility caused by infection associated with sexually transmitted diseases. Some women fail to ovulate as a result of chemotherapy, surgery or other causes. Others do not want to use their own eggs if they are carriers of a serious inherited disorder such as hemophilia. In these cases recourse to donor eggs is less frequent if use is made of preimplantation genetic diagnosis (PGD) which enables couples to select and implant only their own healthy genetic embryos. Male infertility is caused in 30–40 percent of cases by low sperm count (less than 20 million sperm per ml. of semen), low motility, high viscosity of semen, or insufficient semen. A further 10–15 percent of infertility is caused by sperm being impeded from penetrating cervical mucus. The cause of infertility is unknown in about 10 percent of couples.[12]

The sperm count in men is falling at an alarming rate of >2 percent every year. The evidence indicates the likely causes are the effects of environmental chemicals, e.g. pesticides, on the human reproductive system and xeno-estrogens which imitate the action of the female hormone estrogen on male reproductive health.[13] However, an increase in *couple* fertility compensates for any decline in male fertility.[14] There is also evidence of increased mutations in sperm and of more genetic defects in the children of older fathers.[15] The paternal-age effect is less frequent than the maternal-age effect and is more likely to involve inheritable mutation disorders or sex chromosome errors, while the maternal-age effect is more likely to be associated with increased risks of obstetrical complications, perinatal problems or autosomal trisomies.[16]

Treatment

It frequently happens that women who have been unable to conceive for more than a year, become pregnant while awaiting treatment. Some women who have been using contraceptive pills for years may not need treatment, but simply more time for the resumption of ovulation. These possibilities need to be ruled out before undergoing infertility treatment. For some whose work times permit it, all that is needed is for the couple to make use of "timed intercourse" to coincide with natural ovulation.[17] Though infertility is more akin to a disability than a disease, most infertile couples need medical treatment after 12 months of unsuccessful attempts to conceive.[18]

Where there are ovulation defects, or the cause of infertility is unknown, **ovulation induction** may be used with a mild stimulation protocol of superovulation hormones under controlled conditions. Fertilization may then occur following artificial intrauterine insemination and/or normal sexual intercourse, with a pregnancy rate up to 33 percent.[19] Blocked fallopian tubes can also be treated by **microsurgery** with subsequent intrauterine pregnancy rates from about 25–50 percent within two years.[20] Microsurgery is not very effective for women who have been sterilized by cauterization due to the width of destruction of the fallopian tubes. After female sterilization with clips, microsurgical reversal is successful in up to 80 percent of cases. Unsuccessful attempts of reversal of vasectomy is a frequent cause of male infertility.[21]

The most frequently used infertility treatment procedure is the insemination of eggs by sperm by **IVF** followed by embryo transfer to the uterus (ET). Semen may be collected following sexual intercourse and be treated to make it less viscous and sperm more motile. The sperm and eggs, separated by an air bubble, may then be placed in a catheter and promptly injected into the fallopian tube where conception occurs. This procedure is known as *gamete intrafallopian transfer* (**GIFT**). Sperm can also be *injected under the zona pellucida* of the egg to enable fertilization to occur later on when the membranes of sperm and egg fuse. This is called subzonal insemination (**SUZI**) and may be performed in a way similar to GIFT.

Since the pregnancy rate of single embryo transfer is low, *superovulatory drugs* are commonly given to infertile women to induce the maturing of many eggs. These can be harvested transvaginally by ultrasound guidance with little or no anesthesia and several eggs can be fertilized by IVF with ET. The remaining embryos are usually frozen for future pregnancy attempts. Up to 75 percent of frozen embryos survive the freeze–thaw process prior to ET.[22] In an attempt to improve pregnancy rates, reduce the number of embryos transferred and the risk of multiple pregnancies, embryos have been successfully grown in improved cultures up to the *blastocyst stage before implantation*. This avoids implanting up to 50 percent of embryos whose development would arrest prior to the blastocyst stage when implantation begins. In a study 16 morulae and 116 blastocysts were transferred to 56 women with a 43 percent clinical pregnancy rate per transfer. Thirty-three fetal heart beats were detected at 6 weeks gestation giving a 25 percent implantation rate per embryo transferred. If the factors that influence the implantation rate after blastocyst transfer are identified, this may lead to higher ART and natural pregnancy rates.[23]

Sperm that are deficient in number or motility are infertile unassisted. Single sperm can also be micro-injected into the cytoplasm of the egg to achieve a live birth. This is called *intracytoplasmic sperm injection* (**ICSI**).[24] In practice, the problem of male infertility can be overcome because a few sperm can always be aspirated from a man's testis which can give him a reasonable chance to father a child by means of ICSI. If a woman has no eggs, or if they are chromosomally defective, IVF can proceed using donor ova. If her partner has no functional sperm AI with donor sperm can be used. Donor sperm are usually frozen. While this obviates the need for the donor to be present and allows the semen to be tested for HIV, it does reduce the sperm's motility by about half.[25] If both partners have no functional gametes, *donor gametes* could be used with IVF and the resultant embryos implanted in the uterus or an IVF donor embryo could be implanted in the infertile woman's uterus.[26]

When a woman has functional eggs but no uterus, her eggs, fertilized by her partner's sperm, may be transferred to another woman's uterus, who becomes a *surrogate mother* if she gives the child to the commissioning genetic mother after gestation and birth. A similar surrogacy arrangement could involve AI and fertilization of the surrogate mother's own egg by sperm from the infertile woman's partner. Donor sperm and egg may be used to form an embryo for implantation in a surrogacy arrangement.

The cryopreservation of mature human eggs, their thawing and IVF fertilization and development has not been very successful, with about 2 percent of oocytes producing a pregnancy to term.[27] Eggs can be cryopreserved more safely after they are dehydrated in a concentrated glucose solution which is *vitrified*, i.e. becomes glass-like, when frozen and can subsequently be fertilized by ICSI without needing to freeze embryos. Healthy children have been born using this method.[28] Cryopreservation of eggs and even of blastocysts by vitrification offers a promise of healthy ART births.[29]

A woman's frozen immature eggs in an ovarian tissue slice has the potential to be transplanted back to the woman and restore her menstrual cycles as a future clinical and insurance option. In theory this could restore natural fertility without the need of ART for conception.[30] This could enable younger women to freeze their immature eggs with fewer risks of chromosomal abnormalities than with older eggs and to mature them for later use in an ART procedure.[31] It could also benefit women with severe endometriosis or recurrent ovarian cysts and who are at risk of premature menopause. Prior to chemotherapy cancer treatment for a young woman, scientists have already successfully removed, frozen, and, after therapy, transplanted back into a 30-year-old woman her own ovarian tissue.[32] Postmenopausal women can also be treated by harvesting immature eggs from unstimulated ovaries, maturing them *in vitro* and having them fertilized by IVF. Live birth rates of these methods still need to improve and their safety guaranteed with more preclinical trials.[33]

Outcomes of treatment

While there is no confirmed evidence of increased risk of breast or ovarian cancer from the use of fertility drugs, long-term follow-up studies are needed to dissipate fears.[34] Risks of being affected by severe ovarian hyperstimulation and vascular complications are slight. Ovulation induction and intrauterine insemination are not intrusive infertility treatments with about a 33 percent pregnancy success rate per treatment cycle.[35] Since infertile couples seek treatment to have a live baby, ART success is usually given in terms of the number of live births per 100 oocyte retrieval cycles than the number of women treated since some women undergo more treatment cycles than others.

European experience shows the pregnancy rate of ICSI is generally higher than IVF for male infertility and is becoming the preferred treatment option for many infertile couples.[36] In the UK the live birth rate in 1996–7 for IVF and ICSI from 27,288 treatment cycles was 18 percent.[37] In Australia and New Zealand in 1997, the IVF viable pregnancy rate from 6,697 cycles with oocyte retrieval was 13 percent. The ICSI viable pregnancy rate from 6,234 cycles with oocyte retrieval was 14 percent. In the same year the GIFT rate was 20 percent from 1,924 cycles with oocyte retrieval.[38]

Comparisons of pregnancy rates, however, are not very meaningful unless the same definitions and practices are used. Women who have already had a live IVF birth have a higher live birth rate than women undergoing their first IVF course of treatment.[39] A higher pregnancy rate can be obtained by implanting more than three embryos at a greater risk of multiple and preterm births, by including "biochemical pregnancies" in totals, by treating patients with regular cycles below the age of 33 or by avoiding patients in the perimenopausal years.[40] Of 27,981 treatment cycles in the UK, 2,781 had *one*, 10,617 had *two*, and 14,583 had *three* embryos transferred respectively.[41] Of IVF and ET cycles in Australia in 1997, 50 percent involved two and 32 percent three embryos; in GIFT 46 percent had two and 41.5 percent had three eggs transferred.[42] The number of risky and unwanted multiple pregnancies is reduced by transferring no more than two embryos.

In the UK over the two year period 1995–7, of 24,266 treatment cycles only 96 involved women 45 years of age or more (0.4 percent)[43] In Australia and New Zealand in 1997 of 3,488 mothers who gave live births after IVF, 30 (1 percent) were 45 years or more and of 3,488 fathers 336 (10 percent) were 45 years or more. Likewise in 1997 of 505 GIFT pregnancies there were no mothers 45 years or more and 33 fathers (7 percent) were over 45.[44] Since more older women use ART, its birth rate can be expected to be lower than for the general population.

A high proportion of human conceptuses in fertile women is abnormal and do not proceed beyond the 18 cell stage of development and this would also occur in IVF conceptuses.[45] The total *IVF fetal death rate* for pregnancies of at least 20 weeks gestation or birthweight of at least 400g in Australia in 1996–7 was 15 per 1,000 births whereas for all births in Australia in 1997 it was 6.[46] Australia's IVF neonatal death rate was 9 per 1,000 births in 1996–7 whereas for all Australian births in 1997 it was 3 per 1,000 live births.[47] The stillbirth and neonatal deaths per 1,000 births after IVF or frozen ETs in the UK for the year 1996–7 was 10 for singleton clinical pregnancies and 22 for all clinical pregnancies.[48] These figures need to be interpreted in the light of the fact that we are dealing with infertile women, many of whom are at an age when the risk of fetal death and spontaneous abortion is much higher. With two or three embryos being transferred only about 4 percent of IVF embryos become live babies. Success rates for IVF and GIFT are influenced by many factors such as maternal age, the cause of infertility, the quality of the culture medium used, techniques of treatment, and the expertise of practitioners.

In 1996–7 rates for Australian and New Zealand *preterm IVF births* (<37 weeks) were 24 percent overall and 14 percent for singletons, whereas for GIFT it was 23 percent overall and 13 percent for singletons. These rates are much higher than the Australian preterm rate of 7 percent of all births in 1997 and a recent US rate of 11 percent.[49] Low birth weight (LBW < 2,500g) is much more frequent in IVF and GIFT pregnancies than in normal pregnancies. The incidence for Australia in 1996–7 for IVF LBW singleton births was 10.6 percent and for GIFT 9.6 percent, whereas the LBW rate for all singleton births in Australia for 1997 was 5 percent.[50] It is interesting to note that the LBW rate for frozen IVF (16 percent) and ICSI (12 percent) babies is lower than for fresh IVF (32 percent) and ICSI babies (33 percent).[51] The rate of *ectopic pregnancies* is about 2 percent for all pregnancies but after IVF in Australia and New Zealand in 1997 it was 2.6 percent and for GIFT 3.2 percent.[52]

The rate of *major congenital malformations* from 1979–97 for all IVF births and from 1985–97 for GIFT births of at least 20 weeks' gestation was 2.6 percent and 2.4 percent respectively, which is higher than the rate of 1.6 percent given for all births in Australia from 1981 to 1996.[53] Major malformations are generally defined as those leading to functional impairment or needing surgery. What would not count as a birth defect for a naturally conceived child should not count for one conceived by ART.[54] When these figures are interpreted in the light of the older maternal age for ART pregnancies, each couple's reproductive history and the causes of their infertility, the IVF/GIFT abnormality rates are not significantly different.

Evidence is firming that major malformations following ICSI are not highly significant when large numbers are studied for reliable figures. Clarifications over methodology and inclusion criteria for major and minor congenital malformation are needed for both children born after ICSI and for the general population if comparisons are to be helpful. A major Belgian study of 1987 children born after ICSI found there was

no specifically higher incidence of malformations with figures comparable for IVF and natural conceptions.[55] However a statistically significant
increase in sex-chromosomal aberrations was found – 0.83 percent compared to 0.19–0.23 percent. This is not surprising since some fathers of
ICSI children have structural sperm anomalies and, despite screening,
may transmit them as well as infertility to their male children.[56] A slight
increase in autosomal aberrations, mainly trisomies, in ICSI children may
be explained by advanced maternal age.[57] But recent data does not
suggest that ICSI causes a substantial increase in the risk of birth defects
compared to the general population or IVF births.[58]

Intact thawed embryos have a viable pregnancy rate approaching that
of fresh embryos but thawed embryos up to eight cells have a lower
viable pregnancy rate if up to half of their cells perish.[59] Fresh embryos
have a higher pregnancy rate compared to frozen-thawed embryos (9
percent versus 7 percent) and also a lower miscarriage rate (18 versus
21 percent). But frozen–thawed embryos have a lower rate of pathologies after implantation (17 versus 26 percent).[60] The implantation rate of
frozen–thawed embryos is improved by implanting only those which
resume dividing 24 hours after being thawed.[61] The long-term effects of
cryopreservation of embryos need to be monitored in adolescents and
adults.

A recent Australian study showed the general development of singleton children conceived through IVF was appropriate, but that, though
normal, their language development was less than in their control group.
The increased behavior difficulties reported may be more related to their
mothers' concerns.[62] A survey found no independent effect on the growth
and physical outcome of 2-year-old children when matched for plurality
and gestation.[63] An earlier study of 83 IVF children and 93 naturally conceived children matched by age, multiple birth, sex, race, maternal age,
and socioeconomic factors, found no evidence of physical defects or
developmental delay after assessing them at 12–30 months. Long-term
studies are needed to assess ART, including its psychosocial effects in
children so conceived.[64]

Burdens and costs of treatment

It is not easy for a couple to admit that they need treatment for infertility. There is often anxiety over which partner is the cause of the couple's
infertility. This may introduce strains in the relationship and counseling

may be required. Many infertile couples who desire to have children feel unfulfilled if they cannot be parents. Society generates pressure to have children without giving them sufficient socioeconomic support and incentive when they are biologically best prepared to have children. They are frequently made to feel a stigma, be it ever so subtle, and this leads to them making great sacrifices and financial outlays for each infertility treatment cycle.

Some women establish themselves in a career before having children later in life, when there is a higher incidence of natural infertility. It is not easy for a woman to submit to years of tests, internal examinations, having temperatures taken, and having sexual intercourse at prescribed times – to say nothing of enduring investigative and surgical procedures. Women's partners share these burdens and stresses. About a third of infertile couples have a baby after the first treatment cycle and many experience emotional setbacks after a failed pregnancy attempt. It gradually dawns on many couples, after enduring a huge emotional and financial outlay, that they will never be able to have children of their own, and the option of donor gametes is not welcomed by all.

In the UK in 1995 an IVF treatment cycle cost £700–£2,500, depending on the clinic chosen, most of which are private.[65] Based on the Fifth National Survey of the National Health Service (NHS) it was reported in the House of Commons in 1998 that the cost to the NHS of an IVF treatment cycle, including drugs, was £1,500–£1,800, with some units providing it for £1,000. The average cost at private units was estimated to be £2,500.[66] In the USA from 1994 to 1996 the basic IVF cycle cost about $8,000. In 1992 the cost per delivery was $44,200 for IVF. In a more cost-efficient program, including GIFT with their higher pregnancy rates, the overall cost in 1992 for an ART delivery was $30,252, including multiple births, while the cost per infant was $22,991.[67]

Treatment for infertility is well financially subsidized by governments in Spain, Italy, and Australia. The priority given to public funding of ART depends on each nation's evaluation of health services priorities. From 1991, Australia's Medicare subsidized up to six stimulated cycles of treatment, and from November 2000 this limit was abolished. Frozen ET cycles are also covered. Clinics vary in their fees, but generally for each basic IVF treatment cycle in Australia in 1998, an infertile couple paid a minimum of AU$750 while public funds paid about AU$1,800, plus the cost of any additional drugs. The costs for an overseas patient is about AU$5,200 since no subsidy is paid by Medicare. For each basic GIFT procedure, the patient would pay at least AU$600, while Medicare would pay about AU$1,800.[68]

6.2 Artificial Reproductive Technology and Ethics

Utilitarian perspectives

ART in general

In discussing the ethics of ART, sensitivity to infertile couples is required. On utilitarian grounds the benefits of ART have to be weighed against any likely harmful effects for infertile couples, their children, the family, the institution of marriage, and society.[69] Many believe ART does not present great ethical obstacles. Just as science and technology use artificial means to benefit a person's impaired sight, hearing or heart, it would be ethical to use ART to enable infertile couples to have children. The use of artificial means in ART does not per se make it unethical because all medicine intervenes in nature.

Using utilitarian criteria ART is judged to be ethically permissible, subject to professional ethical guidelines. The importance of personal autonomy in making decisions on reproductive choices carries much weight. The freedom of women to decide on what is done to their bodies by ART to have children is taken to be axiomatic. In the name of autonomy it is assumed that a person, endowed with a rational and free nature, a sense of moral responsibility, and a need to express interpersonal love sexually, should not be subordinated to the biological dispositions.[70]

Individual autonomy does not mean other persons may be ignored in making decisions about ART. An evaluation of the social effects and implications of ART need to be made. The state as a matter of public policy may ban some ART procedures or restrict public funding for ART treatments that are not cost effective, e.g. advanced age. The state may also regulate ART in the interests of the dignity and equality of all concerned, including children conceived and born through ART and the protection of marriage and the family as basic social institutions. The interests of all are protected when the law bans any form of exploitation of the weak and vulnerable and requires all involved to be accountable. Within the legal limits of ART, couples make their own evaluation of its ethics and its risks of benefits and harms. Laws differ in each country, depending on the cultural perceptions of the common good, the prevalence of moral pluralism, the relative importance given to personal autonomy and privacy *vis-à-vis* the accepted role of law in society.

Some question whether ART ought to be used for women in their sixties when they would be nearly 80 years of age when they have teenage children.[71] This does not imply that older mothers or fathers cannot care for children as experience attests. It is better to be reared by loving and caring parents of any age than by uncaring and unloving parents. As we have seen above, there is no danger of many elderly people wanting ART, apart from a legal ban on the number of years embryos may be stored to prevent damage to future offspring. Imposing bans may not be wise. Before making a decision older infertile couples should consider the morbidity and mortality risks of pregnancy for postmenopausal women, and the need of children to have at least one parent capable of caring for them in their formative years in addition to having "a stable home with mature caring adults who themselves have a sound relationship."[72]

Donor gametes

The use of **donor gametes** in donor insemination (DI) for human procreation is not new. Resnik sees human gametes as commodities and supports their commercialization while Lockwood sees practical advantages in this over altruistic donor donation.[73] Few women would want to donate their eggs to an infertile couple because they usually receive hormone injections for 12 or more days to ripen their eggs. Due to the shortage of donor ova it has been suggested that eggs retrieved from aborted fetuses could be matured in culture for use in ART.[74] Utilitarian evaluations of the use of donor gametes vary. Many couples opt to use donor gametes to have children even though one or both of them will not be the child's genetic parent(s). This is not seen to be ideal, but an ethical option in the circumstances.

There is ample evidence that social parents who are not the genetic parents of their ART or DI children can be good parents. They can be as loving, dedicated, and caring as natural parents usually are. What is important is the quality of the relationships between parents, children and parents and the security of children's attachment to parents. Susan Golombok rightly says parental responses and love count more than genetic connectedness. There is some evidence that children conceived of donor gametes relate better with their parents than those who have been conceived naturally. It seems that a strong desire of parenthood is more important than the genetic link of natural parents for fostering family relationships. The same applies to single heterosexual mothers with adequate finances and family living circumstances. These children would not miss their genetic fathers as much as children who miss their fathers after divorce. Research also shows that children of lesbian mothers are not disadvantaged in their socioemotional well-being, self-esteem, quality of friendships, or gender development. Partners of lesbian mothers are more involved with the children than are fathers in two-parent heterosexual families.[75] Golombok concludes current findings suggest that

> aspects of family structure such as genetic relatedness, number of parents and the mother's sexual orientation, may matter less for children's psychological adjustment than warm and supportive relationships with parents, and a positive family environment.[76]

On the other hand Golombok admits her conclusions are based on research on children whose average was about 6 years. By utilitarian criteria it seems that once children conceived of donor gametes by ART reach their teens and think of questions of identity it would be preferable to heed their natural desire to know their genetic parents. Not all social parents tell the truth to their children about their genetic origins. An Australian survey found that parents had told only 22 of 420 DI children (5.2 percent) of their genetic origins. Surprisingly 71 percent (182/257) had told others of the origin of their children but 94 percent (24./257) had not told their children. This creates a risk of somebody other than the parents informing these children of their genetic origins. Of 22 children, 21 reacted positively to the disclosure.[77] It is increasingly recognized that nondisclosure causes major emotional and psychological trauma because many adult DI offspring feel they have a right to know of their genetic origins.[78] Once DI children grow and suspect the truth of their origins has been concealed, they experience mistrust in the family and a lack of genetic continuity as they come to grips with their identity as donor offspring.[79] The widespread practice of DI would tend to undermine trust in parents.[80] Growing youngsters need love, trust, and security during their formative years.

Surrogacy

Surrogacy arrangements vary, but Laura Purdy thinks they all are an emotional, ethical, family, and legal minefield. But this does not mean they need always be harmful.[81] She does not give arguments drawn from human nature much credit, denies contract surrogacy involves selling a baby and recognizes "surrogate mothering" could empower some women and enable them to improve their social and/or economic status.[82] On utilitarian grounds, it could be argued surrogacy may be ethical, especially if the commissioning mother supplies her own egg and

it is fertilized by her partner's sperm prior to implantation in the uterus of the surrogate mother. Others say that surrogacy is more socially acceptable now that it is practiced in the USA with approbation of the law and discuss conditions for its ethical practice.[83] Even if donor gametes are used, Charlesworth says there would be no intrinsic immorality involved provided no extramarital sexual act was involved. He holds it would be an act of love and generosity to provide one's womb to gestate a baby for another without any financial return other than remuneration for expenses. He argues that a surrogate mother would not demean herself if, after being warned of all the consequences and taking precautions to lessen the risk of psychological harm to the child, she freely consents. Since it would be against natural justice to oblige the birth mother to give up the child against her will, it would have to be legally permissible for her to keep her child, notwithstanding contracts to the contrary. He thinks fears of harm for the child should not enter the utilitarian calculus unless empirical evidence for obvious harm supports them. He believes altruistic surrogacy ought to be legal since the stability of marriage and the family would not be undermined by the few who want surrogacy.[84]

On utilitarian grounds it can also be argued surrogacy is unethical. Robyn Rowland reports on the nightmares and devastating effects of witnessing the "giving away" of a sibling on the surrogate's young and teenage children.[85] It is hard to justify the needless removal of children from their birth mothers with whom bonding occurs during pregnancy. The lack of alienation experienced by a few children reared by their non-genetic parents does not justify embarking on experimenting with the lives of many children by legalizing surrogacy. In the light of the negative experience of some cases of adopted and DI children, on the balance of probabilities, it may be assumed it would not be in the best interests of children conceived and born of surrogacy arrangements. Ethically, this presumption should stand until the contrary is demonstrated.[86] Most Australian states do not recognize surrogacy contracts, ban the use of ART in all forms of surrogate parenthood and advertisements for it.[87] This lessens the pressure on relatives to volunteer as surrogates.

Where ART is legalized, the birth mother is recognized as the legal mother. It would be anomalous for the law to recognize two legal definitions of *the mother*, the genetic and the birth mother. Consideration also needs to be given to what legalizing surrogacy arrangements would say to society about split motherhood.[88] Commercial surrogacy contracts risk reducing pregnancy to incubation, and children to the status of commodities: they would not be in the public interest.

Cloning humans

Reproductive cloning of children goes a step further than the cloning of human embryos discussed in chapter 4. While cloning human individuals does not have much appeal, it has been defended by Harris in the name of "procreative autonomy" because he does not think it would be contrary to human rights or dignity.[89] Tooley believes it is in principle morally acceptable, though many would prefer the actual world without human cloning. He mentions the benefits of human cloning would include a development in our understanding of human psychology, the social benefit of having many people similar to outstanding gifted persons, the bearing and raising of children with desirable traits, and helping certain infertile couples, including homosexuals, to have a child related to one of them.[90] Pence accepts the cloning of human beings and rightly insists they should be treated as persons with the same rights as others without discrimination.[91] McCarthy holds that human clones would not be worse off than nonclones.[92] Savulescu goes further and claims the cloning of human embryos and fetuses is not only morally permissible but morally required to provide cells, tissues, or organs for therapeutic purposes, followed by eventual abortion of the cloned fetus.[93]

Protection of children's interests

An ethical consideration of importance for all ART procedures must be the best interests of the children. This principle is encoded in law in Victoria and the UK, including a reference to *the need of a child for a father*.[94] Research, based on the responses of both children and parents, shows that children living with their biological parents are likely to thrive in the vast majority of intact families of heterosexual parents who care for each other and their children.[95] Society should allow couples to follow their own informed consciences if the risk of harm to offspring is prevented. Contrary to C. L. Ten, I think parenthood should not be achieved by ART to conceive children destined to be raised without their fathers.[96]

Donor gametes

We have a history and relationships which belong to us as persons and whose origins are genetic. It belongs to our personal identity to have this father and mother, brother and sister, cousin, grand-parents, uncles and aunts. This network of relationships is not chosen but determined from our genetic origins. Unlike animals, we are aware of this and appreciate the importance of genetic family relationships and bonding. Research by social workers strongly endorses the view that the interests of children conceived by DI should take precedence over the interests of their medically or socially infertile parents or the donors of the gametes used for their conception.[97]

It seems unethical to deliberately break the natural tie engendered by nature: the gestational mother and the social father should also be the genetic parents of the child. When the genetic parents are the social parents family bonding and beneficial relations are likely to be strengthened where good family relationships exist. It is regrettable that after adoption due to tragic circumstances, some children are deprived of the knowledge and benefit of their genetic parents. This is not to say adoption is not beneficial. It is one thing to adopt a child whose natural parents are unable to discharge their responsibilities – but quite another thing to engineer anonymity of a child's genetic origins by the use of donor gametes.

It is hard to justify the anonymous, impersonal giving or selling of sperm or eggs to become a genetic father or mother without a care in the world for the resulting child. Human gametes for procreation should not treated as commodities nor their transfer be commercialized. The donation or trading of gametes lacks respect for children who are deprived of the knowledge, love and care of their own genetic fathers and/or mothers during their formative years. The same applies to donor embryos. Parenthood is important, but it should not be achieved to the detriment of children.

If laws are to protect children, they should regulate ART.[98] This occurs for adoption and the use of drugs that might prove dangerous for children, be they born or unborn. Once children born from donated gametes become adults or sufficiently mature they should have a legal right to identifying information about their genetic parents. This has already been done in some states.[99] Such laws go some of the way to protect the legitimate interests of the child and leave scope for parents to use their own discretion when to disclose this information. It is also necessary to know of one's genetic origins for health reasons, e.g. in cases of preventable genetic diseases.[100] It seems obvious that nondisclosure of the relevant information to children conceived by donor gametes is unethical.

It has been suggested that sperm from one's deceased partner could be used to create a child. Timothy Murphy sees no ethical problem with using sperm from dead men in infertility treatment.[101] Others hold that prior explicit or reasonably inferred consent of the deceased man would suffice ethically to retrieve sperm for this purpose in the absence of perceived harm to the child.[102] After a wide public consultation which drew 9,000 responses, the UK Human Fertilization and Embryology Authority "did not consider the use of fetal ovarian tissue was acceptable in the treatment of infertile women."[103] It would be contrary to the dignity of a child to be conceived using gametes from a corpse or an aborted fetus. The use of gametes from corpses and aborted fetuses should be banned by law from use in ART out respect for the inherent worth of children and common human decency.

Surrogacy

Disrupting the natural links between marriage, conception within marriage, gestation, birth, and the rearing of a child conflicts with our understanding of the meaning of marriage and motherhood. It does not serve the long-term interests of children who are conceived and born in this way. It is not helpful to blur one's sense of personal identity by distorting one's concepts of parenthood, family, and relationships.

Motherhood includes the genetic dimension and gestation followed by the rearing of the child together with one's partner. Pregnancy cannot be discounted as having little significance for the mother and child. It constitutes a significant natural interpersonal relationship of dependency of the unborn child for nurture and protection. It places on the mother and father a corresponding duty of care. Gestation and giving birth are of paramount importance in human culture: the mother is the one who bears and gives birth to the child and is presumed to be the genetic mother unless proven to the contrary. The mother's role should not be reduced to that of an *incubator*, divorced of all ongoing maternal relationships with her child. Where donor gametes are legally permitted in ART with the consent of one's partner, common law has usually, and rightly, been changed by statute law to determine that the birth mother is the legal mother of the child rather than the genetic mother.[104] Even the legal sanctioning of altruistic surrogacy would weaken the importance of motherhood.

Autonomy should not be overrated and interpreted in an individualistic way, divorced from personal relationships and responsibilities. Adults involved in surrogacy arrangements cannot act as though they were the only ones involved. An individualistic notion of personal autonomy opens the way to overlook the personal identity and dignity of the child who may be treated as an object. As a result, the notion of harm can be so narrowed as to exclude the psychological damage to the child's sense of personal identity. It is not a question of it being better to be than not to be. Accepting this line of argument could lead to justifying the conception of children from adulterous affairs. Adultery is immoral and ought not be committed even if it gives rise to children who may live happy lives. Respecting the moral beliefs of adults should not go so far as to risk harm to children. Though some private altruistic surrogacy arrangements may sometimes occur, the law should not give them legal standing for the common good, even if it may not be necessary to make them criminal.

Cloning Humans

Cloning a child seems contrary to human dignity and natural justice because it deprives the child of the genetic basis of a father, mother, and other family relations. Being cloned would negatively impact on the child's identity and family relations based on a genetic father and mother. A cloned child would be a human individual, a person, a subject and not an object to be created as a mere means for the benefit of others, such as a source of tissue for transplants. The conditions for the transmission of human life are determined by the natural moral law and may not be deliberately frustrated at will nor be directly subordinated to medical or technological dominion. Furthermore, it would be unfair to place unreal expectations on a cloned child. In addition to the safety concerns of cloning, the President of the European Union was rightly advised that "Considerations of instrumentalization and eugenics render any such acts unacceptable."[105]

Professional ethical guidelines

ART clinicians have to be professional in providing services to infertile couples, maintaining confidentiality of records, and the safe custody of gametes and embryos. It is imperative that infertile couples receive specific counseling in all aspects of infertility treatment as a prerequisite for informed consent, including the prospects of failure to achieve an ART pregnancy and the ethical balancing of their own interests and the well-being of existing and future children. For reasons of privacy and autonomy infertile couples should have the option of access to independent counseling.[106] Couples should be encouraged to seek advice from advisers of their choice on the ethical aspects of their treatment. They need to be given in advance adequate and comprehensive written and oral information on known risks of the short- and long-term harmful effects of ART on the health and psychological well-being of the mother and her ART children, as well as increased risks to their embryos.[107] They should be told of the clinic's relevant success rate and whether the treatment is conventional or experimental.[108] With the consent of the parents, there should be follow up of children born after ICSI. As the children grow older, observations and tests would require the consent of the children concerned.[109]

Doctors practicing ART have their professional ethical responsibilities and they should not be reduced to mere technicians who comply with every wish of their clients. People who are not suited for ART on medical grounds ought to be refused in the same way as for any other unwarranted medical treatment. Apart from the right to try to have a child in the natural way, there is no strict right to a child. Think of a woman suffering from active anorexia nervosa which naturally causes the suppression of ovulation. Before she was cured of anorexia it would be professionally unethical to offer her ART to achieve a pregnancy, including hormonal treatment, simply because she asks for it. It would also be unethical for clinicians to offer ART to a couple whose parenting skills are very deficient. If there is evidence of abuse of addictive drugs, including alcohol, a history of detention in jail, or previous children abandoned, caution is needed. The exercise of professional discretion by ART clinicians should not be confused with unjust discrimination. Firm evidence, however, would be needed before deeming a person unfit for ART on the grounds of a previous unsuitable lifestyle, e.g. a reformed drug addict or prostitute.[110]

Marriage and procreation in the Catholic Christian tradition

From a Catholic Christian perspective, marriage is an "intimate partnership of life and love" grounded in the covenanted relationship of its partners.[111] "Children are the supreme gift of marriage and greatly contribute to the good of the parents."[112] Children should be conceived within marriage and raised with provision for all their basic needs. Catholic teaching says

> The procreation of a new person . . . must be the fruit and the sign of the mutual self-giving of the spouses, of their love and of their fidelity. The

fidelity of the spouses in the unity of marriage involves reciprocal respect
of their right to become a father and a mother only through each other.[113]

Referring to ART techniques in general Pope John Paul II said

they are morally unacceptable since they separate procreation from the
fully human context of the conjugal act.[114]

Marriage enshrines a right for a couple to try to have a child by a conjugal (marital) act whereby spouses seal an irrevocable commitment to
each other and their children, including their responsibilities to bring
them up in a suitable environment. Children of the marriage are equal
and genetically related members of the family with a right to be cared
for and loved. These are some of the reasons why Christians generally
believe marriage is needed for human procreation and Catholic teaching
rightly insists that out of respect for the personal nature of a human
being the child ought to have a fully human origin, i.e. ought *"to be conceived and to be born within marriage and from marriage."*[115]

On account of its social importance marriage has been, and should
be, legally recognized and protected. Society needs to identify legally the
parents of children and their respective obligations.[116] These ethical and
legal requirements protect children by providing a firm basis for the
family, parental duties and the good of society. Many states require marriage or a stable relationship of a man and a woman for access to ART.[117]
Catholic teaching also says that conception by ART

brought about outside the bodies of the couple by the actions of third
parties . . . establishes the domination of technology over the origin and
destiny of the human person . . . contrary to the dignity and equality that
must be common to parents and children.[118]

But it is not obvious that ART necessarily involves the domination of
technology if its purpose is to facilitate the fusion of sperm and egg for
conception, without discarding or harming human embryos. The fact
that some embryos are discarded in some ART procedures does not imply
that this need always happen. To the extent that the use of ART veers
from offspring being conceived and born within marriage and from marriage, it is deemed to be immoral by many in the Christian tradition,
especially Catholics.[119]

Recourse to ART does not imply that the child cannot be a child of
the marriage. Catholic teaching says that if ART

facilitates the conjugal act or helps it reach its natural objectives, it can be morally acceptable.[120]

This would obviously morally permit *assisted intrauterine insemination* within marriage. If semen collected following a marital act were used to fertilize the wife's egg *within her body* using GIFT it would seem to be assistance to the marital act to enable sperm and egg to meet in the fallopian tube. The object of the assistance is to enable conception to occur at the normal site. Before judging this to be unethical one would need to be certain that the assistance given by GIFT, and a procedure similar to it, SUZI, prevents the child being conceived within and from marriage.[121] Catholic teaching has not pronounced on the moral permissibility of GIFT. In practice, GIFT is permitted in Catholic fertility clinics.

While the Church does not approve IVF, she does admit, however, that IVF for a married couple

is not marked by all that ethical negativity found in extra-conjugal procreation; the family and marriage continue to constitute the setting for the birth and upbringing of the children.[122]

The Church, of course, holds that all newborn children should be accepted as living gifts of God's goodness.[123] I think it is necessary that any morally permissible ART procedure to assist infertile couples to have children would need to protect the dignity of the couple, the children, and marriage. In practice, this means that children should be *conceived and born within marriage and from the marriage*, i.e. *within the fully human context of the conjugal act*. I do not believe any ART technique would be morally acceptable if it could be shown to be inconsistent with the moral values enshrined in the above principle, bearing in mind the couple's infertility. While many disagree with Catholic teaching on ART, it is helpful to understand its underlying reasons.

Challenges ahead

The suffering caused to infertile couples by their condition and its treatment warrant more research on its causes and how its incidence may be reduced. Governments world-wide need to address the issue of the causes of female and male infertility. Better public education is required to avoid preventable infertility in men and women, including sexually transmitted diseases. There is a need to create a society where infertile couples can freely choose to remain childless without feeling compelled to have recourse to ART.[124] There is also a need to research and address the societal causes of couples seeking to begin their families later in life when there is an increase in the natural incidence of infertility, miscarriages and genetic abnormalities in newborns. The risks of any eventual negative impact on children conceived by ART, natural family formation, society or culture should be monitored. ART clinicians should promote prospective studies on the long-term effects of ART on its offspring. Comprehensive and thorough evaluations need to be conducted because ART clinicians "do not repair an organism, they help to create a new being."[125]

Far from being enslaved to ART, we should assert ourselves as its morally responsible masters. ART should be at the service of persons, not young persons at the service of ART.

7

Prenatal Screening
and Diagnosis

7.1 Prevalence of Fetal Congenital Malformations

The prevalence of major abnormalities at birth is about 2 percent but it varies according to country, culture, ethnicity, and the efficiency of recognition and reporting criteria. The rate may rise to 5 percent if minor abnormalities are included.[1] The prevalence of congenital malformations in the State of Victoria, Australia, for 1998 for all infants of birth-weight at least 400g or 20 weeks' gestation and terminations of pregnancy before 20 weeks was 4 percent. This figure includes both structural defects and chromosomal abnormalities.[2] The rate of *major* congenital malformations for Australia in 1996 was 173.4 per 10,000 births (1.7 percent).[3] This includes chromosome abnormalities (0.23 percent), which occur when there is a net gain or loss of chromosomal material caused by a rearrangement of chromosomes. In the case of Down syndrome there are three instead of the usual two copies of chromosome 21, hence its name trisomy 21. This is not usually inherited from the parents but occurs at fertilization if the egg or sperm has two instead of one copy of chromosome 21 due to an error in their formation. Maternal age may cause this in the eggs in 96 percent of cases.[4] For 1983–95 the Victorian prevalence of trisomies was 21.2 per 10,000 births.[5]

Inherited single-gene defects occur in about 1 percent of births. A gene is a large DNA molecule and forms part of a chromosome. There are some 40,000 to 50,000 genes strung along the two sets of 23 human chromosomes. Each gene functions as a unit of inheritance for a characteristic. Inheritance of genetic disease may be dominant or recessive. With dominant inheritance only one parent needs to have a defective gene for the offspring to have a 1 in 2 chance of inheriting the genetic condition, e.g. Huntington's disease. For recessive inheritance, both parents need to have the defective gene for an offspring to have a 1 in 4 chance of being affected, while there is a 1 in 2 chance of being an unaffected carrier. If only one parent has the defective gene none of the offspring are affected by the disease but there is a 1 in 4 chance of an unaffected carrier. In the case of an X-linked disease, sons have a 1 in 2 chance of being affected, the daughters are not affected since they have two copies of the X-chromosome but they have a 1 in 2 chance of being unaffected carriers. Examples of X-linked diseases are haemophilia and Duchenne muscular dystrophy. Usually the expression of polygenic defects is modified by environmental factors, e.g. alcoholism, coronary heart disease, some cancers, neural tube defects, etc. There may be a genetic predisposition for them but they usually need to be activated by an appropriate environmental trigger before people can be affected by them. One who never drinks alcohol cannot develop alcoholism.[6]

About one-third of congenital anomalies are caused by known genetic factors, mutant genes (7–8 percent) and a combination of genetic and environmental factors (20–5 percent), while chromosomal abnormalities account for another 6–7 percent. Causal environmental factors account for 7–10 percent of congenital defects from fertilization. These include infections, chemicals, drugs, dietary deficiencies, hormonal imbalance, viruses, and bacteria. Chromosomal disorders, single-gene defects and developmental malformation syndromes account for about 43 percent of individuals with an IQ less than 50; accidents at birth, prematurity, substance exposures, and unknown factors account for the remaining 57 percent.[7]

The risk of a live-born child with Down syndrome increases with maternal age: 1 in 1,560 at 20 years of age, 1 in 1,350 at 25 years, 1 in 890 at 30 years, 1 in 355 at 35 years, 1 in 97 at 40 years, and 1 in 23 at 45 years.[8] The incidence at conception is much higher, but greater than 60 percent miscarry and about 20 percent are stillborn.[9] Hence the frequency of trisomy 21 is higher earlier in the pregnancy when prenatal diagnostic tests are done than at birth.[10] These facts ought to be recalled when analyzing the impact that prenatal diagnosis may have on the increase above the background rate of spontaneous abortion due usually to congenital anomalies. Its rate from 8 to 19 weeks is about 7 percent and after the first trimester it is 2 percent.[11] Most chromosomal and other non-inheritable congenital malformations arise unpredictably at, or after, conception, and the offspring affected are born to women who are not in recognizable risk groups.[12]

7.2 Pregnant Women's Anxieties

Judith Searle has analyzed why pregnant women feel at risk and fear the worst outcome for their unborn children.[13] Her research was on routine screening tests for blood infection, diabetes, ultrasound (U/S), and also screening tests for Down syndrome. She found women's perception of risks of fetal abnormalities are higher than the objective epidemiological risks. Of 367 participants questioned 242 (66 percent) reported that they felt anxious sometimes, or a lot, about having an abnormal baby. Searle found that while these women hoped that confirmation of fetal normality would result from prenatal screening tests, they feared abnormalities would be revealed. She found that detection of abnormality is consistent with the medical model of pregnancy with its focus on abnormality and that this model powerfully influences the perception of women receiving prenatal care. Society's attitudes towards abnormality and disability, along with the desire to avoid burdens and sufferings for their child and themselves, were potent considerations in women's perception of risk. The role of the media in focusing on negative outcomes has also influenced pregnant women's perceptions of pregnancy and its risks. This is not insignificant when research shows that maternal stress is associated with abnormal patterns of blood flow through the uterine arteries – which may explain the known association between maternal stress and low birth weight.[14]

Searle's survey showed that greater than 96 percent of 367 postnatal women believed that routine prenatal screening tests would benefit all pregnant women. She found greater than 93 percent thought that all pregnant women should have routine prenatal screening tests and that these were a necessary part of normal pregnancy.[15] She also found that participants identified routine prenatal screening tests (53 percent) and support/advice from healthcare professionals (40 percent) most helpful in reducing their anxiety during pregnancy whereas only 4 percent found antenatal classes helpful.[16] An international survey answered by 682 medical geneticists shows that 73 percent would perform prenatal diagnosis for maternal anxiety or refer the woman.[17]

The reasons for pregnant women's perception of risk of having an abnormal child were based on a sociocultural, rather than a medical, definition of risk and this creates anxiety. This anxiety, however, can be reduced by prenatal screening tests which are sought for reassurance and perceived certainties amid fears and uncertainty. Hence, there has been a rise in the number of women who have prenatal screening tests. The problem is that when providers of prenatal screening inform pregnant women of the true epidemiological risks of anomalies, disproportionate fears may be generated.

Prenatal diagnostic tests cannot guarantee that there are *no risks* of abnormality, but only that the specific abnormalities tested for are present or absent. Anger may be felt if a defect occurs for which a prenatal screen or test was not given. In such cases compensation may be sought through the courts, driven by false perceptions of a certainty of normality. Granted that not all pregnant women will avail themselves of all prenatal screening and diagnostic options, Dorothy Wertz rightly says children will "still be born with genetic conditions or congenital malformations (unsuspected inborn errors of metabolism, new mutations, etc.)."[18]

In their review of the literature on the psychosocial aspects of prenatal screening and diagnosis, Green and Statham referred to research which compared women who did not have amniocentesis and those who did, but received negative results. It was found there were no significant differences between them by mid-pregnancy. It was believed that "differences between the two groups are likely to relate to pre-existing characteristics, which is a recurring theme in this area."[19] Green and Statham concluded that women undergo prenatal screening and diagnosis because they feel the need to seek reassurance that their baby is healthy; that positive screen results generate considerable anxiety which is not always relieved by subsequent negative results; that women find waiting for results of diagnostic tests quite stressful and finally that what is communicated, and how this is done, is very important.[20]

7.3 Current Procedures

New advances in diagnostic techniques, coupled with the advent of legal abortion in most countries over the last 25 years, have increased pressures to extend the availability of prenatal screening and diagnostic testing. Prenatal screening differs from prenatal diagnosis in that screening is applied to individuals without any known physical risk to identify those at a higher than average risk of a genetic defect or carrier status, whereas diagnostic testing is done to detect a defect in individuals with a known risk based on family history or age.[21] Since most birth defects are not genetic, interest has grown in recent years for maternal serum screening for other disorders. Costs are not usually a consideration for couples since prenatal screening and testing are provided in many countries by their healthcare system.[22]

Maternal serum

Maternal serum screening (MSS) is now offered to pregnant women between 15 and 18 weeks' gestation to detect pregnancies which are *screen positive*, i.e. with a risk of 1 in 220–300 or greater of being affected with Down syndrome, other trisomies, or a neural tube defect.[23] MSS checks the levels of three or four markers which may be a sign of the presence of these defects. A diagnostic test is required to obtain a definitive result after MSS. Many women are unnecessarily made anxious for days as they await definitive results.

Quadruple MSS is now commonly used and can have a detection rate of about 75 percent for Down syndrome pregnancies if gestational age is estimated by a scan, with a 5 percent false screen positive rate.[24] Of 503 women in Victoria who had a diagnostic test prompted by raised MSS in 1999, there were 10 fetuses (2 percent) with trisomy 21 detected. It is to be noted that of the 503 women retested, 298 were less than 35 years of age, and 8 of the 10 fetuses with trisomy 21 belonged to this age group.[25] Universal MSS, then, is more effective than maternal age alone as an indicator for selection for prenatal diagnosis. Again, MSS is more economical than an age criterion alone for diagnostic testing since it cuts the detection costs per affected pregnancy by up to two-thirds.[26]

Cystic fibrosis

Cystic fibrosis (CF) is a recessive genetic disease affecting the lungs and digestive systems for which 1 in 20 perfectly healthy persons in the UK is a carrier. A simple DNA screening test for CF based on a mouthwash sample detects 85–90 percent of carriers.[27] Testing pregnant women for CF carrier status can be done by general practitioners and it can be planned from the first consultation provided adequate explanations are given and information leaflets are supplied.[28] A screening trial of 3,000 women for CF carrier status without any family history for it found 100 carriers. They all appreciated the opportunity of being screened, even though there was some anxiety until their partners had also been

screened.[29] Being a recessive genetic disease, the scientific validity of
prenatal screening of couples for CF depends on their partners being
the genetic fathers of the unborn children. The nonpaternity incidence
in the general population is difficult to determine. The accuracy of the
oft-quoted 10 percent for the general population in the UK has been
questioned, while 2.8 percent has been suggested in France.[30]

Thalassemia

In countries where there is a known high risk of thalassemia in the
general population there has been a successful switch from prenatal
testing to premarital screening. The Greek Orthodox Church in Cyprus
requires screening for this common recessive genetic disease if couples
wish to marry in the Church, but there is no requirement for them to
make the results known and they are free to marry even if they know
they are both carriers of the gene for this disease.[31] This enables engaged
couples to make their own informed and morally responsible decision
about marriage and parenthood.

Nuchal translucency

Fetuses develop a fluid under the skin of the nuchal or neck area. An
abnormal nuchal thickening appears black on an U/S screen from 10–13
weeks' gestation. This has been found to be associated with Down syndrome. This early U/S scan is known as a *nuchal translucency scan* (NTS)
and it can be indicative of *an increased risk of* Down syndrome. Its
sensitivity is good with an expert operator: it can identify up to 84
percent of pregnancies at an increased risk with a false positive rate of
6 percent.[32] It decreases the need for women at a low risk to have CVS
or amniocentesis at a later date. Anxious mothers are now more frequently asking for NTSs. Of a recent NTS of 3,550 pregnancies only 172
(5 percent) were reported to be at a higher risk of Down syndrome.[33]
Clearly the results of NTS are not definitive and need a diagnostic test
for confirmation.[34] By integrating the results of NTS with MSS markers
of the first and second trimester the false-positive screen rate falls to 1
percent for an 85 percent detection rate in a single Down syndrome
screening result. This reduces the number of women having unnecessary
amniocenteses.[35]

Ultrasound

The most widely used prenatal diagnostic technique is *U/S imaging or scanning* which is non-invasive, safe and usually performed at 16–20 weeks' gestation. Images of the deep structures of the fetus are projected on a screen. This is done by recording the echoes of sound impulses which reflect off the planes and densities of the various tissues. U/S is important for determining accurate pregnancy dates and is able to detect multiple pregnancy and many anatomical fetal defects.[36] Difficulties may arise in interpreting the results, especially by less expert operators, leading to failure of detection of abnormalities or the diagnosis of an abnormality where there is none. U/S results may indicate further prenatal testing for a definitive result, and this can increase uncertainty and anxiety for mothers.[37] U/S may detect so-called soft markers such as nuchal thickening and echogenic bowel. When soft markers were included in reporting results of 33,376 U/S scans, the number of false positives rose from 14 to 174 (04 percent to .54 percent). One reason for this is that some soft markers are transient appearances, not structural defects, but this information still generates anxiety in prospective parents.[38] Using soft markers without associated fetal structural malformations is an unreliable indicator for amniocentesis and results in four times as many fetal losses than cases of Down syndrome detected.[39] Expert fetal anomaly scanning is a specialized form of U/S that may be offered to women at 18–20 weeks' gestation. It can detect 70–80 percent of major malformations, e.g. neural tube defects such as spina bifida and anencephaly.[40] However, the detection rate of internal structural abnormalities such as congenital heart disease or congenital diaphragmatic hernia is about 50 percent.[41]

Amniocentesis

From the fifteenth to sixteenth week of gestation *amniocentesis* can be performed and its results are definitive.[42] It involves the withdrawal of 15–20 mls of fluid from the amniotic cavity using a syringe under U/S guidance. This fluid contains fetal cells shed from the skin and they can be grown in culture for chromosomal examination to test for Down syndrome and other trisomies or used for DNA and biochemical analysis for many common inherited and developmental disorders. It may take up to two weeks to obtain definitive results of an amniocentesis test and this usually makes pregnant women anxious.

Although it is hard to prove amniocentesis causes fetal losses, it is generally agreed its procedure-related fetal loss rate within two to three weeks of the test ranges from 1 percent down to about 0.5 percent for expert operators. Mid-trimester amniocentesis is the safest invasive procedure, especially if the women follow the advice given for prenatal healthcare.[43] Amniocentesis done at 14 weeks' gestation has been found to have a higher fetal loss rate (2.5 percent) for women aged 37 years or over compared to women who have it at about 16 weeks' gestation (1.1 percent). However, there was a lower rate of premature rupture of membranes following early, compared to later, amniocenteses.[44]

The test may be medically indicated for mothers greater than 35 or 37 years of age according to local practice; for those who have had a previous child with a congenital defect; for carriers of an inheritable disorder, when there is a history of chromosomal problems; and when there are unexpected results from U/S, NTS of MSS. The frequency of detection of a fetus with Down syndrome for a woman aged 37 years at the time when amniocentesis is usually performed is 1 in 190 (.53 percent) – about the same as the risk of miscarriage due to the procedure.[45]

Chorionic villus sampling

Chorionic villus sampling (CVS) entered into medical practice in the mid-1970s. It is usually performed between 10 and 13 weeks of gestation and involves taking a sample of placental tissue which is usually genetically identical to the cells of the fetus. This is done using U/S guidance with little discomfort. CVS is almost as accurate as amniocentesis if enough tissue is sampled to allow for several cultures to be examined for double checking. CVS has a higher risk of error because not all placental tissues are equally representative of the genotype of the fetus. CVS results can be available in 6–10 days if cells need to be cultured or within 48 hours by short-term analysis.[46]

CVS is performed before fetal movements are felt. This may also give rise to what is known as the "tentative pregnancy," where a woman is reluctant to bond with her fetus and acknowledge she is carrying *her* baby before she receives results showing her baby will not be born with the defect for which a test was done.[47] It is not surprising that a survey found that 76 percent of 83 women who participated in a mid-trimester screening program would have preferred to have had the test in the first trimester mainly because early termination of pregnancy is easier or because of the earlier reassurance.[48]

The maternal risks of morbidity from CVS are not substantial and resemble those of amniocentesis, including bleeding, infection and rupture of the membranes. Research has shown that severe fetal limb reduction abnormalities are associated with CVS performed at about 8 weeks' gestation, e.g. limbs have been found missing. When performed a couple of weeks later the abnormalities are less severe, such as finger or toe abnormalities. After 10 weeks the risks are much lower.[49]

More serious is CVS's procedure-related fetal loss of 1–2 percent, depending on the number of attempts to obtain the placental biopsy and the gestational age. The earlier an invasive procedure is performed the higher the fetal loss rate will be because the pregnancy with time becomes more stable. The spontaneous miscarriage rate falls by 3 percent between the normal testing period for CVS and amniocentesis.[50] Results of an American trial of 2,308 pregnancies intended to continue after CVS showed 48 (2.1 percent) resulted in miscarriage less than 20 weeks and only 13 (0.6 percent) from 20 to 28 weeks.[51] The frequency of Down syndrome for women aged 37 years when CVS is usually performed is 1 in 130 (0.77 percent), whereas the risk of miscarriage due to the procedure is about 1 percent.[52] Research shows that even when amniocentesis and CVS are offered at no cost to women aged 37 years or over, most women had no diagnostic testing.[53]

Testing fetal blood and cells

Fetal cells have been detected and isolated in cervical mucus and maternal bloodstream.[54] More importantly cell free fetal DNA has also been found in maternal plasma. Using this is simpler and more robust than testing fetal cells in the blood. This *non-invasive* method is safe for the fetus and has been used in prenatal diagnosis to detect fetal rhesus D status, sex-linked, and other paternally inherited disorders. An increased level of fetal DNA has also been found in maternal plasma in pregnancies affected by Down syndrome.[55] This new prenatal diagnosis technique will improve and replace testing fetal blood drawn from the fetal cord with about 2 percent risk of fetal loss.[56]

Testing pregnant women for HIV

In most developed countries routine prenatal screening of infectious diseases is offered for the prevention of perinatal transmission of hepatitis

B and C, and syphilis.[57] The global tragedy of HIV and AIDS has brought new anxieties to some pregnant women who are concerned that they may have contracted HIV infection and may then risk passing the virus on to their children (vertical transmission). Each year in the USA up to 7,000, and world-wide about 2.3 million, HIV infected women give birth to children, most of whom are not HIV infected.[58] Where the availability of antiretroviral therapy is scarce or unavailable, the estimated rates of vertical transmission vary from 15–20 percent in Europe, 15–30 percent in the USA, and 25–35 percent in Africa.[59] Up to 70 percent of cases of vertical HIV transmission occur during labor and delivery and 14 percent result from breastfeeding.[60] The challenge of prenatal care is now to prevent as well as identify HIV pregnancies.[61]

7.4 Sex-selected Insemination

Some success has been achieved in selecting X and Y sperm based on their relative size because statistical analysis shows that human X sperm are larger and longer than Y sperm. Males are conceived by Y sperm and females by X sperm since the egg always has an X chromosome. This raises, for example, the possibility of having *sex-selected insemination* with X sperm to prevent the conception of male offspring at risk of an X-linked disease. Since females have two X chromosomes, if one is defective the other makes up for the deficiency. Recent reports indicate a separation success rate of about 90 percent for X and 65–70 percent for Y sperm has been achieved by staining sperm heads with a fluorescent dye. This enables X sperm to be selected because they have about 3 percent more DNA content than Y sperm.[62] Following selection of X sperm using flow cytometry (MicroSort) 13 of 14 pregnancies with known fetal or birth gender were female (93 percent).[63] In time techniques to identify defective sperm may be improved.

7.5 Therapeutic Benefits

The results of prenatal tests reduce the anxiety and fears of most pregnant women and this is also a benefit for the fetus. If an untreatable defect is detected the parents, with appropriate genetic and pastoral counseling, may be able to prepare themselves mentally for the birth of a disabled baby. Prenatal information may also be of benefit to obstetricians for the better management of the pregnancy, and the prevention of an unnecessary caesarean delivery. It provides an indication for specialist neonatal staff to be at hand in case of need after birth.

Unless certain fetal defects are specifically sought, routine prenatal diagnosis does not usually provide information that could lead to fetal therapy. But it can give information that may help provide *medication or therapies* for the benefit of some fetuses, with the exception of chromosomal and neural tube defects.[64] It is possible to provide fetal therapies for a few conditions discovered by amniocentesis. It enables an evaluation of pulmonary maturity, fetal hemolysis and anemia for therapy *in utero*. Fetal conditions such as anemia or Rh incompatibility can be treated by intrauterine blood transfusions. Some anatomical and developmental fetal defects, e.g. variations in heart beat, discovered by U/S can be treated by drugs or repaired by fetal surgery.[65] Better detection rates of treatable abnormalities could lead to fewer neonatal deaths by arranging for delivery at a level 3 hospital or by means of appropriate fetal therapy.[66]

HIV infected pregnant women who receive AZT have a *HIV vertical transmission* rate of 9 percent compared to 15 percent for those who do not have AZT.[67] The rate can be reduced if AZT is given in the last trimester and during labor; it is better still if it is given before the onset of labor and the bag of forewaters is intact in conjunction with elective caesarean section. This lessens risks of infection from contaminated blood and cervical discharge in the presence of ruptured fetal membranes.[68] To reduce risks of teratogenic effects in the developing fetus due to antiviral therapy, AZT should be administered after fetal organs are formed.[69]

7.6 Ethical Evaluation of Prenatal Screening and Diagnosis

Prenatal screening and diagnosis *per se*

Nature is not perfect. Natural selection is propelled by errors which are part of the given natural order. While one could question whether it is worth having prenatal tests for defects for which a cure is not yet available, this is only known after the test. In the meantime valuable information may be gained for the benefit of the mother and her fetus. Pregnant women have a right to seek accurate information on the state of the health of their fetuses for reassurance.[70] A survey of 376 postnatal women shows that over 95 percent of them perceived routine prenatal diagnosis to be beneficial.[71] There is also some scope for intrauterine fetal therapy for some pathologies. U/S is safe for the mother and fetus and useful for verifying dates, fetal health and growth as well as being inexpensive. Prenatal screening and diagnosis are *per se* ethically permissible, under certain conditions, if their purpose and methods used are respectful of the life and dignity of the pregnant woman and her fetus, and provided the requirements of informed consent, due sensitivity for persons with disabilities, and social justice are satisfied. But this does not imply that pregnant women are in duty bound to undergo prenatal screening or diagnostic tests.

Respect for the life of the fetus

An ethical concern arises over prenatal diagnostic tests that involve risks to the life or health of the fetus. Fetal losses due to prenatal tests are greater when amniocentesis and CVS operators perform too few tests per year to acquire and maintain their expertise.[72] Operators should train under the supervision of experts and the profession should set minimum standards.[73] Amniocentesis done at the normal time of about 16 weeks, and CVS performed at 10–12 weeks, come under moral scrutiny due to their procedure-related fetal loss rate up to 0.5 percent and 1–2 percent respectively. This increased risk of miscarriage of normal fetuses is not intended, but results indirectly as a side-effect of the test. John Paul II stated the following ethical principle:

> When they do not involve disproportionate risks for the child and the mother, and are meant to make possible early therapy or even to favour a serene and informed acceptance of the child not yet born, these techniques are morally licit.[74]

Under these conditions amniocentesis with a fetal loss risk of 1 percent to 0.5 percent could be deemed to be ethically permissible by a pregnant woman and her doctor if a safer test is not available. More serious reasons would be required to justify CVS with its fetal loss risk of 1–2 percent. Amniocentesis currently would be the safer and ethically preferred invasive prenatal test until a reliable test is available which poses no risk of fetal loss, e.g. the use of fetal DNA from maternal plasma.

On account of its invasive nature, its fetal risks, and costs, in addition to giving information, there is no need to recommend routine amniocentesis to all pregnant women. One could not objectively justify the routine administration of such tests to pregnant women without proportionate reasons. The use of U/S for recommending amniocentesis that results in four miscarriages to every case of Down syndrome detected is unnecessary and unethical. At the same time the assessment of these risks necessarily involves both objective and subjective elements, especially for the mother, who may be enduring great stress and anxiety over her fetus's health, which is also enhanced by the mother's own good health. The fetus benefits from allaying the mother's fears and anxiety, which are not isolated from the family situation and community pressures.

It is the pregnant woman herself in the midst of her fears and anxieties and in the context of her family situation who is properly entitled to evaluate the risks involved provided she is well informed. The responsible taking of risks is an inevitable part of parents' lives. It is interesting to note that 28.5 percent of the women who requested genetic counseling at the Medical School of the Catholic University in Rome between 1977–80 eventually decided not to undergo amniocentesis either because they were not convinced they needed it or because they could not morally agree with the slightly increased risk of fetal loss or of having an induced abortion.[75] Doctors performing prenatal tests also have a personal ethical responsibility to evaluate the risks. A reasonable evaluation may go either way. It is necessary for genetic counselors and doctors to respect the conscientious evaluation of pregnant women as well as their own consciences. It is not right to engender unwarranted feelings of guilt in pregnant women for their conscientious decisions. What is required for ethical conduct is that the risks involved in prenatal tests must not be disproportionate to the benefits reasonably expected.[76]

Finally, granted there are therapies to prevent or substantially reduce the risk of HIV perinatal infection, pregnant women should be informed of these risks and the available antiretroviral therapies. It is imperative that all pregnant women, after adequate counseling, be offered access to HIV testing to prevent, or greatly reduce, the risks of HIV infection to their fetuses or newborn infants. An HIV infected pregnant woman should be informed of the risks her child would have of perinatal HIV infection, the benefits and risks of delivery options, and of an HIV infected baby's risk of a painful death within a few years of birth.

Anonymized testing for HIV in pregnant women can scarcely be justified where preventive treatment for both HIV infected pregnant women and their fetuses is available. Very few pregnant women would choose anonymized HIV screening if they knew HIV screening with its undoubted benefits was an alternative. It reflects badly on health professionals to ask a pregnant woman to have an anonymized HIV test which would prevent them from offering preventative treatment if her fetus was HIV infected. The arguments in favor of anonymized HIV by now have lost their credibility.[77]

Informed consent, counseling, and pastoral care

Mothers and fathers should both be responsible for seeing the pregnancy through to birth and beyond. Women are under some social pressure to undergo prenatal screening and diagnosis. There is evidence that those who agree to participate in screening programs only do so as a response to an invitation and may not feel free to decline if the request is made by doctors.[78] Pregnant women and their partners need practical freedom to consent to, or decline, prenatal screening tests and diagnosis without any undue pressure. There is no ethical duty to have them nor should women be made to feel guilty if they don't. Women's decisions to undergo or forgo prenatal screening tests and diagnosis need to be informed and free.

Before they choose to have prenatal screening or diagnostic tests, pregnant women should be adequately informed by doctors or qualified genetic counselors about the purpose of the tests, their risks, the available treatment options with their likely outcomes and their implications for themselves and their children.[79] The autonomy of pregnant women does not require counselors to refrain from alerting them to family and social consequences of prenatal screening and diagnosis so that they may make free, informed and responsible decisions. Genetic counseling that is dialogical and interlocutory promotes a deliberative process that is aware of alternatives and free of manipulation and coercion.[80] Pregnant women need to consider the consequences of both having, and of not having, these tests, including the possibility that their fetuses may, or may not, be affected by a congenital anomaly. Risks, be they genetic or not, are better presented in different forms: "proportional (1 in 4) by percent (25 percent), and in a verbal form (higher than the average for the general population)."[81] Pregnant women should be given the required information on prenatal screening tests and diagnosis in plain language by doctors or genetic counselors.[82]

There is evidence that for many mothers the requirements of informed consent are not always adhered to for MSS and prenatal diagnosis, even if the mothers concerned thought it was sufficient at the time.[83] Doctors and genetic counselors should respect women and their partners as persons – their dignity, integrity, levels of knowledge, autonomy, and privacy. They are to help pregnant women make their own decisions, not to make decisions for them. They should give the time needed to listen to their concerns and help them work through their fears, doubts, and anxieties on their options by providing accurate and easy to understand answers to their questions. It is their role to point out to women and their partners the relevant scientific and medical facts, the range and degrees of risks involved, and their correct interpretation.[84] Consent should not be sought until the required counseling has been given and sufficient time has elapsed for consulting their partners and making a responsible decision. It should be made clear that they may withdraw from the prenatal screening and diagnosis program at any stage.

It is necessary to ensure that pregnant women are informed of positive diagnostic results for an abnormality with great cultural sensitivity and by offering to make contact with the relevant support groups.[85] A dialogical nondirective style of counseling is of great value to present test results objectively and the available options to both parents if possible. They need all the help required to make the right decision that they will have to live with all their lives. Proper protocols are needed for all staff who communicate with parents to guarantee that accurate results are given to them with emotional support to cope with their distress. There is evidence that this is not always the case.[86] A couple's grief for the child they desired is not to be mistaken for grief for the child they will have. No direct or indirect attempt is to be made to persuade a pregnant woman to have recourse to selective termination of pregnancy if the test for a congenital defect is positive.

It is not usually the role of genetic counselors to give ethical advice. Pregnant women, however, should be made aware that they are free to seek ethical advice from the genetic counselor or other qualified persons on the hospital's staff. They should be given the opportunity to discuss their ethical concerns with their partners and respective pastors, chaplains, or personal advisers. Advisers should not give advice contrary to their own conscience, but they should respect pregnant women who may choose to make different, informed ethical decisions. With pregnant women's consent, genetic counselors and pastoral care workers may liaise to help them to cope with, and accept, an abnormal baby.

In secular public hospitals pro-life medical staff and genetic counselors need not feel they should exclude themselves from involvement provided they are prepared, if asked, to present both sides of the ethical debate on selective abortion and they adhere to the relevant guidelines of their hospitals. By replying to pregnant women's requests for information about prenatal diagnosis or test results they need not compromise their own ethical principles.[87] In a hospital administered by a religious organization genetic counseling should be given in accord with the hospital's ethical framework and, in one of their first interviews, pregnant women should be informed of the hospital's ethical policy of not providing selective abortion. A woman attending, say, a religious hospital who decides to seek an abortion after she learns that she is carrying a fetus with a disability should be treated with courtesy, be given a copy of her medical records and test results, and be advised to seek further counseling since the hospital is unable to refer her for an abortion.

Prenatal diagnosis and selective abortion

A serious ethical dilemma may arise when pregnant women are informed that their fetus is affected by an abnormality, e.g. Down syndrome or a neural tube defect. A decision to have an abortion is likely to derive from the fear of being unable to cope with the long-term implications of raising a child with a disability, especially when society condones abortion. Advance warning of future prospects allows them time to prepare to make their decisions. Chris Goodey says abortion could not be for the benefit of Down syndrome children since their physical conditions can be treated and they themselves do not seem to suffer.[88] Where prenatal diagnosis is designed to help women to abort abnormal fetuses it is ethically flawed. Concerns of eugenics have been raised about the funding of genetics clinics tied to their cost effectiveness, i.e. an increase in the number of terminations of pregnancies affected by disease.[89] John Paul II comments:

> Such an attitude is shameful and utterly reprehensible, since it presumes to measure the value of a human life only within the parameters of "normality" and physical well-being, thus opening the way to legitimising infanticide and euthanasia as well.[90]

It would be unethical to decide to have an abortion if a fetal abnormality is detected.[91] Likewise, from a pro-life perspective, it would be unethical for a health professional to try to persuade a woman to have the test for this purpose, or who made consent to abortion, a condition for having the test.

In a survey of 20 papers it was found that termination rates after diagnosis of Down syndrome varied, with the highest being 92 percent.[92] Clearly there is a link between information about abnormal fetuses and selective abortion. Positive results change parents' anxiety of incertitude to the trauma of knowing their fetuses are affected with a defect. In South Australia, where abortion is legal and MSS is offered to all pregnant women, about 75 percent of women whose fetuses are confirmed to be affected by Down syndrome have an abortion.[93] A survey at a Melbourne hospital over a 5-year period found that 3 of 179 women decided to continue pregnancy after a diagnosis of Down syndrome – equivalent to a selective termination rate of 98.3 percent of affected fetuses.[94] But there is another side to the coin. In Victoria in 1999, of the 5,268 women whose fetuses were given diagnostic tests, 233 or 4.4 percent were affected by a major chromosome abnormality.[95] These results were reassuring for the vast majority of the women concerned and for whom abortion was not the outcome of prenatal diagnosis.

Another ethical problem is whether prenatal diagnosis *per se* amounts to material cooperation with the subsequent abortion of abnormal fetuses. A survey was conducted of 1,000 participants aged 16–44 in a cystic fibrosis (CF) carrier screening program in which they were asked what they would do if their *future* pregnancy were affected by CF. Their replies to the question whether they would consider terminating an affected pregnancy were: 26 percent yes, 17 percent no, but 57 percent replied they did not know what they would do.[96] This showed that only a minority of participants would consider terminating a future, and presumably wanted, pregnancy if the fetus was found to be affected by CF. An intention to terminate a wanted pregnancy would not be formed before it was *confirmed* the fetus was abnormal. Prenatal diagnosis, then, is not always, *nor necessarily*, linked to abortion. It provides information which women have a right to seek. Unless a woman intends to abort a fetus detected with an abnormality, prenatal diagnosis is ethically distinct from any subsequent decision to have an abortion.

There is, however, a remote material link to abortion in at least 4.4 percent of cases of prenatal diagnosis where the results indicate that the fetus is affected by a major chromosome anomaly.[97] Since most women have an abortion once it is confirmed that their fetuses are affected by Down syndrome, one could argue that prenatal diagnosis involves sufficient material cooperation with abortion to constitute collusion with it. On the other hand, more weight should be given to the fact that in about 95.6 percent of cases, the results of prenatal tests indicate that fetuses are not affected by the major chromosome abnormalities for which they are tested. This shows that in the vast majority of cases prenatal diagnosis is not *per se* materially linked to abortion. It is ethical, then, to perform prenatal diagnostic tests to provide accurate information on the health of their fetuses to women who request it. This is not changed by the fact that most prenatal tests that detect Down syndrome have a material link to abortion.

The above discussion on cooperation applies to institutions as well as to individuals. Hospitals which respect human life should not *adopt a policy* that *formally* permits cooperation in abortion after prenatal diagnosis. Their staff should take the necessary steps to guarantee that prenatal screening and diagnosis are guided by ethical principles without condoning selective abortion.

Genetic screening and responsible parenthood

The information gained from genetic screening and testing which confirms carrier status for a genetic disease has serious moral implications for responsible parenthood. One may learn of this after one is already married and a parent, or before one marries or becomes a parent. There is a difference between screening to enhance the exercise of morally responsible parenthood, and screening designed to prevent the birth of fetuses affected by severe congenital defects.[98] While it would be wrong to put pressure on a couple not to have children once they find out they are both carriers of a serious recessive genetic disease with a 1 in 4 risk of having an affected child, there are good reasons why such a couple might consider refraining from accepting this known risk. But I do not think there is a moral duty for such couples to avoid having children.

People who are known carriers of a major recessive genetic defect need to consider carefully the implications of entering committed relationships that could lead to marrying partners who are carriers of the same defect. One who is in love is not required to enter marriage while turning a blind eye to what could negatively affect the well-being of their future children and their marriage relationship. Parents' obligations towards children with disabilities cannot be set aside.[99] If they marry noncarriers, none of their children would be affected but there would be a 50 percent risk of them being carriers. One of the reasons why Catholic Church law forbids marriage between close blood relatives, e.g. first cousins, is to prevent the inheritance of diseases by children.[100] Without implying a lack of regard for people with disabilities, for the sake of the future children, it would show a mature sense of responsibility for a carrier to marry a partner who does not share the same genetic defect.

People who are already affected by a serious dominant genetic disease need to consider whether to choose to assume the responsibility of marrying and having children with a 1 in 2 risk of having the same disease. It is not a question of it *being better to be or not to be*. An existing child with a genetic disability is of inestimable value. It is not a question of telling a person with a disability that they should not have been born. This would be extremely offensive. Nor would it be a case of unjust discrimination against a possible disabled child. An act of injustice can only be committed against an existing child. Morally responsible family planning implies that a couple ought not risk conceiving a child with a dominant disease unless they are prepared to love and raise their child with care. Prior to making their decision, couples in this situation need to be adequately informed of the 1 in 2 risk of their child being affected, the age of its usual onset and the degree of likely suffering their child would have to endure. To choose to have a child with a 1 in 2 risk of having to endure much suffering for most of their life would involve assuming an awesome responsibility.[101]

Sex-selected insemination

Mary Anne Warren holds that sex selection is integral to women's reproductive freedom, is ethical, and that the risk of harm resulting from a slight sex ratio imbalance is negligible.[102] Likewise Julian Savulescu thinks that the ethical objections against sex selection carry little weight in Australia.[103] On the other hand, sexist selection of Y or X sperm for the conception of a male or female child for cultural, social, or economic reasons are not health-related matters and as such ought not to be part of the practice of medicine or prenatal diagnosis.[104] Being male or female is not pathological. There is evidence that readily available sex selection would "foster the already existing bias against the female child, and create an overall imbalance in the male to female ratio worldwide."[105] Sexism ought to be eliminated by sociocultural development and legal reform rather than by implicitly endorsing sexist practices by recourse to sex selection of offspring.[106]

The natural probability for procreating a girl or a boy is integral to the Creator's plan. Parents should accept their child as a personal gift and natural endowment of the expression of their love for each other. This relationship should not be jeopardized at conception by manipulation and discrimination against one or other gender.

The use of sex-selected insemination to try to prevent the conception of a boy with an X-linked disease, e.g. hemophilia, would not be *sexist* and it would be better from a pro-life perspective than an abortion of an affected male fetus or discarding a male embryo following PGD.[107] Sex-selected insemination to increase the chances of the birth of a child without a sex-linked disease would be ethical provided it assists a marital act to achieve its purpose, as discussed in chapter 6.

Professional confidentiality

The common good requires the presumption in favor of professional confidentiality until the contrary is proven. At the same time, the social nature of the human person obliges a doctor, but especially a family doctor, not to undertake an obligation that conflicts with a prior duty to prevent serious injustice to other members of a family, other persons, or the common good. If necessary, a doctor may have a duty to disclose to the relevant authorities a patient's certain HIV positive status in order to prevent one or more persons being unjustly infected with a lethal virus. In this case community trust in doctor–patient confidentiality would not be eroded.

The results of prenatal tests are personal and should be kept strictly confidential between the woman and her doctor and only shared with other health professionals if treatment so requires. In general, doctor–patient confidentiality also applies to minors, provided they are mature enough to understand the issues at hand and can cope responsibly without undue risk of harm being done to themselves or others. Doctors may well need to advise them to tell their parents about the consultation.

When information is obtained about oneself, but which may also be true of another family member, family solidarity morally requires that an offer be made to share this information with the relative concerned, especially if this knowledge would influence this relative's decision about having children, with a high risk of them inheriting a serious disease. The doctor should try to convince the person of their duty in such a case. Consider the rare case of a doctor who discovers that a fetus has a dominant paternally inherited single-gene defect like Huntington's disease, informs the mother and then finds out her partner is not the father of the child. This information should not be shared with other health professionals without the woman's consent. The genetic father ought to be advised of this fact so that he may make morally responsible decisions about fathering more children. The doctor should try to persuade the mother to inform the genetic father, but it is the mother's responsibility to act, not the doctor's, unless the doctor has been asked by the mother to do so.

Another ethical issue is about the right of access to non-identifying aspects of genetic registers and medical records for health purposes and *bona fide* epidemiological research on fetuses and newborns requiring cross-referencing of symptoms, indications, and success of treatments. At first glance, one would be inclined to say this could not be done without the informed consent of each patient. But if we recall that public funds bear the bulk of the financial burden of delivering health services to the community and that it is in the interests of public health and cost-effectiveness to have access to such records without asking each person for permission, one sees things differently. What is essential is that all direct and indirect identifying references be excluded from access. With computer technology this could be done. Limited disclosure of medical records of this sort does not seem to pose any reasonable threat to the legitimate right of privacy of parents or their children. The underlying reason for the presumption of professional confidentiality is to protect the privacy, reputation and general interests of patients and their children. Of course, these research projects would have to be approved by an appropriate ethics committee to guarantee the interests of public health are being served without jeopardizing persons' rights of privacy.

Sensitivity for people with disabilities

The inevitable presence of congenital defects does not diminish the dignity nor inviolable rights of the persons so afflicted. They deserve love and care from their families and dedicated service from health professionals. People who care for persons with disabilities find their own lives enriched. Some couples, however, are only too acutely aware of the strain put on their marriages and families by the presence of a child with a disability. They are afraid that they might not be able to cope over the years with few prospects of respite. We cannot underrate the stress caused by the realization of the consequences that the long-term presence of a child with a disability may have on the family's daily life, its income, and life plans. These are a few of the reasons why some pregnant women have recourse to prenatal screening and diagnosis. They want to be reassured their fetus is normal, to seek any available fetal therapies, or to prepare themselves to care for a child with a disability. This is not the same as saying that there is a right to a child without defects. Italy's Health Minister, Pia Garavaglia, put it well when he said: "Desires are not rights. A child is not a consumer good."[108] The myth of the possibility of the perfect child for all must be dismissed.[109]

The long-term impact on the community's consciousness of the social approval of the deliberate taking of the lives of defective fetuses so that subsequently others may be born to enjoy lives free of congenital disease is a cause of concern to people with a disability and cannot be ignored in policy-making in this regard. Liz Hepburn aptly remarked:

> Paradoxically, we seem to be prepared to eliminate the very people before birth whom anti-discrimination legislation seeks to protect after birth.[110]

Priscilla Alderson reports that people with Down syndrome say that

> discrimination is their worst problem in preventing them from contributing to society as they can and want to.[111]

Christopher Newell questions

> the dominance of a perspective which believes that a likelihood of a disability is so significant that it acts as a trump card regarding abortion.[112]

Referring to the social nature of disability and genetics he laments

> such technology will perpetuate the oppression and control of people with disability, especially if the knowledge of people with disability is not utilized in bioethical debates.[113]

Ani Satz has argued that prenatal diagnosis with the option of abortion of a disabled fetus does not discriminate against disabled people on the dual grounds of fetuses lacking moral standing and of women's right to reproductive freedom. She admits, however, that there could be a perception of indirect discrimination in this situation if there are not sufficient material supports provided for the disabled.[114] Lyn Gillam also argues prenatal diagnosis is not *per se* discriminatory against disabled people, but the way it is practiced should eliminate or reduce its potential negative effects on people with disabilities.[115]

One could hardly disagree with Wertz, who said: "the availability of genetic tests must not be allowed to create an illusion that most disabilities are preventable and therefore unacceptable to society."[116] Kaplan admits disabilities are associated with social-economic disadvantages, but suggests that "these disadvantages can be eliminated without persons with disabilities being eliminated."[117] Prenatal screening and diagnosis may be ethical, but attention still needs to be given to how the prevention of disease may be achieved sensitively and without hurting people who are disabled. It is up to prenatal healthcare professionals to ensure that prenatal screening and diagnosis do not send a message of intolerance to people with a disability.[118]

Justice and public policy

Many of the ethical positions espoused in this chapter would find support among consequentialist thinkers, especially in regard to distributive justice and public policy. Public funds for prenatal screening and diagnosis should not be provided unless other higher health priorities are already met to the satisfaction of the community. In countries where the deaths of most infants and children are not caused by congenital abnormalities but are a result of poverty, infection, malnutrition and a lack of basic medical care, it would be inequitable to publicly fund the general availability of prenatal diagnostic services before the major causes of infant deaths were addressed. Before making policy decisions on the provision of prenatal diagnostic services, provision should be made for nonmonetary and nonquantitative factors such as emotional, psychological, and social costs and benefits to individuals and families. Distributive justice requires there should be no arbitrary discrimination on nonmedical grounds for the provision of prenatal diagnosis and genetic screening services.[119] Due regard should also be given to the rights of fetuses as well as of pregnant women.

Where allocation of scarce health resources is a real issue, it would seem equitable that access to publicly funded prenatal diagnosis should be limited to pregnant women who have a greater need of reassurance, i.e. those in the medically indicated categories for testing, and to others known to be in an advanced risk category, e.g. those over 37 years of age. Priority also needs to be given to those prenatal screening and testing procedures which potentially confer greater benefit in addition to being more cost-effective.

8

The Fetus

The fetus occupies a prominent position as medicine's youngest patient. Prenatal diagnosis is ever expanding the number of conditions that may be detected and which may be treated successfully *in utero*.[1] Fetal therapy, as we shall see, aims to benefit the fetus directly and may reduce the number of induced and spontaneous abortions. In cases of threatened premature labor, respiratory distress syndrome (RDS) can be prevented, or reduced in severity by good *obstetric management* and maternal administration of corticosteroids, unless infection is present.[2] Here I shall mention just a few examples of fetal therapies.

8.1 Fetal Therapies

Medication

For some years it has been known that fetal metabolic diseases or deficiencies may be treated before birth by transfusing needed substances into the fetal peritoneal cavity.[3] Some fetal conditions may be treated by injecting medications or deficient nutrients into the amniotic fluid for the fetus to swallow. Therapy for other fetal deficiencies or inherited metabolic diseases requires the administration of the vitamins or medications to the mother.[4] An untreated maternal metabolic disease like phenylketonuria may have teratogenic effects on fetuses unless mothers follow a prescribed diet to control it. Dietary therapy may be adopted for prenatal treatment of genetic fetal metabolic defects. Pharmacological treatment may also be given to mothers whose fetuses suffer from fetal arrhythmias.[5]

Intravascular therapy

Severe anemia secondary to Rh incompatibility in fetal blood can be treated by blood transfusions. Risks decreased once prophylactic antibiotics were used. Access to the fetal circulation opened the way for direct intravascular transfusions. The technique of choice most widely used is percutaneous ultrasound guided intravascular fetal blood transfusion.[6] Its results in tertiary referral centers are excellent, often with a survival rate up to 90 percent with only 2 percent fetal loss per transfusion.[7] It may also be used together with percutaneous intraperitoneal transfusion to increase the total amount of blood given to the fetus.[8] Fetal transfusion is now a well established life-saving therapy for some fetal conditions, but caution is needed for transfusions after 32 weeks' gestation to avoid risk of bradycardia.[9]

Fetal surgery

Human fetal surgery has been in use for some 20 years at a couple of centers in the USA.[10] It is "the act of opening the gravid uterus, surgically correcting a fetal abnormality, and returning the fetus to the uterus for postoperative recovery and continued gestational development."[11] It increases our knowledge of developmental pathophysiology of fetal anomalies, the healing of fetal incisions without a scar, the natural history of wound healing and how this may be imitated; it also has the immunological and biological advantages of fetal tissue for transplantation.[12] Expert clinical judgment is to determine if defects are best corrected at term, during birth, before birth, or after induced preterm delivery.[13] Fetal surgery can be performed to correct lethal defects in organs which, if repaired, would be able to develop normally and give the fetus a chance to survive after birth. Only a few life-threatening conditions are currently judged suitable for fetal surgery. All such interventions are approached from the perspective of the maternal-fetal unit with the avoidance of maternal deaths and maternal safety given priority over fetal therapies. Fetal surgery is indicated if it can enable fetal organ development and growth to resume.[14] Maternal deaths resulting from fetal surgery are practically non-existent, but some morbidity may occur, primarily related to preterm labor, infection, amniotic fluid leaks and mild accumulation of fluids in the lungs. Deliveries following fetal surgery are usually by caesarean section.[15] With techniques ever improving, fetal surgery may become a more cost effective and humane approach to a number of otherwise tragic fetal disorders.[16]

Fetal urethral obstruction impedes the development of the fetal kidneys and the passing of urine into the amniotic sac. This creates a build-up of fluid inside the fetal body instead of in the amniotic sac. The swallowing of amniotic fluid is necessary for fetal lung development. For some fetuses, the result is fatal without treatment. If both kidneys are damaged it may be necessary to remove the fluid by a catheter shunt. Pringle's Law of the Uterus sums up the seriousness of this abnormality: "If you don't pee *in utero*, you don't breathe when you're born."[17] If obstructive uropathy is associated with a deficiency in the amount of amniotic fluid, experience suggests that, if the fetus is otherwise normal, shunting would be warranted to restore amniotic fluid after 24 weeks' and before 32 weeks' gestation to avoid futile surgical intervention.[18] Fetuses with bilateral hydronephrosis due to urethal obstruction and with oligohydramnios need treatment.[19] However, over 90 percent of these cases are best treated after birth. For the few fetuses that need prompt attention, minimally invasive treatment is now the preferred treatment.[20]

Congenital cysts of the lungs can be fatal for the fetus, especially if they lead to the development of hydrops and underdeveloped lungs.[21] Of 134 cases of congenital cystic adenomatoid malformation cases, 14 women had selective abortions, 101 women were managed expectantly, 13 women had fetal surgery, and 6 fetuses received a shunt. All the babies survived when the cysts were not associated with nonimmune hydrops. Of the 13 hydropic fetuses who had fetal surgical resection of the tumors, 8 were successful leading to survival after birth. Most cases can be given prenatal care and maternal transport for planned term delivery and postnatal surgical resections.[22]

Congenital diaphragmatic hernia is the absence of a membrane which lets internal organs rise and constricts lung development. It is difficult to predict the outcome of fetal surgery to correct it. Liveborn babies have been treated by surgical intervention to remove protruding viscera from the chest region to their proper place in the abdomen and the hernia in the diaphragm is repaired. This gives the lungs a chance to develop normally, but still many babies die after treatment due to underdeveloped lungs.[23] Despite good postnatal care, up to 60 percent of newborns with this defect die. Repair before birth seems to make physiological sense and is technically possible since the fetal lungs can grow after repair. Success of surgery to a great extent depends on the size of the herniation. Premature labor risks fetal lives and remains a great challenge for the medical team. Postnatal treatment is the preferred option unless the liver is herniated.[24] Doubts, however, have been raised whether the failure of lung development results from pressure or from a broader defect involving the lungs since repair of the hernia has not always resulted in lung growth and suggests postnatal therapy may still be advised.[25]

Hydrocephalus is a condition where cerebrospinal fluid accumulates in the ventricles of the brain. This causes them to expand unduly and generates great pressure which inhibits normal brain cell development and neurological function. The usual result is mental retardation, cerebral palsy, general weakness, blindness and premature death. The condition affects the central nervous system and there is a serious risk of deterioration of a severe defect in a fetus that might otherwise abort spontaneously. The condition is highly problematic for the management and outcome of the pregnancy and is dangerous for the mother unless expert obstetrical assistance is available. For a time shunts were surgically inserted to drain the excess fluid but they did not always remain patent. There is a moratorium on shunting for hydrocephalus until shunting techniques and selection criteria improve.[26]

Experimental fetal surgery has been successful in repairing severe **open spina bifida** and saving neurological function. Prenatal repair may enable rearrangements of function due to the plasticity of developing neural tissue.[27] In the meantime experiments with animal models continue to see how methods can be improved for human application. Trials with sheep show that fetoscopic and open transumbilical cardiac catheterization are feasible and provide potential alternative approaches for human fetal cardiac surgery.[28] Visualization through small "needlescopes" is already in use and technical advances in *videofetoscopic* surgery make it possible to perform major fetal surgery through small puncture sites in the uterus. A laser procedure may be performed by video in a fluid environment. This lessens the need for full hysterotomy and minimizes the risks resulting from uterine incisions such as preterm labor, hemorrhage, uterine irritability, etc.[29] Up to 75 percent of fetuses with left congenital diaphragmatic hernia are saved by the fetal endoscopic method for some conditions.[30]

Fetal tissue transplants *in utero*

Infants and children often are unable to be treated once a disease has progressed beyond a certain point. There would be no need to seek scarce whole organs to transplant after birth if diseased organs could be successfully treated by cell transplants before birth.[31] It is easy to do, enables healthy, fresh, cultured or cryopreserved cells to be transported and placed in the recipient's body at a physiologically beneficial site for development near host fetal cells and growth factors. It would be good if cell transplants were done at fewer than 15 weeks' gestation, before the fetal immune system is fully developed and so lessen the risk of rejection of transplanted cells.[32] This would eliminate or decrease the need to use immunosuppression drugs with their risks for the baby after birth. Rather than use cells from adults, it would be better to use early fetal donor cells because they graft more readily. If they are derived from a preimmune, recently aborted fetus, there would again be less risk of rejection and of graft-versus-host disease. The effect would resemble the permanent chimerism that naturally occurs in twins who share a common placental circulation. The *uterus* also provides a sterile environment for transplants with little risk of infection. Fetal therapy could be more successful if enhanced vascular access was available to allow repeated injections and sampling.[33]

Blood disorders due to malformation of hemoglobin in the bone marrow and immunodeficiencies are inherited genetic defects which are currently treated postnatally by transplanting healthy donor bone marrow cells to the baby. Bone marrow contains hematopoietic stem cells (HSCs) which are capable of specializing further to become blood cells. The progeny of the donor's normal cells colonize the recipient's organism, and once engraftment occurs, can make up for the genetic defects in its cells and correct the anomaly. This raises possibilities for intrauterine transplantations performed with bone marrow. One successful case has been reported.[34] Fetal bone marrow is a safe source of HSC's for transplantation which can be used to treat diseases diagnosed prenatally and prevent irreversible harm before birth.[35]

Up to 1996 only 21 *in utero* transplants had been reported, and of these only four were successful, two of which used fetal donor cells to treat immunodeficiency disease. Interest has continued in transplants which are helped by advances in prenatal diagnosis and fetal intervention.[36] These transplants of fresh and later on cryopreserved fetal liver stem cells were performed to treat metabolic or blood disorders and immunodeficiency diseases. There were only five successful outcomes, including one which used cryopreserved liver cells, but none with a metabolic disorder.[37] Four fetuses were treated successfully with reconstitution of immunity, with three aged 4 years.[38] It is estimated that the risk of a miscarriage for *in utero* HSC transplantation is about 2 percent.

Fetal stem cell transplants *in utero* have also been used to treat inborn errors of metabolism. Following more transplants after birth, the number of cells deriving from the earlier transplanted cells was found to increase. The overall results of fetal stem cell transplants *in utero* are >60 percent due to a higher rate of graft take and the enhanced possibility of transplanted cells proliferating within the fetal host with less risk of graft-versus-host disease. *In utero* stem cell transplants are a real alternative to postnatal transplants and to abortion after prenatal diagnosis.[39]

Fetal cells from umbilical cord blood could be cultured and stored to provide cells for transplantation as fetal and postnatal therapeutic needs arise. Human HSC or other adult immunologically incompetent stem cells could be transplanted *in utero* to induce immunotolerance in a fetus who is diagnosed to suffer kidney or liver failure soon after birth so that postnatal kidney or liver organ transplantation could safely be done. T-cell-depleted HSC from a relative could be transplanted to prepare the fetus for a postnatal kidney transplant from the same relative. Fetal metabolic liver diseases could be corrected by cell transplants since fetal bone marrow is primed to receive migratory stem cells from the liver. For diseases which need a high proportion of a donor relative's cells, tolerance could be induced in the fetus with timely postnatal booster injections from the same relative.[40] A similar procedure to induce tolerance could even be done with an animal for the xenotransplant of a heart or liver.[41]

Fetal gene therapy

Many serious neurologic, metabolic, immunologic, and hematologic genetic diseases can now be diagnosed early in gestation for which gene therapy *in utero* would be most beneficial because fewer cells would be needed to reconstitute the fetus than a newborn.[42] Primitive stem cells abound in the fetus and therefore transferred therapeutic genes would be more readily multiplied throughout the entire fetus. The fetus at less than 15 weeks' gestation is immunologically incompetent and this would prevent rejection. Viral vectors derived from adenovirus can be made replication incompetent by replacing their essential genes with the desired therapeutic genes. The same can be done with retroviral vectors. The modified therapeutic vectors can still integrate themselves into a cell and deliver the new genes and complement the original cell's genome for ongoing replication. A drawback after birth is that these vectors are somewhat unstable in expressing their therapeutic genes. This could change with improved design in vectors or even new vectors and in preimmune fetuses inflammation could be less.[43] A tiny engineered minichromosome has recently been constructed from a human chromosome to act as a large capacity gene vector for entry into a patient's target cells or stem cells with only the needed gene sequences retained for therapy and stable propagation. It would be nonmutagenic and non-disruptive because it contains only naturally occurring human DNA and it would autonomously replicate in target cells. It offers great promise for future gene therapy.[44]

Genetically engineered retroviruses with the therapeutic gene could be injected into the fetus through the pregnant woman's abdominal wall. There is a slight risk the altered genes could affect fetal eggs and sperm and be passed on to the next generation.[45] The seeding of fetal bone marrow with transfused genetically altered stem cells extracted from fetal liver may soon become a reliable therapy, but the limits of fetal tolerance for foreign substances could be as low as 15 weeks, as mentioned above.[46] Either way the inserted genes could multiply throughout the fetal body as a therapy for specific organs or systems. Gene therapy offers great possibilities and hopes for the treatment of some diseases of the lung and liver, cystic fibrosis, and some congenital hematological disorders, etc.[47] What needs to be known is how long a particular gene therapy will be effective, whether the transferred gene, once expressed, will provide clinical benefit, and whether *in utero* or postnatal treatment is better in the long term.[48]

French Anderson recently proposed a trial to treat fetuses with severe combined immune deficiency by giving them healthy copies of a gene for an enzyme needed for the development of the immune system. He also proposed similar *in utero* therapy for fetuses with alpha-thalassaemia, an inherited blood disease which could cause the death of the fetus, before or after birth. It could also cause the pregnant woman to develop life-threatening pre-eclampsia which involves high blood pressure and fluid retention. If the therapy is not fully effective the fetus could live longer before dying and increase risks for the pregnant woman. Hence it was suggested the trials begin on fetuses with alpha-thalassaemia for whom abortion had already been decided. However, not all problems would go away because the researchers and women, to their regret, might discover a cured fetus had been aborted.[49]

There is a concern to protect the germ line. Preimmunine sheep fetuses have been injected with engineered retroviral vectors and the offspring followed over 5 years. Expression of the engineered gene was found in many hematopoietic lineages. The introduction of retrovirally packaged gene constructs *in utero* showed the potential for safe long-term expression, without modifying the germ line of the recipient sheep fetuses.[50]

Twin abnormalities

The risks of major malformation in identical twins is 10.7 percent whereas it is 8 percent for fraternal twins and 7 percent for singletons. Risks of mortality or long-term neonatal morbidity for the normal twin are higher when monozygotic twins share a common placenta and chorion and more so if both twins share one amniotic sac. This information may give rise to indications for selective abortion in cases of twin pregnancies where one twin is normal and the other is not. Instead of aborting both twins, parents often prefer to selectively abort the abnormal twin rather than let both go to term. It is estimated that in the selective termination of an anomalous twin there is an 80 percent probability of a live birth for the remaining twin.[51]

A serious situation arises in the monochorionic twin – twin transfusion syndrome where abnormal chorionic blood vessels in the placenta link the blood circulation of two normal fetuses. These cases are associated with perinatal mortality as high as 75 percent, especially when the syndrome develops before 27 weeks' gestation.[52] Only 5–17 percent of twins sharing one chorion are affected by this syndrome. An extreme case of this syndrome which endangers the lives of both twins occurs when one is growth retarded and virtually without any amniotic fluid and stuck to the wall of the uterus while the other is affected by excessive amniotic fluid. No one therapy has prevailed as yet but serial amniocenteses has been tried to draw off excess amniotic fluid. Selective feticide has been used for the abnormal twin by means of an intracardiac saline injection. Delivery of the perfused twin has been reported in 7 pregnancies, with 6 neonatal survivors.[53] Another remedy is to block vascular communications between the fetuses. Four out of six infants survived with this technique which is the least invasive and an effective treatment.[54] In the rarer case of the *acardius acephalus* twin which lacks a head, a heart and thoracic organs, the normal and larger "pump" twin supplies blood to the nonviable parasitic "perfused" twin. Delivery of the *acardius acephalus* twin by incision of the uterus has succeeded at 22.5 weeks' gestation followed by the delivery of the normal twin at 33 weeks. Mortality for the *acardius acephalus* twin is 100 percent and 50 percent for the normal pump twin. Fetal reduction by injection is not medically indicated in this case due to the risk of blocking blood vessels.[55]

Multiple pregnancy

Multifetal pregnancies usually occur as the result of infertility treatment, e.g. ovulation induction or the transfer of many embryos to the uterus. The incidence of chromosomal abnormalities for such pregnancies in a 25-year-old woman rises from 1 in 476 for a singleton, to 1 in 238 for a twin and 1 in 150 for triplets. Special problems occur in cases of multiple pregnancies where a higher number of normal fetuses may put the whole pregnancy at risk. To enhance the birth of one or two viable infants the number of live fetuses is at times reduced by a lethal intracardiac injection of potassium chloride for two or more fetuses. This immediately causes death and they may at times be absorbed. This is known as *multifetal pregnancy reduction*. The choice of fetuses for the injection is random unless some have been already diagnosed as defective.[56] A study has shown that of 140 triplet pregnancies, 106 were managed expectantly, of which 21 percent resulted in the loss of the entire pregnancy before 25 weeks; of the remaining 34 pregnancies there was a 9 percent loss rate of the entire pregnancy due to the procedure.[57] It saves more lives in higher order multifetal pregnancies: of 93 septuplets, only 13 percent of entire pregnancies were lost.[58]

8.2 Use of Fetal Tissue

Fetal tissue transplants to children and adults

From 8 to 12 weeks' gestation the fetal liver's HSCs do not induce graft-versus-host disease after transplantation because T-lymphocytes have not yet matured. The HSCs, together with thymic cells, have been transplanted to treat 24 infants and young children with severe combined immunodeficient diseases, 12 (50 percent) of whom were cured of their otherwise lethal disease. The failures were mainly due to infections present prior to transplantation. Liver stem cells from fetal donors at a more advanced gestational age have also been transplanted to 34 children suffering from various inborn errors of metabolism. About 64 percent of all patients are alive, enjoying a full cure or significant benefit from the treatment. Infections apart, failure was due to insufficient graft take in patients capable of rejection. Without the benefit of cell transplantation 80 percent of these afflicted children would have died within three years.[59] There are patients whose livers are sound but suffer from some treatable defects like an enzyme deficiency or a clotting disease. These may benefit from the transplantation of fetal or postnatal liver cells but they do not need a whole liver transplant.[60] HSCs from stored placental blood have also been transplanted successfully to hundreds of patients world-wide aged less than 2 years to adulthood without histocompatible donors.[61]

A common cause of morbidity and early death is diabetes mellitus. Type I diabetes mellitus (insulin dependent) may be treated with insulin but the proper control of glucose levels in the blood to prevent blood disease and other complications can only be obtained by functioning pancreatic islet cells which produce insulin. There is great interest in perfecting techniques for islet cell transplantation for the treatment of diabetes. Early fetal cells may be less immunogenic but their functional capacity would be reduced unless they develop and grow to function normally in their host. The use of fetal and postnatal islet cells for transplantation as an experimental therapy may benefit patients with Type I diabetes mellitus.[62]

Parkinson's disease is a neurological disorder manifesting itself by abnormally diminished motor activity, tremor and rigidity. Most likely it is caused by the degeneration of the cells in the brain's substantia nigra. These cells produce dopamine which acts as a neurotransmitter in the central nervous system (CNS). Following successful transplantation trials in rodents and in nonhuman primates clinical trials of transplants of fetal neural tissue in human adults have shown diminished symptoms of Parkinson's disease in the USA and in Sweden. Transplanted fetal neurons differentiated sufficiently to adopt the characteristics of the host neural tissue.[63] Clinical progress is slow and better functional recovery requires long-term survival and integration of grafted fetal dopamine neurons in the host brain.[64] Clinical trials show that significant symptomatic improvement is found in patients with Parkinson's disease who are less than 60 years of age but not in those over 60 years, but 15 percent of patients developed uncontrollable writhing as a result of unregulated and excessive production of dopamine.[65] Furthermore there was no reversal of the neurogenerative disorder.[66] Only time will tell if fetal transplants will have therapeutic potential for other brain diseases and brain lesions in the future.

Source of fetal tissue

It is necessary that the fetal tissues and cells used for fetal therapy be available and healthy, i.e. cytogenetically normal, free of infection or contamination. The procuring of fetal cells must be done at the medically requisite gestational age for a specific transplant, i.e. the donor fetus must be old enough to have a sufficient quantity of the required tissue or cells and these must be mature enough to be functional. Provided they are medically suitable, fetal tissues and cells could be derived from miscarriages, ectopic pregnancies or induced abortions. Up to 90 percent of induced abortions occur in the first trimester and about 10 percent in the second trimester usually for maternal and/or fetal health reasons. Later induced abortions are more likely to be contaminated if the fetal abdominal wall or other surfaces are ruptured. Clinicians seek intact fetuses from first trimester abortions.

Prostaglandins used in abortions could induce damage to tissues resulting in a reduced supply of oxygen and restricted blood flow. The use of chemical methods for early abortions, e.g. mifepristone, will eventually limit the supply of suitable fetuses for transplantation in some countries. It may be necessary to actively seek suitable fetuses from miscarriages and ectopic pregnancies. It is a matter of selecting fetuses that have not been damaged and can provide suitable tissue. Miscarriages do not usually occur in a medical or sterile environment and should not be used if the tissue shows signs of degeneration, bacterial contamination or chromosomal abnormalities. Exceptions occur and tissue from some miscarriages is safe. The medico-scientific debate on this issue is far from over.[67]

For the safety and success of fetal transplants, tissue screening and high quality control is required. Cytogenetic, viral, and HIV screening are being recognized as necessary in spite of the delays caused and the urgency of therapeutic bone marrow transplantation. The tissue of the dead aborted fetus needs to be tested, not that of the mother. Tissues and cell lines may be frozen to prolong their availability in time and facilitate transport to where they are needed. Research suggests that fetal liver HSCs can survive the freeze–thaw process better than mature progenitor cells (63 percent versus 35 percent) – which means they are suitable for storing.[68] HSCs can be obtained from noncontroversial cord blood and, along with fetal tissue and cell lines derived from culture, can be stored in central banks to guarantee a safe supply.[69] The media report that multipotent stem cells can be derived in abundance from the placenta after child birth. But it will not be known if they resemble adult or embryonic stem cells until scientific papers are published.[70]

8.3 Fetal Pain

There is much debate about when the human fetus acquires the capacity to feel pain. Stuart Derbyshire puts the beginning of the experience of pain well after birth:

> In terms of the conscious development of the fetus it is reasonable to suggest the fetus has nociceptive responses but no pain experience. The conscious conceptual system begins from 12 months of age.[71]

Some argue that a fetus could experience pain from 28 to 30 weeks' gestation.[72] Others, relying somewhat on comparisons with what occurs in adult experience, conclude that a human fetus first becomes conscious from 30–5 weeks after conception.[73] Most experts believe a fetus could not experience pain, as distinct from a reflex response to a stimulus, until 24–30 weeks' gestation.[74] Peter Singer thinks it is unlikely a fetus could feel pain before 18 weeks' gestation, when the cortex is sufficiently developed to enable pain signals to be transmitted through synaptic connections.[75]

Earlier gestational estimates for the experience of pain should not, however, be uncritically dismissed. Pain has been defined by the International Association of the Study of Pain as "an unpleasant sensory and emotional experience associated with actual or potential tissue damage."[76] This definition suits pain in adults rather than in fetuses. Apart from U/S evidence of fetuses of 9 weeks' gestation moving away from a possible pain stimulus, there are reasons to believe that the sensation of pain prior to the formation of the cortex is mediated by the brain stem. Peter McCullagh believes it has not been demonstrated that a functioning cortex is necessarily required for pain sensation.[77]

The scientific literature reports the case of an apparently normally functioning 21-month-old child who, after death, was found to lack a cortex.[78] It is known that infants without a cortex, e.g. anencephalic infants, are more similar to normal infants who can feel pain than to adults. Their behavior resembles normal newborns in many ways – they suck, swallow, cry, and recoil from painful stimuli. The brain stem of newborns seems to perform certain neurological functions that are subsequently subsumed by the cortex.[79] The main difference between normal newborns and those without a cortex is not their present capacities but their potential for future cognitive development. Criteria for the perception of pain based on adult experience should not be used for fetuses or newborns. Since the brain stem of anencephalic infants is usually intact and functioning we cannot dismiss the possibility of them experiencing pain.[80]

There is mounting evidence that the anatomical structures required for the experience of pain may be present and functional by 10–14 weeks' gestation and that pain could be experienced before the fetus has the capacity to move.[81] Experiments involving injury to decerebrate rats suggest fetal pain could be experienced before the cortex is formed.[82] Sensation and reflex movements are not mutually exclusive.[83] But since sensation is unobservable it cannot be excluded simply because reflexes are observed.[84] More research is needed to determine with confidence when a fetus can first experience pain because the fetus cannot communicate this to us nor is there evidence that adults can remember pain experienced when they were fetuses.

8.4 Care of the Fetus and Ethics

Pregnant woman responsible for her fetus

Both parents must be responsible and do what is reasonable and possible for the safety and well-being of their unborn child. The pregnant woman is the natural trustee of her fetus and for whose health she is primarily responsible. To fulfill this duty she seeks advice from doctors who are bound to assist her in discharging her duty of reasonable care. It is up to her to accept or decline medical treatment for her fetus after having been informed of the relevant risks and implications for herself and her fetus.[85]

The fetus has a moral right to reasonable life-saving or life-enhancing therapy. The doctor acts on behalf of the pregnant woman to provide reasonable therapies for her fetus. She may have a duty to permit a reasonable fetal therapy, but this does not imply that doctors or the state are morally entitled to use force to make a competent pregnant woman take medications or undergo invasive fetal therapies against her will.[86] Not every moral right is legally enforceable but criminal neglect is a matter for the courts. Maternal–fetal conflicts concerning therapy are better resolved by discussions involving both parents, and possibly consultation with other suitable persons such as a counselor, a psychologist, or a moral adviser. As a matter of public policy it would be in the best interests of the fetus if pregnant women's autonomy was respected rather than run the risk of pregnant women in need of help being afraid to consult doctors. It would be different for an infant, since invasive intervention on the mother would not be required. Life-saving blood transfusions should be given to save the lives of infants even if their parents refuse consent.

Doctors should not be surprised if some pregnant women do not accept their advice, since they also have to be satisfied beyond reasonable doubt that a decision to proceed with fetal therapy is justified. An objective medical evaluation of slight maternal risk of a therapy might not appear slight to the pregnant woman from the perspective of her fears, anxieties, and family situation. Pregnant women differ in their perceptions and reactions to information received on known risks and consequently in good faith make different evaluations and decisions in similar cases. Pregnant women are less likely to want aggressive treatment for their fetuses than new mothers for their babies.[87] The subjectivity of each pregnant woman is unique: this is part of the human predicament. It is helpful for mothers to realize that choices involving some risk to themselves may be more than balanced by their unborn children's greatly enhanced prospects for a normal life. Fetal therapy may also lessen the hardships of raising children by correcting malformations or curing diseases.

Doctor's duty to the mother and her fetus

Fetal therapy is a highly specialized field of medicine where it is becoming increasingly difficult to apply the principle of the duty of reasonable care for the pregnant woman and her fetus. The drawing of the line between when fetal therapy is futile and unwarranted and when it would be beneficial and warranted, and at what time during pregnancy, is one of the most difficult dilemmas that doctors and pregnant women have to face. More than one evaluation of risks by doctors and the mother could be reasonable without any being unreasonable. Clear-cut medico-moral answers are not frequent since in fetal therapy answers cannot always be given in advance. Ethical principles need to be applied case by case with an eye to the likely short- and long-term effects of intervention on the fetus, the mother and the family.

A doctor's professional expertise is called on to evaluate the risks for the mother and fetus before making a judgment on whether intervention is needed or what is the best medical fetal therapy in each case. Successful fetal therapies require accurate diagnoses and knowledge of the relevant fetal pathophysiology. This requires a careful evaluation of the fetus in addition to a clear anatomical understanding of the relevant malformation. Since it is known that malformations often occur as part of a syndrome, a search for associated abnormalities would be necessary to avoid delivering a neonate with one anomaly corrected, while still affected by another unrecognized life-long and severely disabling abnormality.[88] The timing of intervention should not be so early as to endanger the fetus nor so late as to make it futile. Again the mother should not be subjected to unnecessary invasive surgery. Most fetal defects are best treated after birth by the appropriate medical and/or surgical therapy. Other defects detected *in utero* may require early induction if continued gestation would have a progressive ill effect on the fetus or if correction of the defect is best left until after birth or delivery by elective caesarean section. The fetal age selected for premature delivery and treatment ought to be in the best interests of the health of the mother and fetus.[89] Consultation among colleagues may facilitate the task of assessing the risks to the fetus from fetal therapy, against the burden of malformation for a lifetime if treatment is not given. The probability of success would need to be fairly high to justify fetal therapy where the risk to the life of the fetus was substantial. Under no circumstances, not even at the request of the mother, should doctors act against their conscientious judgment in the medical care of a pregnant woman and/or her fetus. Often a mother or family members, for peace of mind, ask for what is unwarranted or even futile treatment in the hope that doctors will somehow put things right. Doctors may need to reassure them that not all interventions are in the best interests of both mother and fetus. If required, the doctor should act as a fetal advocate.

Fetal surgery

Some abnormalities warrant surgery *in utero*, subject to some ethical conditions. The services of a multidisciplinary team should be available, including a perinatal obstetrician, an ultrasonographer, a neonatologist, a paediatric surgeon, and a geneticist if required. It is necessary to avoid fetal surgery that saves a child who would have died naturally but who would instead survive with an enduring defect that causes much suffering. As a general rule, fetal surgery should only be used for singletons. The pregnant woman's informed and free consent is required, hopefully, with the involvement of her partner and doctor. Although there is an ethical duty to avoid preventable harm, surgery is not at present warranted for a fetus with hydrocephaly nor one affected by multiple defects. What needs to be known is how certain and great is the benefit of surgery for the fetus, if it is harmful for the mother, and what is the gain or loss in delaying it until after birth.[90]

Fetal surgeons should only routinely use surgery for those anomalies where it offers reasonable hope of success. They should review their work and shelve surgical procedures that would have poor outcomes. At the same time it would not be unjustified, with the mother's informed consent, to attempt an innovative therapeutic fetal surgical procedure to save the life of the fetus, when other remedies are likely to fail. Such surgery could lead to new therapies, preventive measures and knowledge of fetal pathologies for the benefit of other defective fetuses. But nontherapeutic fetal research that risks harming the fetus is unethical, even if it is done with parental consent. Experimental surgery in search of a subject should not proceed.

Fetal surgery is ethical if it poses no undue risks to the mother, is directed to improving the health of the fetus, the risks of intervention are considered less than withholding treatment until after birth, and the risks to the integrity, health, and life of the mother and fetus are proportionate.[91] Consider the risks of a fetus with urethral obstruction and severely damaged kidneys. The benefits of probable correction would have to weighed against the trauma of surgery for the mother, risks of perinatal death, severe disability from renal failure, and the emotional stress of prolonged, costly, and sometimes burdensome treatment of chronic renal failure after birth.[92] It would be pointless to treat *in utero* obstructive uropathy if the kidneys are already ruined, or to attempt surgery for hydrocephalus if brain damage is irreversible.

The risks of surgical intervention should be outweighed by the risks of non-intervention. One needs to consider the risks of surgery to both mother and fetus which may include perforation of the uterine wall, loss of blood, inadvertent injury to adjacent organs, the trauma of a misguided catheter or placental abruption. Infection could induce premature labor and delivery which would be detrimental to both mother and child. Less serious risks include the possibility of a caesarean section for all subsequent deliveries as well as the trauma of everything being suffered in vain. The medicoethical dilemma is magnified when we recall that diaphragmatic hernia in conjunction with excess amniotic fluid is 90 percent fatal without successful treatment.[93] Expert diagnosis is crucial to determine which fetus will die without surgery and which fetus will have a better chance of survival with it.

The risks of a therapy for a fetal malformation should be weighed against the probability of its correction and objective improvement. The possible benefit to be derived from the surgery would depend on the severity of the malformation, its likely degree of correction, the prospects for survival without severe disabilities and the need of ongoing treatment. In a case of obstructive hydrocephalus, if the choice were between no intervention with certain severe cerebral palsy and a premature death or intervention with a poor chance of correction, an infant with severe cerebral palsy and some risk of loss of life, all other things being equal, the balance would probably be against intervention. In a case of confirmed congenital diaphragmatic hernia it would be a matter of judging whether no intervention would mean a high risk of loss of life after birth or whether correction would allow the lungs to grow enough to support life at birth. Surgeons at times need the wisdom of Solomon to determine whether the odds warrant intervention or not.

At present, fetal surgery should normally be regarded as an *extraordinary* means of medical treatment to preserve life and improve the quality of life.[94] It needs to be justified in the sense that the normal presumption favors postnatal treatment. At times it is preferable to let death occur by allowing nature to take its course than to intervene and prolong a life of suffering and distress. It would seem better not to intervene if it could cause a child to survive in a permanent unconscious state. Fetal surgery may become an extremely beneficial therapy and reduce healthcare costs. Priority should be given to fund research on laboratory animals, without unnecessarily subjecting them to pain, to gain the required competence and success rates before using innovative fetal therapies on human subjects.

Fetal surgery, by focusing attention on the fetus as the subject of therapy, may raise timely questions in the public conscience on the moral status of the fetus as an unborn patient if not as a legally recognized person. It is certainly anomalous to find some doctors using their skills to save their unborn patients whilst others fail to recognize them by terminating pregnancies. This highlights the inadequacy of decisions on the value of life depending on the choice of parents or others. The likely correction of fetal defects through surgery might save fetal lives by persuading some pregnant women not to proceed with a planned induced abortion when their fetus is diagnosed with an abnormality.

At centers of excellence, however, fetal surgery is rightly a part of clinical practice for only a few anomalies amenable to correction for carefully selected fetuses.[95] It may significantly lessen degrees of disability and suffering and the need for life-long therapies. These reasons may justify it, irrespective of the costs saved. The savings over the years would be enormous for an outlay comparable to the cost of open heart surgery or coronary artery bypass if treatment of spina bifida *in utero* were to enter clinical practice. It could be a healthy baby may be born, capable of enjoying a normal life expectancy. Account must also be taken of factors arising from the culture and the socioeconomic situation of each country. What might be routinely available in a developed country might be unrealistic to expect in a developing nation.

Fetal tissue transplants

There should be strict compliance with the requirements of informed consent in relation to all known benefits and risks for the pregnant woman and her fetus. The pregnant woman, after receiving the necessary information, may need counseling before consenting to *in utero* fetal transplants. She would have a moral right to be informed if the transplant tissue was taken from a directly aborted fetus and to refuse to allow it to be transplanted into her fetus. Consent would be given more readily for *in utero* transplants than for fetal surgery because the former are less invasive and risky. The same conditions would apply to parents of children before allowing them to receive fetal tissue transplants. Informed consent is also required of the donor's mother if the tissue is to be used for the benefit of a third party for therapeutic or research purposes. Depending on the relationship, the father's consent should also be obtained, especially if transplantation is preceded by prenatal diagnostic testing since this could provide information about his genetic constitution as well as that of the mother.[96] It is important that adults over and below 60 years of age be fully informed of the risks and benefits before receiving fetal tissue transplants for the treatment of Parkinson's disease.

The same moral respect should be given to the life and dignity of mothers, fetuses, the donor, and the recipient. Fetal tissue should be donated, not sold as a commodity for commercial gain generated by market forces. Guarantees of success would be needed from research with animal models before beginning clinical trials.[97] Moral respect for the donor fetus absolutely demands that tissue should not be procured for therapeutic purposes before the fetus is dead, whether the fetus came from a miscarriage or an induced abortion. Death should be verified by the irreversible cessation of vital signs like heart beat, spontaneous respiration, movements of voluntary muscles, or pulsation of the umbilical cord as distinct from transient or reflex movements.[98] Consideration should be given to the possibility of known reversible factors, such as the effects of hypothermia, drugs, or metabolic disorders in the mother, to avoid a mistaken diagnosis of the fetus' death.[99]

Subject to taking reasonable precautions and compliance with all the above conditions, *in utero* transplants of fetal or adult stem cells may be ethical in selected clinical programs as also the use of fetal tissue for transplantation to children and adults. The funding for research to treat the symptoms of Parkinson's disease by fetal tissue transplants would be ethically warranted. There is a need for innovative and ethical therapeutic trials on human subjects to verify and perfect these techniques and increase our understanding of neural transplants. Since it would be unethical to risk "personality transfer" only small fragments of neuronal tissue or neurons should be transplanted to any recipient.[100]

Collusion with induced abortion

The major ethical objection to the use of fetal tissue for transplantation is its link with induced abortion if this is the source of the tissue. It is unethical to have an abortion, or to persuade a woman to have one, in order to obtain fetal cells for therapy. The same would also apply to a mother who becomes pregnant to abort her fetus so that the tissue could be used for an older sibling. It is unethical for the perpetrator of an immoral deed to profit from it, but not necessarily for others who were not party to the immoral deed. There is no intrinsic ethical objection to the therapeutic use of organs from murder victims nor for undertakers to profit from burying them. The use of aborted tissue need not *per se* imply approval of abortion nor complicity with the institution where the abortions are performed. The ethical problem is to find a way to avoid collusion between abortion and the use of aborted fetal tissue. An ethical barrier is needed to separate to the community's satisfaction the therapeutic use of tissue from induced abortions.

Some believe that the ethically required separation between consent for abortion and the therapeutic use of aborted fetal tissue is possible, subject to certain conditions.[101] They hold there should be no direct or indirect financial advantages nor other inducements offered to the pregnant woman nor the abortion clinic in exchange for consent to allow the aborted fetal tissue to be used. People who need fetal organs should not contact potential donors in any way to avoid exercising undue influence on the decision to abort. After a decision to have an abortion is made, clinicians using the tissue may not ethically influence the management of the pregnancy, the timing nor the method of abortion to better suit transplantation purposes. Transplant team members who prolong life still extant in an aborted fetus by medical treatment to improve prospects for procuring tissue would be in collusion with abortion. Finally the donor should not control the destiny of tissue donated for medical use, know its beneficiary nor profit financially from the future production of a cell line from the aborted fetus.[102]

Where transplant techniques are established, it is argued, it may be possible for an independent agency to arrange the transfer of tissues from aborted fetuses to clinicians who use them or to fetal tissue banks. The transfer of any necessary medical or genetic information about the mother and fetus would be done only through this intermediary. It is claimed that this could guarantee the ethically required separation between the users of the fetal tissue and the decision to abort by the mother and the abortion clinic staff. It is of interest to note that a survey of Europeans professionally involved in reproductive health found half of those opposed to elective abortion supported the therapeutic use of aborted fetal tissue. Though only 37 percent believed elective abortion was morally acceptable, 66 percent believed it was morally acceptable to use human tissue obtained from elective abortions.[103]

There would be the problem of knowledge in the community that fetal tissue from induced abortions was being used for the benefit of third parties. This practice, however, would hardly influence women to have abortions if there were no financial inducement. Legal abortions have been available long before the therapeutic use of fetal tissue began. Powerful personal factors influence a woman's decision to have an abortion, not abstract considerations of generosity for the benefit of anonymous fetuses or patients with Parkinson's disease.[104] Provided there is strict compliance with all the conditions and medical procedures described above, it is argued that the required moral separation could be achieved. Granted that aborted fetal tissue is available in any case, therapeutic benefit may be sought for third parties without any ethical compromise with the decision for an abortion.

On the other hand, I do not believe those who are morally opposed to induced abortion can consistently raise an ethical barrier between abortion and a policy to make aborted fetal tissue available for therapeutic use. Such a policy would implicitly condone abortion by the transplant team, the recipient, and the tissue provider. It would be ethically indistinguishable from collusion with abortion and the reduction of one human being to the status of a means for another's benefit. No respected independent agency could broker the supply of organs for transplants retrieved from the civilian victims of massacres in a war without moral taint and causing offense. It is one thing for a doctor not involved in a termination of pregnancy to use aborted tissue in a one-off emergency situation, but quite another to institutionalize and regulate its practice as a policy.[105] Use, however, may be made of suitable fetal tissue obtained from a source beyond moral reproach, such as a fetus who died as a result of ethical intervention to save the mother, a miscarriage in a sanitary environment, umbilical cord blood, or from cell lines cultured from these tissues.[106]

Fetal gene therapy

At present a justification is required for fetal gene therapy rather than postnatal therapy. Its risks of germ line transfection and of altering the human genotype of individuals and their offspring need to be addressed. It is ethically imperative for this risk to be absolutely excluded. When adult gene therapy is improved it would be timely to look to fetal trials in animals. The next step would be trials on preimmune primate fetuses to verify its efficacy and safety for the fetus and also the mother's cells. The ethical problems and social concerns about altering the genotype of adults and children need to be critically debated and settled before clinical trials of human fetal gene therapy start. Its safety, efficacy and its likely short- and long-term risks must be rigorously tested and verified to the community's satisfaction before it is allowed in clinical practice.[107] To date it is too early for fetal gene therapy to begin clinical trials.

In time, it may be deemed safe for experimental trials with human subjects. But following prenatal diagnosis of severe diseases it is likely anxious parents may not sufficiently grasp the implications and risks of fetal gene therapy for mothers and their fetuses. Selecting only fetuses with otherwise untreatable lethal diseases in the perinatal period would make the risks involved more tolerable. However, this would not be justified if the modifications entered the germ line unless their activation could be blocked to prevent their transmission in future offspring, as discussed in chapter 4.[108]

There is no ethical problem with *fetal gene therapy* in principle pro-vided the necessary trials with animals have been successfully completed and the pregnant woman has been fully advised of its safety and any known low level risks for herself and her fetus before freely giving consent. But the use of gene therapy trials on fetuses destined for abor-tion is unethical because it would be experimentation on human fetuses, not therapy. Genetically engineered minichromosomes offer promise as safe and effective vectors of therapeutic genes for target cells which can populate the required sites of the body. In the meantime morally respon-sible research must continue. Successful fetal gene therapy could even-tually become an alterative to termination of pregnancy when lethal or severe diseases are diagnosed prenatally.

Monochorionic twin abnormalities

In the case of monochorionic identical twins affected by twin–twin trans-fusion syndrome, including the case of the *stuck* twin, it would be ethical to attempt to save both by blocking vascular communications between them, even though this has a 33 percent risk of mortality and a 66 percent probability of success.[109] If nothing is done the risk of mortality is at least 75 percent for both as mentioned above. It would be ethical to perform serial amniocenteses when medically appropriate. On the other hand, there would be no ethical problem to remove the *acardius acephalus*, a parasitic twin without a heart and head since, unlike the anencephalic fetus, it could not be deemed a living human individual. In general, it would be ethical to surgically remove a nonviable "stuck" twin whose functioning was objectively threatening the life of the viable twin if this was necessary to save the viable twin. The viable twin would be saved by the removal of the life-threatening twin, not *per se* by the twin's death which is foreseen and permitted as an unwanted side-effect. The lifesaving *object* of removing a nonviable fetus from the uterus is crucial for interpreting its morality, even though the outcome is the same as a direct induced abortion.

Success for the treatment of lethal twin anomalies by surgery has not been high. The question arises as to whether the use of a lethal intrac-ardiac injection for an abnormal fetal twin who constitutes a threat to the life of the viable twin could ever be ethically justified when a live birth would otherwise be most unlikely and no other safe remedy is avail-able. By utilitarian criteria it would be deemed morally acceptable to do this, especially if it is believed the fetus is not a person. This would be deemed preferable to risking the lives of both. On the other hand I believe it would not be ethically justified because the viable twin would be saved by directly killing the abnormal twin.

Multifetal pregnancy reduction

The situation of a higher order multifetal pregnancy of six or more normal fetuses is somewhat similar to the previous case. In some cases an ethical problem arises from the well founded prognosis that if nothing is done, the whole pregnancy will be lost. It is unethical in the first place to risk creating this situation by implanting an excessive number of embryos in a woman as part of an ART procedure or by giving an infertile woman too high a dose of fertility drugs.[110] The ethical dilemma, however, still remains because higher order multifetal pregnancies occur naturally. *Multifetal pregnancy reduction* has been suggested to save one or more fetuses rather than lose the whole pregnancy.[111] But again it would be unethical to *deliberately* kill some fetuses *in utero* to give one or more of their siblings a chance of surviving. This would be *direct* abortion. One may not directly choose to kill some fetuses so that others may live, even if the alternative is the probable death of them all. One may not drown some infants to ensure sufficient food for the survival of others in a tragic situation. I do not agree with the usual utilitarian solution for multifetal reduction.[112]

Fetal pain

In therapeutic interventions on the fetus, there is an ethical duty to avoid inflicting unnecessary pain. The subject on whom pain is inflicted influences the degree of the disvalue of the harm inflicted. It is bad enough to hurt a sheep fetus without necessity, but worse to do so to a human fetus. From the time in gestation when there are good reasons to believe a human fetus could experience pain, the *benefit of the doubt* should be given by the clinician to a human fetus to avoid inflicting unnecessary pain, even by using an anesthetic if this is warranted. It seems the burden of proof in relation to fetal sentience lies with those who exclude it as a possibility rather than with those who have good reasons for claiming it is possible. Researchers on animals are bound by the following guideline in Australia:

Unless there is specific evidence to the contrary investigators must assume fetuses have the same requirements for anaesthesia and analgesia as adult animals of the species.[113]

It would be reasonable to expect no less a standard should apply to all medical procedures on human fetuses.

9

Newborns

9.1 Breastfeeding

Both parents should be involved in the well-being of their newborn child by way of support and the sharing of responsibility in caring for the child. It is important for mothers to breastfeed their newborn babies for the first months after birth, unless they are HIV-infected. Due to the maternal antibodies in breast milk, breastfeeding protects the baby against debilitating diarrhea, fatal inflammation of the small intestine and bowel, gastroenteritis, some allergies, immunological deficiencies, a shortage of specific nutrients required for postnatal brain development, and respiratory infections. There are also benefits for the mother: it significantly reduces her risk of breast cancer and carcinoma of the ovary later in life. Society's attitudes need to improve to facilitate breastfeeding in view of the benefits for children, but without making impositions on mothers.[1] Also the levels of organochlorins passing from the environment and water ways into breast milk need to monitored.[2]

9.2 Perinatal Mortality

There was a perinatal mortality rate (PMR) of 6.9 for Australia and 7.5 for the UK per 1,000 births in 1995 based on deaths between 28 weeks' gestation and one week of age.[3] The mortality rates of infants during the first year of life per 1,000 live births in 1998 were 6 for Australia, 8 Greece, and 7 for the UK and the USA.[4] These figures represent a great leap in perinatal survival compared to earlier years.[5] In Australia the

Table 9.1: Causes of Australian neonatal deaths

Cause of death: main condition	Percentage
Respiratory conditions – hypoxia, birth asphyxia etc.	17.0
Congenital anomalies	32.4
Slow fetal growth and fetal malnutrition and immaturity	15.0
Infections specific to newborns	5.8
Unspecified	1.5

Source: modified from Australian Bureau of Statistics *Causes of Death Australia 3303.0 – 1998.*

neonatal death rate from 400 g birthweight or 20 weeks' gestation fell from 10 per 1,000 live births in 1975 to 3.0 in 1998.[6] The main conditions that caused Australia's 754 neonatal deaths for 1998 are given in table 9.1, although respiratory defects would apply to other categories as well. The figures are comparable to other countries and are useful for ethical reflection.[7]

9.3 Low Birthweight Babies

Terminology

Full-term delivery occurs from 37 to 42 weeks' gestation and postterm delivery is after 42 completed weeks. A preterm infant is one who is born at less than 37 weeks' gestation, calculated from the date of the last menstrual period. About 7 percent of infants are born preterm in the UK and Australia and 6 percent are postterm. A low birthweight (LBW) baby is one born weighing less than 2,500 g. About 6 percent of babies are LBW in developed countries. These may be preterm or may not have grown sufficiently in the uterus and are said to be small for gestational age (SGA). Very low birthweight (VLBW) babies weigh less than 1,500 g and represent about 1 percent of all live births. Extremely low birthweight (ELBW) infants weigh less than 1,000 g and are 0.04 percent of all live

Table 9.2: Mean fetal weights according to
gestational age, Australia

Gestational age in weeks	Weight in grams
20–1	420
22–3	552
24–5	690
26–7	874
28–9	1,206
30–1	1,441
34–5	1,988
38–9	2,892

Source: modified from *Journal of Paediatrics and Child
Health* 26 (1990): 102.

births.[8] Infants born about 16 weeks' premature are sometimes called
"micro-prems." In Australia for 1995–7 the PMR of twins was 4.4 times
more than for singletons and 8.5 times more for higher multiple births.[9]
Though not identical, LBW may be used as a crude indicator of immaturity. Table 9.2 shows mean fetal weights according to gestational age.[10]

Causes

The causes for SGA babies in the UK include chromosomal and other
congenital anomalies (10 percent), maternal and fetal infections (less
than 5 percent), placenta and cord defects (less than 5 percent), vascular disease in the mother including diabetes and heart disease (35
percent), drugs, medications, and smoking (5 percent), and other causes
(32 percent).[11] In the USA abuse of cocaine, opiates, and cannabinoids
has been found to be associated with a high perinatal morbidity.[12] In
urban populations the incidence of cocaine abuse has been reported to
be as high as 10 percent during pregnancy: it has harmful effects on prematurity, intrauterine growth, first trimester miscarriage, premature
labor, intracerebral hemorrhage, and some overt teratogenic effects.[13]

Early induction of labor for the benefit of the health or life of the
mother and/or fetus accounts for about one third of LBW babies. The

Table 9.3: Neonatal intensive care unit, Loyola University Medical Center, survival rates, 1990–4

Gestational age, weeks	Survivors %
22–3	19
24–5	63
26–7	88

Source: modified from "Neonatal Survival Rates" in *Cambridge Quarterly of Healthcare Ethics* 8 (1999): 162.

reasons for early induction of labor include pre-eclampsia, essential hypertension, intrauterine growth retardation, multiple pregnancy, premature rupture of the membranes, maternal infections, and uterine bleeding. To these may be added risk factors such as low socioeconomic status, maternal age less than 18 or greater than 35 years, excessive maternal activity, and cigarette smoking.[14]

VLBW babies may experience trauma and distress during labor and birth due to prematurity or its cause, e.g. premature detachment of the placenta. They often suffer from respiratory distress syndrome (RDS) and need resuscitation, even though antenatal steroids are usually given to the mother and surfactant to the baby after birth.[15]

Neonatal intensive care

Survival rates of newborns are usually given by birthweight or gestational age. Neonatal survival rates have improved dramatically since the 1940s when newborns less than 1,000 g did not generally survive in England and Wales and when world average survival rates for newborns less than 1,500 g was about 38 percent and 50 percent in the 1960s.[16] Risk-adjusted survival for VLBW babies is the best basis for comparison. It involves taking into account birthweight, gestational age, congenital malformations, and other clinical risk factors.[17] By the mid-1990s 85–90 percent of ELBW newborns survived.[18] From 1990 to 1994, the neonatal intensive care unit (NICU) survival rates of the Loyola University Medical Center were better; see table 9.3.[19]

Table 9.4: Survival rates by gestational age, 1994–6

Gestational age (weeks)	Live births	Survivors percentage
23	31	35.5
24	36	65.6
25	46	73.9
26	64	85.9
28	75	96.0
32	262	98.1

Source: modified and calculated from data in the Royal Women's Hospital in Melbourne, *Medical Journal of Australia*, June 7, 1999.

A recent major study of *all live births* in the UK and Ireland over 9 months in 1995 showed that of 138 newborns at 22 completed weeks' gestation, 2 (1 percent) survived to discharge, of 241 newborns at 23 weeks' gestation, 11 percent survived to discharge, of 382 at 24 weeks 26 percent survived, and of 424 newborns at 25 weeks 44 percent survived.[20] It is to be noted that neonatal mortality rates would be lower if all ELBW babies were transferred for birth to a center with a level-3 neonatal intensive care unit (NICU). Survival rates of live preterm newborns in a hospital with a NICU over the three years 1994–6 are given in table 9.4 by gestational age.[21] It is worth noting that 14 percent of 154 deaths in NICU of newborns of 23–7 weeks' gestation was caused by infection during 1983–90, whereas it was 44 percent of 80 deaths in the same NICU for the same gestational age during 1992–6.[22]

Survivors with disabilities

About 7–8 percent of VLBW babies have chronic neuromotor impairment of varying severity and 40 percent of all children with cerebral palsy are preterm babies. Estimates for VLBW babies give a 50 percent minor impairment rate, e.g. cognitive reductions, learning disabilities, speech and language disorders, persistent neuromotor abnormalities including difficulties with balance and coordination, and problems with emotional maturity.[23] In Victoria in 1979–80 of 129 infants weighing 500–749 g at birth about 6 percent survived two years, of whom about 88 percent had a disability – 25 percent severe, 13 percent moderate, and 50 percent mild. In 1991–2 of 169 newborns of the same weight, 32 percent survived two years and of these about 39 percent had a disability – 9 percent severe, 9 percent moderate, and 20 percent mild.[24] Of 316 live births at 24–6 weeks' gestation over two years in Victoria 1985–7, 30 percent survived to 5 years of age, of whom 60.6 percent were unaffected, 7.4 percent had a severe disability, 7.4 percent a moderate disability, and 24.5 percent a mild disability.[25] Though most VLBW babies do well, longitudinal studies show functional disabilities of varying severity appear in the first 5 to 7 years of life, e.g. adaptation, interaction with the environment, and information-processing strategies.[26]

Severe disability rates of survivors at 30 months in the major study in the UK and Ireland mentioned above for newborns at 23, 24, and 25 weeks were 30.8 percent, 24 percent, and 21.5 percent respectively; the rate of other disabilities in the same group of survivors was 23 percent, 28 percent, and 23.7 percent respectively. Severe disability was defined as unable to walk without assistance, unable to sit, to use hands to feed self, no head control, blind, hearing impaired even with hearing aid, and not communicating by speech. Other disabilities included abnormal gait, unstable sitting, difficulty in using both hands, vision needing correction, and speech defects.[27] Of newborn survivors of less than 800g in the University of Washington, major impairments were found in 22 percent born in 1986–90, 21 percent born in 1983–5, and 19 percent born in 1977–80. The rates of cerebral palsy, mental retardation, blindness, and deafness have remained stable in the 1980s and 1990s.[28] While more preterm infants survive in good health, there are also more surviving with difficulties – neurological, emotional, and intellectual as well as physical disabilities and an excess of neurocognitive and behavioral problems in adolescents with respect to their controls.[29] Low survivor and severe disability rates for ELBW newborns have some relevance to the ethics of treatment decisions for borderline ELBW newborns.

Costs

The cost for caring for ELBW babies in Britain in the early 1990s ranged from £10,000–15,000 per survivor.[30] The overall cost per day of assisted ventilation in NICU was estimated at AU$1,140. The costs per surviving newborn weighing 600–699g and 700–799g in 1985–7 were AU$131,690 and AU$113,080 respectively. The cost effectiveness ratio of NICU care of ELBW babies is, however, better than that of some high-technology operations for coronary care and organ transplants as well as for some low-technology procedures, such as treatment for hypertension.[31] After surfactant was used in NICU the economic outcome improved considerably.[32]

9.4 Delivery for HIV-infected Pregnant Women

As we saw in chapter 7, if maternal antiretroviral therapy is used in conjunction with elective caesarean section delivery, the HIV vertical transmission rate is reported to be reduced to 2 percent compared to 7.3 percent with other modes of delivery; if it is not used the transmission rate is 10.4 percent for elective caesarean and 19 percent for other modes of delivery.[33] Researchers in Britain have confirmed European and American conclusions that antiretroviral therapy and caesarean section delivery, combined or separately, significantly reduce vertical HIV transmission to less than 2 percent in some cases. A "bloodless caesarean section" technique in which the baby is not exposed to maternal blood or bodily fluids, has been found to further reduce the risk of HIV transmission.[34] It has also been suggested that therapy consisting of a combination of antiretroviral agents reduces HIV vertical transmission almost to zero without the need of a risky caesarean delivery.[35] It has been reported however, that HIV-infected pregnant women have a greater risk of postoperative morbidity and complications after caesarean section delivery, regardless of antiretroviral therapy.[36] Finally the rate among nonbreastfeeding HIV-infected women fell from 19.6 percent in 1993 to 2.2 percent in 1998 after the use of maternal antiretroviral therapy significantly increased.[37]

9.5 Neonatal Transplants

Thanks to advances in pediatric surgery, abnormalities in many newborns can be successfully repaired.[38] Over half of 404 of babies who received surgery for major congenital malformations were born at term.[39] The cause of death of newborns is often an untreatable congenital defect of the heart, liver, or kidneys. Recourse to organ transplants is often the only chance to save infants. Many newborns and infants die waiting for a suitable heart or liver to become available. The use of the immunosuppressive agent cyclosporin has increased the success rate of transplants. To lessen the risk of rejection, the blood type of donor and recipient are matched and often tissue typing is also done. Once donor infants die, their organs need to be transplanted within 4 to 6 hours of removal to lessen blood and oxygen deficiency which jeopardizes the success of transplants.[40] As we shall see, the quality of all organs obtained from deceased anencephalic infants needs to be monitored to verify that they are suitable before using them for transplants.[41] It is to be noted that success rates normally refer to survival rates, but seldom is mention made of quality of life considerations, i.e. capability for normal activities, severe disability or frequent need of hospital care.

Heart

Heart transplants from newborns and infants offers hope of life for other newborns and infants with congenital heart defects, e.g. hypoplastic left heart syndrome, a defect which has an early mortality rate of about 50 percent and few prospects for long term survival. In the USA and Europe the number of heart transplants has increased and been more successful since the early 1980s. Over 300 pediatric heart transplants have been done at California's Loma Linda University Medical School, where the survival rate of newborn recipients was 77 percent at 11 years.[42] At Giessen, Germany, the overall survival rate for heart transplants into 39 infants from 1988–97 was 82 percent, all in excellent condition, and up to 96 percent in 24 infants from 1994–7.[43] Naturally the survival rate of newborns following heart transplants is not as high as in older children.[44]

Liver

Liver transplants in newborns are usually performed for biliary atresia, a progressive obliterative process involving the bile ducts. Its onset is in the newborn period and unless treated it is fatal. Liver transplants can improve survival and quality of life.[45] The 1-, 5- and 10-year survival rates for 20 newborns from 0–6 months of age who had liver transplants in the USA from 1984–95 were 85 percent, 79 percent, and 79 percent.[46] In the UK 5 out of 9 younger newborns, mean age 6 weeks, were alive with good graft function at a mean follow-up of 22 months.[47] Bone marrow or liver transplantation offer a chance of definitive treatment for lysomal storage disease. Liver transplantation may also help newborns suffering from inborn errors of metabolism or a liver-specific enzyme deficiency.[48]

Kidney

The outcome of kidney transplants into newborns varies: it is less successful than in adults but age disparity in donors and hosts is less important. Adults' kidneys have also been successfully transplanted into newborns. There is a greater probability of success when transplants are received by infants after their first year of life.[49] A study of 101 pediatric recipients from 1984–93 found that kidneys from donors less than 4 years in the UK lowered the one-year graft survival rate to an unacceptable level (63 percent versus 85 percent).[50] In the USA the 1- and 5-year survival rates for 537 recipients of kidney transplants aged 0–2 years were 71 percent and 60 percent. In this group, the survival rate with living donors was 84 percent compared to 66 percent with cadaveric donors.[51]

Umbilical cord blood

Umbilical cord blood (UCB) with its hematopoietic stem cells (HSCs) has clinical advantages and a higher success rate than bone marrow transplants for allogenic recipients with blood disorders.[52] From 1989–98 over 500 UCB stem cells transplants have been performed, mainly in USA and Europe. UCB has about 10 times the repopulation potential of bone marrow and HSCs are likely to be less immunologically active than those found in blood or bone marrow and so cause fewer problems with graft-versus-host disease. In the UK the costs of each procurement and banking of UCB is approximately £2,500.[53] A study of UCB transplants from sibling donors into 44 children to reconstitute their hematopoiesis shows the success rate was 85 percent after 50 days for patients who had a fairly perfect graft match, and the probability of graft-versus-host disease after 100 days ranged from 3–6 percent. The probability of survival for these recipients with a median follow-up of 1.6 years was 72 percent. This shows that closely matched UCB from sibling donors is a good source of transplantable HSCs for the treatment of children with a low risk of graft-versus-host disease.[54] Advantages of UCB include its non-invasive collection, low risk for viral infection and immunologic naiveté. Little wonder that UCB banks have been established for the children's future use or for donation.[55]

Brain death and neonatal transplants

There is no agreement on whether whole brain death (brain stem and cortex) criteria are reliable and safe for full-term newborns in the first 7 days of life.[56] The reliability of these criteria are uncertain in predicting nonrecovery in the case of newborns since brain death criteria, designed for biologically and physiologically mature adults, do not necessarily apply to newborns without modification. In the UK the traditional criteria of spontaneous cessation of heart beat and respiration have been retained by medical authorities for all newborns in their first week of life, for newborns of 37 weeks' gestation during the first two months of life, and for newborns of less than 37 weeks' gestation. Whole brain death criteria, however, could be applied reliably to comatose infants older than two months, who are supported by a respirator and when there is compliance with the medical preconditions of structural brain damage or the cause of coma is known and the influence of drugs, hypothermia, endocrine, or metabolic disturbances have been excluded.[57] A UK medical authority has approved of organs being removed from anencephalic infants after two doctors who are not members of the transplant team declare spontaneous respiration has ceased or apnea is verified, even within the first week of life.[58]

There is a drastic shortage of neonatal and infant organs to meet the ever growing demands for transplants. Doctors have looked to anencephalic infants as an alternative source of organs. However, organs from deceased anencephalic infants are not likely to be very suitable for transplantation because the oxygenation of their organs is below the physiological level required due to their likely deficient cardiorespiratory functions. An attempt to solve this problem at Loma Linda in California failed and doctors decided to resort back to their original source of organ donors.[59]

9.6 Ethical Issues in the Treatment of Newborns

General principles and criteria

Improved neonatal survival rates do not console those parents whose babies are at risk because they are born extremely premature or with severe birth defects. Ethics requires that all that is necessary and reasonable ought to be done in the best interests of the newborn baby to preserve life and restore health. It is not a matter of saying one life is worth more than another, nor of being guided only by vague generic quality of life criteria. Doctors have the difficult task to determine when the benefits of treatment outweigh expected burdens and risks of harm. Neonatologists are qualified to make these assessments. Medical treatment should serve the true good of the person and not merely prolong life. The British Bishops wrote:

> One should not expect doctors to strive to prolong the lives of newborn babies who cannot achieve at least that degree of well-functioning which would be sufficient to enable them to share in some of the goods of human life. . . . [e.g. communication . . . or especially relevant to babies, some form of play or the sheer appreciation of one's own vitality].[60]

This is close to John Wyatt's criterion of the "capacity . . . for loving and interactive human relationships."[61] However, provided a distressing dying process is not prolonged, treatment in NICU may continue until parents and close relatives can come to see and cuddle the child before death, and perhaps time should be allowed for the baby to be christened if the parents so wish.[62]

Alleviation of distress is a priority in neonatal care. Even if a clinically appropriate dose of morphine represses respiration in a newborn and may shorten life, it would be ethical to do so if this was the only effective remedy to alleviate distress of a dying baby.[63] But it would be unethical and criminal to administer to dying newborns a lethal drug as some physicians' self-reported practices indicate for France (73 percent) and the Netherlands (47 percent).[64] On the other hand Peter Singer and others believe incurable severely disabled and/or infants dying in distress may be painlessly killed with their parents' consent.[65]

The medical practitioners responsible for newborns with serious health problems should decide what treatment options to recommend to the parents bearing in mind the availability of any necessary follow-up medical care. It must be admitted that not all doctors would recommend the same treatment in the same case. This is not problematic provided the treatment is properly evaluated, reasonable in the circumstances and not contrary to ethical values.[66] The law should only intervene in cases of homicide, manslaughter, negligence, or unjust discrimination. I agree with the ruling of Lord Donaldson, Master of the Rolls, in the UK Court of Appeal in 1992 when he said:

> there will be cases in which . . . it is not in the interests of the child to subject it to treatment which will cause increased suffering and produce

no commensurate benefit, giving the fullest possible weight to the child's and mankind's desire to survive.[67]

Since it is not always possible to assess fully and immediately the true condition of newborns with *severe congenital diseases or malformations*, NICU treatment should be commenced to allow time for consultations so that accurate diagnoses and reasonably confident prognoses can be given. Once it is known a baby is suffering from an incurable fatal condition it would be unethical to provide futile treatment which could cause the infant to experience intractable pain or distress. Life for the newborn is a gift, not a life sentence. Kluge rightly disapproves of treatments given in good faith whereby "severely disabled newborns are tortured to life."[68] For example, it would be futile to treat an infant with surgery for a lethal defect that was part of a syndrome which included other untreatable lethal defects. In these cases, decisions not to treat should not be ethically equated with killing the infant. Parents may need counseling to understand these ethical distinctions for their peace of mind. But if there are reasonable doubts concerning a child's condition being fatal, the benefit of the doubt should be given to the child and aggressive treatment should continue until the situation is clarified.

Most *conjoined twins* can be safely separated. In the case of conjoined twins where both will die unless they are separated and it is likely only one twin could be saved if separation were to proceed, it would be unethical to save one by *deliberately* and *directly* killing the other. If a life-saving procedure has reasonable prospects of saving one twin but has the foreseen and inevitable, but *unwanted* side-effect of causing the death of the other twin, this could be deemed to be ethically defensible. If the prognosis for both was very poor after separation, it would be ethical to provide normal nursing care without attempting to separate them.

Whenever parents are not available and medical treatment cannot be delayed, doctors should proceed with the indicated treatment in virtue of their professional responsibilities. If parents refuse consent for necessary and reasonable life-saving treatment, doctors should give it and not simply provide palliative care since their primary duty of care is to their infant patients, not the parents. If necessary, an application may need to be made for the appointment of a legal guardian. Usually these problems can be avoided by good communication between doctors and parents.

Caution is needed if newborns with a disability are also affected by a life-threatening condition which requires treatment. They should be given the same medical treatment and care that would be given to infants without a disability. In the case of a baby with Down syndrome, who has a blocked bowel or a life-threatening infection, failure to remove the blockage or administer appropriate antibiotics would be unethical. However, if treatment itself may severely lessen quality of life, and most likely would do so throughout life, this would be ethically significant in decision-making. The life-saving treatment that would be given to a sick infant without a disability, all other things being equal, should also be given to one with a congenital disability. Adults need to be wary about judging the severity of a newborn's disability solely from their own perspective. The experience of one who has a congenital disability cannot be compared to the loss experienced when a competent adult becomes disabled.

Once it is determined that the baby's condition is not fatal, the likely benefits, burdens and risks of treatment options and their short- and long-term outcomes, including quality of life, should be discussed with the parents before obtaining their informed consent. A therapy may be tried if it offers a reasonable hope of curing a serious disability, even if death might result, provided no other alternative is at hand and the risks are not disproportionate to the expected benefits. A society that requires aggressive treatment be given to keep a severely defective newborn alive should also contribute substantially to the costs of caring for the child for life and not leave the burden to the parents alone.[69]

Doctors should not act against their judgment to comply with parents' wishes by aggressively treating newborns to save their lives when the outcome would result in prolonging a distressing dying process. But in cases where doubts persist the parents, as their child's natural trustees, may assume more responsibility in making the decision between the various treatment options, bearing in mind the likely benefits, risks, short- and long-term prospects for the child, including the burdens of physical and psychological suffering and the capacity of the family to cope. The prospects of a burdensome existence should not be lightly dismissed when making these decisions. In such gray zones subjective factors play a role in decision-making. Parents may then have no less expertise than doctors in making the right decision and doctors should normally defer to the judgment of the parents in such cases.[70]

It could be that the reasonable and morally permissible option, on the balance of probable benefits over burdens, is equally poised between treatment and nontreatment, provided normal medical and nursing care continue. The benefits of pediatric surgery could also be offset by some fatal risk caused by it. If a newborn baby with a severe cerebral hemorrhage had a prognosis of 20 percent survival with respirator treatment in NICU and a 75 percent risk of a serious disability after survival, I do not think continued therapy would be ethically necessary because the harm would outweigh the benefit. In a Danish survey on this case where the parents favored continuing treatment, 43 percent of the sample surveyed agreed, 49 percent disagreed and 8 percent were undecided, whereas when the parents opposed continued treatment 77 percent agreed, 14 percent disagreed and 10 percent were undecided.[71]

Delivery options and HIV transmission

About a third of South Australian women had not been involved in the decision to have a caesarean section delivery and one fifth reported they were not given sufficient information on their options.[72] Recently a Senate Report in Australia recommended lowering an unacceptably high national caesarean section rate of 20.3 percent of all births in 1997 to 15 percent.[73] It is reasonable for women to have a choice in the matter provided they have been given unbiased information about their birth options.[74] When complications during delivery are anticipated, the mother should be given an informed choice on delivery options. HIV-infected pregnant women should be allowed to choose vaginal or caesarean section delivery for their children after they have been given up to date information on the likely risks and benefits.[75]

After the use of antiretroviral therapy was significantly increased in the British Isles in 1994, the rate of HIV-infected newborns progressing to AIDS within the first six months of life fell from 18 percent to 7 percent. In this study, after six months it was found about 5 percent of children who had not developed AIDS did so each subsequent year.[76] In the light of these figures, and others mentioned in chapter 7, non HIV-related conditions in newborns at risk of HIV should be treated the same as others who are not at risk of HIV and without any unjust discrimination. This point is worth making as it has been found that 98 percent of neonatologists would recommend cardiac surgery for a newborn not at risk for of HIV, 93 percent for a child of an HIV-positive mother and only 50 percent for a newborn known to be HIV infected. The corresponding percentages for chronic dialysis were 91 percent, 61 percent, and 26 percent.[77]

Artificial nutrition and hydration

There is a clear duty to provide appropriate nutrition and hydration because it is a basic need to sustain life for newborns whether they are normal, abnormal or affected by a fatal condition. The same applies to normal comfort care. Though newborns can survive without nutrition for a few days after birth, artificial nutrition and hydration should be given as needed to an abnormal newborn infant whose condition is treatable until such time as it is no longer required. The same applies in a doubtful situation until a certain prognosis for life can be made. One may not deny food and fluids to newborns with the intention of causing or hastening death on account of a poor quality of life prognosis. Medically assisted nutrition and hydration should be continued to avoid a newborn's distress, but not if "nutrition itself aggravates the state of a dying child."[78] It would be ethically permissible to give a dying infant analgesics and/or sedatives needed to relieve pain or distress even if this meant a demand for food would not be expressed. In this situation there would be no need to initiate medically assisted nutrition and hydration. By the same token there would be no duty to initiate ventilation or artificial nutrition and hydration for a newborn baby with no long-term prospects of surviving without them.

Treatment of extremely low birthweight babies

As a preliminary remark, anticipated premature deliveries should, as far as possible, be prevented by early admission to a level 3 hospital for therapy aimed at stabilizing the pregnancy to delay birth. In the light of the facts of NICU deaths caused by infection mentioned above, it is ethically imperative to monitor infection control in NICU in relation to procedural practices and the avoidance of overcrowding in NICU itself.

A fair presumption is that ELBW babies should be treated aggressively unless a proper assessment determines it could not save life, prolongs the dying process, results in untreatable distress, or would be futile without any reasonable hope of permanently maintaining spontaneous respiration. Treatment would be virtually futile if it is linked to intractable pain for a disproportionate potential benefit. While refusing to initiate treatment without good reasons may be compared to "obstetrical soothsaying," there is no ethical duty to resuscitate an infant at birth if it is clear that the prognosis is one of ongoing severe pain and suffering; however obstetricians should be cautious to refuse to involve a pediatrician and the NICU team.[79] Where it is not possible to transport the child to a center with NICU facilities ELBW babies should be given normal nursing care and kept comfortable until they die naturally.

Parents should be reasonably and honestly informed and helped to share in making treatment decisions for their ELBW babies where death or life with serious disabilities are likely outcomes. Counseling may be needed and obstetricians are probably the best suited to do this because they already know the family situation of the mothers who have to care for their child, with or without significant neurological or other disabilities. To this end, if an ELBW baby is expected to have very poor prospects an action plan should be discussed with the parents prior to delivery. Decisions to forgo, or withdraw, NICU treatment should be made in the best interests of the child and in consultation with the parents.[80] Once babies arrive in NICU reasonable allowance must be made for variations in assessment by the NICU team before a firm diagnosis can be reached. However, when reasonable doubts persist about continuing treatment in NICU they should be resolved in favor of life.

National ELBW and gestational age survival rates are only indicative and from them alone absolute cut-off points for NICU cannot be determined. Congenital abnormalities and other relevant complications should always be considered together with the hospital's current survival rates by gestational ages and birthweights, as both are important when determining if NICU treatment should continue. The human factor for all concerned cannot be neglected. The benefits of continuing NICU have to be proportionate to the burdens likely to be caused to newborns, their parents, the community and the distress endured by NICU staff.[81] Kluge's criteria of the likely degrees of long-lasting severe pain, distress, and disability for life-saving treatment decisions for severely disabled newborns could also be considered in the case of some ELBW babies.[82] A recent study has shown that parental education, a sound family financial situation, family and geographic stability and rearing by both parents are better predictors of school performance than early perinatal complications.[83] Parents might be reassured by these findings. Continued NICU treatments would not be ethically necessary if, in the words of John Paul II, they

> no longer correspond to the real situation of the patient, either because they are by now disproportionate to any expected results . . . It needs to be determined whether the means of treatment available are objectively proportionate to the prospects for improvement.[84]

Traditionally, treatment that is too burdensome to the patient has always been accepted as ethical grounds for refusing it. In this sense pain and suffering are in a high-level category of quality of life criteria with ethical significance. Risks of lower-level quality of life criteria like deafness, blindness, or mental impairment should not alone determine whether NICU treatment should be discontinued. ELBW Down syndrome babies should be given NICU treatment to enable them to survive. It would be quite another matter if the prognosis of an ELBW baby was survival with considerable pain or with frequent burdensome invasive treatment for life or with life-long severe physical and mental disabilities.[85] It is to be noted that severe intellectual disability in ELBW babies is rarely found in isolation from severe physical disability, e.g. cerebral palsy.

Assessments of viability at the margins and of NICU treatment for ELBW infants should be made case by case as the combination of maturity, condition, weight, sturdiness and prior maternal administration of steroids to accelerate fetal lung development is unique for each infant. It has been said "two 24-week-gestation infants are no more alike than two 12-year-old children entering puberty."[86] It would be decided at birth that NICU treatment would be futile for a newborn of 20 weeks' gestation and weighing less than 350g. Clearly a healthy baby born at 28 weeks' gestation and weighing 900g would be viable and should certainly receive NICU treatment. Drawing the line for the birthweight and gestation age of viability when NICU may, but need not be, and when NICU should be used is more difficult. This is a gray area where the professional judgment of neonatologists may legitimately differ.[87] Kraybill calls it the zone "of uncertain viability."[88] Painstaking clinical judgments are required to determine those ELBW babies for whom continued treatment is warranted in the light of the probabilities of survival, the proportionate benefits received and any likely severe disabilities the child may have over the years. A survey of neonatologists' attitudes found one third of them as parents would not give their own ELBW infants the same aggressive treatment they as physicians give to others ELBW infants: this may suggest that treatment of some ELBW babies may be going too far.[89]

Newborns of 22 completed weeks' gestation and less than 400g birthweight should not be resuscitated since their prospects of surviving would be extremely poor. In general it would be ethically permissible, but not necessary, to initiate NICU treatment for newborns of 23 completed weeks' gestation and weighing at least 400–500g at birth. After assessment and consultation with the parents, a decision could then be made whether continued NICU treatment for these babies is warranted granted their very poor prospects, survival rates of about 30 percent and likely disabilities.[90] This would satisfy the duty of reasonable care and allow a more equitable allocation of NICU facilities for a greater number of older preterm babies for shorter periods of time.

By 24 completed weeks' gestation and a birthweight of 500–600g I believe the presumption should favor a duty to resuscitate and provide NICU treatment unless it is confirmed by assessment that the baby is not responding well and the parents are in agreement.[91] Where NICU is available, from 25 completed weeks' gestation and a birthweight greater than 600g, barring other complications, it would be ethically required to resuscitate and treat all newborns in NICU in the light of survival rates greater than 70 percent.[92] In the same Danish survey mentioned earlier, a majority (57 percent) favored life-prolonging treatment after 25 weeks even if the parents were reluctant to do so.[93]

Neonatal transplants

Neonatal transplant programs can only succeed with the support of the wider community. If there is a perception that something in the program is ethically amiss parents will be reluctant to be generous and donate the organs of their deceased infants. Organ donations, however, should only be made with the informed consent of the recipient's parents in relation to its likely success, benefits and risks of rejection as well as the effects of immunosuppressive therapy. Counselors may need to help the donor's parents resolve their anxieties or moral dilemmas by pointing out the benefit that may come to another child from their own tragic loss. Though help may be needed for parents to freely consent to the donation of an organ of their deceased infant, they must not be made to feel guilty if they refuse to donate their baby's organ. Once the parents have been duly informed, their eventual decision should be respected by the medical team. Support and gestures of thanks should be shown by the relevant medical and/or hospital staff to parents who donate their deceased babies' organs. This needs to be done lest they feel doctors only care about obtaining their consent to use their babies' organs. Support should also be shown to those who have cared for the children before they died as well as their families.

Newborns' own interests should dictate the kind of care given to them before they die, not the needs of the recipients of their organs. No human being should be reduced to the status of mere means for another's benefit, and much less should newborn infants be subjected to the risk of enduring pain. This ethical concern is worth raising since there is an unfounded belief that anencephalic newborns cannot experience pain, as we saw above in chapter 8.

It is ethically necessary that prior to the removal of organs, newborn infants must be brain dead, certified by qualified doctors who are not involved in the transplant procedure and in accord with legal requirements. Some parents may need to be reassured that the death of a person occurs once the criteria for whole brain death have been met, even if the infant is still breathing with the help of a respirator and maintains a heart beat. Where there are reasonable doubts about the reliability of brain death criteria for certain newborn infants, it is ethically imperative to give them the benefit of any reasonable doubt. The criteria for whole brain death should not be used to declare the death of full-term newborns: the traditional criteria of spontaneous cessation of heart beat and respiration should be used for all newborns in the first week of life. It is also necessary to use these same criteria for newborns at or below 37 weeks' gestation.

Granted the shortage of organs for neonatal transplants one can understand why some doctors and others would like cortical death to be accepted as the death of the person, both for adults and newborns, including anencephalic infants, even though the brain stem is still functioning and the heart is beating.[94] There are no convincing reasons to claim that anencephalic infants, or other living individuals whose cortex is permanently nonfunctional, should be ethically or legally deemed to be dead in order to permit removal of their organs for transplants. Anencephalic infants are dead once their heart beat and spontaneous respiration have ceased. An anencephalic infant should not be stripped of human rights to provide transplant tissue for another.[95] As discussed in chapter 1, to be a person it is necessary for a human individual to have a rational nature, but not an acquired capacity to perform rationally self-conscious acts. Hence, it would be unethical and inhuman to remove organs from living, severely defective newborns.

Transplants for infants should only be done in centers which have the services of a full transplant and pediatric team. Short- and long-term follow-up studies are needed for the benefit of each child and there should be pooling of knowledge to learn from experience and to improve transplant techniques. Vital organs should not be taken from any living human individual. Other organs may be donated by a competent person for just and proportionate reasons, provided there is no serious harm to the donor's life or personal identity. Out of a sense of solidarity and love for one's neighbor a competent person may donate a kidney or a lobe of liver to a newborn in need.[96]

Resource allocation and neonatal treatment

Governments and hospital administrators may decide on the level of funding for publicly financed NICUs and other therapies for newborns, including transplant programs. This in its turn depends on the community's evaluation of priorities in healthcare and non-health-related budgetary factors, especially in developing countries. In developed countries costs for NICU treatment of ELBW babies should not be judged in isolation from public health resource allocation for other routine costly forms of treatment such as coronary artery bypass operations and dialysis treatment for kidney failure. It is worth recalling the costs per survivor for babies at 23–4 weeks' gestation and weighing greater than 600 g compare favorably with kidney transplants or coronary bypass surgery in terms of "health related quality of life" criteria.[97] All other things being equal, there is greater benefit gained by paying a high price to save a newborn baby whose life is yet to be lived compared to prolonging the life of one who has already lived three score years and ten. This is readily understood if one reflects on the benefits gained by ELBW babies over a lifetime compared to operations that prolong life for the elderly for a few years. Still, costs are a factor when deciding whether the likely benefits of treatments, are, on balance, out of proportion to the risks of harm and the responsible allocation of scarce resources.

At the same time, we need to remember that today's routine successes would not have been possible without the pioneering attempts of neonatal staff over recent decades, despite their initially high mortality and morbidity rates. Neonatal centers of excellence should continue to try to lower the prematurity threshold for saving newborns without continuing futile treatment or causing them ongoing pain. Transplant procedures that once were experimental are now routine and benefit thousands. Money spent on research in the past is now paying dividends. Research into innovative transplant procedures and trials on animal models should be funded and precede clinical practice on humans. Progress in medicine should be monitored, not halted.

Notes

Chapter 1 Morality for Persons

1 Peter Singer, *Rethinking Life & Death: The Collapse of Our Traditional Ethics* (Melbourne: Text Publishing Company, 1994 and Oxford: University Press, 1995), 1.
2 Ibid., 189.
3 Ibid., 105.
4 Ibid., 130–1.
5 Ibid., 189, 221.
6 Peter Singer, *Practical Ethics*, 2nd ed. (Cambridge: University Press, 1993), 10.
7 Ibid., 11–12.
8 Ibid., 12.
9 R. M. Hare, "A Utilitarian Approach," in Helga Kuhse and Peter Singer, eds., *A Companion to Bioethics* (Oxford: Blackwell Publishers, 1998), 82.
10 Singer, *Practical Ethics*, 13.
11 Ibid., 14.
12 Ibid., 326.
13 Ibid., 327–9.
14 Ibid., 331.
15 Ibid., 332.
16 Ibid., 332–5. For more on Singer's views on ethics see Peter Singer, "A Response," in Dale Jamieson, ed., *Singer and his Critics* (Oxford: Blackwell Publishers, 1999), 269–332.
17 Ibid., 87.
18 Ibid., 151.
19 Ibid., 171–2; 190.
20 H. Kuhse and P. Singer, *Should the Baby Live? The Problem of Handicapped Infants* (Oxford: University Press, 1985), 133.

21 Mary Anne Warren, "On the Moral and Legal Status of Abortion," in Robert M. Baird and Stuart E Resenbaum, eds., *The Ethics of Abortion: Pro-Life vs Pro Choice* (Buffalo, NY: Prometheus Books, 1993), 231.

22 Michael Tooley, *Abortion and Infanticide* (Oxford: Clarendon Press, 1983), 123; 123–34; 146; 303; 419–20; "Personhood," in Kuhse and Singer, *A Companion to Bioethics*, 120–1.

23 Michael Lockwood, "When Does a Life Begin?" in M. Lockwood, ed., *Moral Dilemmas in Modern Medicine* (Oxford: University Press, 1985), 10.

24 Singer, *Practical Ethics*, 117.

25 Singer, *Rethinking Life & Death*, 182.

26 Singer, *Practical Ethics*, 169.

27 Lockwood, "When Does a Life Begin?," 10.

28 Ibid., 13.

29 Ibid., 19.

30 Ibid., 23 and n. 19, 212–13; M. Lockwood, "Of Persons and Organisms: A Reply to Howsepian," *Journal of Medical Ethics* 23 (1997): 42–4.

31 Walter Glannon, "Genes, Embryos, and Future People," *Bioethics* 12 (1998): 190.

32 John Locke, *Essay Concerning Human Understanding*, Book II, ch. 27, para. 9, first published in 1690. Singer quotes this same definition in *Practical Ethics*, 87 and *Rethinking*, 162.

33 Boethius, *Liber de Persona et Duobus Naturis*, cc. 2,3. See also Norman Ford, *When Did I Begin? Conception of the Human Individual in History, Philosophy and Science* (Cambridge: University Press, 1988, p/b 1991), 84.

34 John Hymers, "Not a Modest Proposal: Peter Singer and the Definition of Person," *Ethical Perspectives* 6 (1999): 126–38.

35 See Leslie Stevenson and David Haberman, *Ten Theories of Human Nature*, 3rd ed. (New York: Oxford University Press, 1998).

36 Much of the inspiration for this section was derived from the works of the following personalist philosophers: Martin Buber, *I and Thou*, trans. with intro. by Walter Kaufmann (Edinburgh: T. & T. Clark, 1970); Paul Tournier, a medical practitioner turned philosopher, *The Meaning of Persons* (London: SCM Press, 1957, 1974), the whole book, but especially part I, "The Personage"; Emmanuel Mounier, *Personalism* (Notre Dame/London: Notre Dame Press, 1952), the whole book; Joseph Donceel, *Philosophical Anthropology* (New York: Sheed and Ward, 1969), ch. 1.

37 Buber, *I and Thou*, passim.

38 Tournier, *Meaning of Persons*, 123–40.

39 Mounier, *Personalism*, 17–32.

40 Jenny Teichman, "Wittgenstein on Persons and Human Beings," *Royal Institute of Philosophy Lectures* (London), 7 (1972/1973): 140.

41 Jenny Teichman, "Humanism and Personism," *Quadrant* 36/12 (1992): 19.

42 See Norman Ford, "P. F. Strawson's Concept of Philosophy," *Salesianum* 34/3 (1972): 532–3.

43 For more on this see Ford, *When Did I Begin?*, 16–17, 38, 59, 73–5, 130–1.

44 For more on when the human soul is created see Ford, *When Did I Begin?*, 42–4, 50–2, 58, 61, 172, 175, 193–7.

45 See also Thomas J. Bole, III, "Zygotes, Souls, Substances, and Persons," *Journal of Medicine and Philosophy* 15 (1990): 637–52.

46 Lockwood, "When does a life begin?," 23–4; see also Tooley "Personhood," Kuhse and Singer, *A Companion to Bioethics*, 122.

47 For more details see Ford, *When Did I Begin?*, 68–72.

48 See also John F. Crosby, "The Personhood of the Human Embryo," *Journal of Medicine and Philosophy* 18 (1993): 399–417; Kirkland Young, "The Zygote, the Embryo and Personhood: An Attempt at Conceptual Clarification," *Ethics & Medicine* 10/1 (1994): 2–7.

49 Werner Wolbert, "The Kantian Formula of Human Dignity and its Implications for Bioethics," *Human Reproduction and Genetic Ethics* 4 (1998): 18–21.

50 Aquinas, *Summa Theologiae*, I-II, Q 94, a 2.

51 John Paul II, *Veritatis Splendor*, Encyclical Letter (Vatican City: Liberia Editrice Vaticana, 1993), N. 78. See also the Latin text, *Acta Apostolicae Sedis* (1993), N. 78: "Rectus ideo est actus, cuius objectum cum bono personae convenit atque bona ipsi moraliter potiora servat"; idem. NN. 72–3; *The Catechism of the Catholic Church* (Vatican City: Libreria Editrice Vaticana, St. Pauls, 1998, corrigenda incorporated), NN. 1749–52; Norman Ford, "The Meaning of Intrinsic Moral Norms for Persons," *The Australasian Catholic Record* 60 (1983): 186–7.

52 *Veritatis Splendor*, N. 50.

53 Aquinas, *Summa Theologiae*, I-II, Q 94, a 2, shows how the *good* is the foundation of practical reason's judgments in the natural moral law.

54 *Veritatis Splendor*, N. 78.

55 Richard Holloway, *Godless Morality: Keeping Religion out of Ethics* (Edinburgh: Canongate, 1999), 2.

56 Alfred J. Ayer, *Language, Truth and Logic*, 2nd ed. (London: Victor Gollancz, 1946), 107–8.

57 Aquinas, *Summa Theologiae*, I-II, Q 90, 1; Q 91, 2.

58 *Veritatis Splendor*, N. 80.

59 Josef Fuchs, "Innovative Morality," *Moral Demands and Personal Obligations*, 114–19.

60 Joseph Boyle says something similar, "An Absolute Rule Approach," Kuhse and Singer, *A Companion to Bioethics*, 76–7.

61 Aquinas, S.T. 2-2, Q 43, a 3; S.T. 1-2, Q 20, a 3.

62 See Aquinas on self-defense, S.T. 2-2, Q 64, a 7, ad 4, where he shows that adultery has no necessary link with saving one's life as killing sometimes can have in one action.

63 Aquinas, S.T. 2-2, Q 64, a 7.

64 Ford, "The Meaning of Intrinsic Moral Norms," 190.

65 For a simple account of proportionalism see Richard M. Gula, *Reason Informed by Faith: Foundations of Catholic Morality* (Mahwah, NJ: Paulist Press, 1989), 265–82; for scholarly words see Richard A. McCormick, "Ambiguity in Moral Choice," *Doing Evil to Achieve Good*, eds. Richard A McCormick and Paul Ramsay (Chicago: Loyola University Press, 1978), 7–53; *Readings in Moral Theology No.1 – Moral Norms and Catholic Tradition*, eds. Charles E. Curran and Richard A. McCormick (New York: Paulist Press, 1979); for a critical view see John Finnis, *Fundamental of Ethics* (Washington, DC: The Catholic University of America Press, 1983).

66 See Richard McCormick's comment on *Veritatis Splendor*, *The Tablet*, Oct. 30, 1993, 1410–11.

67 See Aquinas, S.T. 1-2, Q 18, a 2, a5; Q 19, a l, a 3.

68 Aquinas, S.T. 1-2, Q 19, a 3.

69 Aquinas, S.T. 1-2, Q 18, a 2.

70 Aquinas, S.T. 1-2, Q 18, a 5.

71 Aquinas, S.T. 1-2, Q 19, a 1.

72 Aquinas, S.T. 2-2, Q 64, a 7, ad 4.

73 Ford, "The Meaning of Intrinsic Moral Norms," 192.

74 See the following works on the natural moral law: R. George, *In Defence of Natural Law* (Oxford: University Press, 1991); John Finnis, *Natural Law and Natural Rights* (Oxford: Clarendon Press, 1980); "The Natural Moral Law and Faith," *The Twenty-Fifth Anniversary of Vatican II – A Look Back and a Look Ahead. Proceedings of The Ninth Bishops' Workshop Dallas, Texas* (Braintree, Mass: The Pope John Center, 1990), 223–38; Germain Grisez, "Natural Law and the Fundamental Principles of Morality," *The Way of the Lord Jesus: Christian Moral Principles* (Chicago: Franciscan Herald Press, 1983), 173–204.

75 John Paul II, *Veritatis Splendor*, N. 50.

76 Ibid., N. 50.

77 Literal translation of the Latin text John Paul II, *Veritatis Splendor*, N. 79: "Haec sunt bona, quibus praesidio sunt leges divinae, quae totam legem naturalem continent."

78 Ford, "The Meaning of Intrinsic Moral Norms for Persons," 195–6;

79 Joseph Fuchs, "Historicity and Moral Norm," *Moral Demands and Personal Obligations* trans. Brian McNeil (Washington, DC: Georgetown University Press, 1993), 91–108.

80 James F. Keenan and Thomas R. Kopfensteiner, "Moral Theology out of Western Europe," *Theological Studies* 59 (1998): 128–30; Josef Fuchs, "'Epikeia' Circa Legem Moralem Naturalem?" *Periodica De Re Morali, Canonica Liturgica* 69 (1980): 264–70; see its English translation in "Epikeia Applied to Natural Law?," *Personal Responsibility and Christian Morality* (Washington, DC: Georgetown University, 1983), 191–9.

81 John Macquarrie, *Three Issues in Ethics* (London: SCM, 1970), ch. 4, "Rethinking Natural Law," 82–110, at 107.

Chapter 2 Life, Health, Ethics and the Bible

1 I have relied on the following sources for much of this biblical section: F. J. Moloney, "Life, Healing and the Bible: A Christian Challenge," *Pacifica* 8 (1995): 315–34; *Beginning the Good News: A Narrative Approach* (Biblical Studies I; Homebush: St. Paul Publications, 1992), 19–42.
2 Moloney, "Life, Healing," 320.
3 A. Kelly, "The Historical Jesus and Human Subjectivity: A Response to John Meir," *Pacifica*, 4 (1991): 202–28.
4 Moloney, "Life, Healing," 318 and B. Byrne, *Reckoning with Romans: A Contemporary Reading of Paul's Gospel* (Good News Studies 18; Wilmington: Michael Glazier, 1986), 57–60.
5 The Hebrew ADAM is usually translated as "man," but it might be better to render it as "humankind"; Gerhard Von Rad, *Genesis: A Commentary* (London: SCM Press, 1963), 55–9.
6 Claus Westerman in *Genesis 1–11: A Commentary*, trans. J. Scullion SJ (Minneapolis: Aubsburg Publishing House, 1984), 233–4, where he accepts the usual meaning of "one flesh" as the loving union of a man and a woman in sexual intercourse; but Von Rad, in *Genesis*, 82–3, interprets "one flesh" as the child of their union.
7 O. A. Piper, Art. "Life," in *The Interpreter's Dictionary of the Bible*, ed. George Arthur Buttrick (New York/Nashville: Abingdon Press, 1962), 124–30.
8 J. L. McKenzie, "Life," in *Dictionary of the Bible* (London: Geoffrey Chapman, 1968, 1978), 507–8.
9 Moloney, "Life, Healing," 324–5; A. F. Campbell, *The Study Companion to Old Testament Literature: An Approach to the Writings of Pre-Exilic and Exilic Israel*, 2nd ed. (Collegeville, Ill.: Liturgical Press, 1992), 139–251; B. W. Anderson, *The Living World of the Old Testament* (London: Longman, 1988), 183–4.
10 R. K. Harrison, Art. "Medicine," in *The Interpreter's Dictionary of the Bible* 331–2. For more details see Howard Clark Lee, "Medicine and Healing" in *The Anchor Bible Dictionary* 4, eds. David Noel Freedman et al. (New York: Doubleday, 1992), 659–64.
11 R. K. Harrison, "Healing, Health," *The Interpreter's Dictionary of the Bible*, 542.
12 For more details on preventive medicine prescriptions in the Mosaic code see Harrison, "Healing, Health," 542–7 .
13 Harrison, "Healing Health," 542.

14 McKenzie, "Sheol," 800–1; for more details see Theodore J. Lewis, "Abode of the Dead," *The Anchor Bible Dictionary* 2 (1992), 101–4.
15 For a critical presentation of the figure "Luke" see R. Maddox, *The Purpose of Luke-Acts* (Edinburgh: T. & T. Clark, 1982), 6–9.
16 Piper, "Life," 127–8.
17 I am aware that there is much scholarly discussion concerning the historicity of many of the narratives which I report here. For a detailed historical survey of Jesus' miracles see J. P. Meier, *A Marginal Jew: Rethinking the Historical Jesus* (3 vols., The Anchor Bible Reference Library; New York: Doubleday, 1991, 1994), 2:509–1038. My use of the Gospels respects that scholarship, but I report these stories as they convey the Church's memory of something fundamental to that memory of Jesus' ministry.
18 For more details see Harrison, "Healing, Health," 546–7.
19 Much of what follows is drawn from R. E. Brown, *Responses to 101 Questions on the Bible* (London: Geoffrey Chapman, 1991), 68–9.
20 Ibid., 69.
21 Moloney, "Life, Healing," 334.
22 McKenzie, "Life," 507–8.
23 "Pastoral Constitution of the Church in the Modern World," *Vatican II: The Conciliar and Post Conciliar Documents*, ed. A. Flannery (Dublin: Dominican Publications, 1975), N.18.
24 See also N. Frye, *The Great Code: The Bible and Literature* (London: ARC Paperbacks, 1983).
25 Richard Holloway, *Godless Morality: Keeping Religion out of Ethics* (Edinburgh: Canongate, 1999), 2.

Chapter 3 Ethical Principles for Healthcare

1 Tom L. Beauchamp and James F. Childress, *Principles of Biomedical Ethics*, 5th ed. (New York: Oxford University Press, 2001).
2 "Pastoral Constitution of the Church in the Modern World," *Vatican II: The Conciliar and Post Conciliar Documents*, ed. A. Flannery (Dublin: Dominican Publications, 1975), N. 19.
3 The Second Vatican Council's "Decree on the Church's Missionary Activity," *Vatican II*, ed. Flannery, N. 3.
4 Terence, *Heauton Timorumenos*, I, i, 25.
5 "Pastoral Constitution of the Church," *Vatican II*, N. 41.
6 The Congregation for the Doctrine of the Faith, *The Reality of Life after Death* (1979), *Vatican Council II: More Post-Conciliar Documents*, ed. A. Flannery, 500–4.
7 "Pastoral Constitution of the Church," *Vatican II*, N. 18.

8 Francis F. Moloney, "Life, Healing and the Bible: A Christian Challenge," *Pacifica* 8 (1995): 229–30.

9 John Paul II, Encyclical Letter *Evangelium Vitae* (Vatican City: Libreria Editrice Vaticana, 1995), N. 57; on the value of life as God's gift see J. Kleinig, *Valuing Life* (Princeton: Princeton University Press, 1991), 63–9; for a Catholic philosopher sympathetic to voluntary euthanasia see M. Charlesworth, *Bioethics in a Liberal Society* (Cambridge: University Press, 1993) 30–5.

10 Peter Singer, *Practical Ethics*, 2nd ed. (Cambridge: University Press, 1993), 135–217; Michael Tooley's views are in *Abortion and Infanticide* (Oxford: Clarendon Press, 1983).

11 Singer, *Practical Ethics*, 182–91.

12 Carol A. Tauer has argued that the theoretical doubt about the person-hood of the early embryo could "permit some early abortions": "The Tradition of Probabilism and the Moral Status of the Early Embryo," *Theological Studies* 45/1 (1984): 3–33.

13 Congregation for the Doctrine of the Faith, *Declaration on Euthanasia* in *Vatican Council II: More Post Conciliar Documents*, ed. Flannery, 515–16.

14 John Paul II, *Veritatis Splendor*, Encyclical Letter (Vatican City: Liberia Editrice Vaticana, 1993), NN. 78 and 45; James J. Walter, "The Meaning and Validity of Quality of Life Judgement in Contemporary Roman Catholic Medical Ethics," in J. J. Walter and T. A. Shannon, eds., *Quality of Life – The New Medical Dilemma* (New York: Paulist Press, 1990), 78–88.

15 Moloney, "Life, Healing and the Bible," 331.

16 John Paul II, *Evangelium Vitae*, N. 65; *Declaration on Euthanasia*, 515–16.

17 For a brief account and more references see Jorge L. A. Garcia, "Double Effect," *Encyclopedia of Bioethics*, vol. 2, eds. Warren Thomas Reich et al. (New York: Simon & Schuster Macmillan, 1995); *Double Effect: Theoretical Function and Bioethical Implications*, Thomas J. Bole III, Issue Editor, *Journal of Medicine and Philosophy* 16 (1991): 467–585.

18 Norman Ford, "The Meaning of Intrinsic Moral Norms for Persons," *The Australasian Catholic Record* 60 (1983): 187–91.

19 John Finnis, *Natural Law and Natural Rights* (Oxford: Clarendon Press, 1980), 120.

20 Benedict Ashley and Kevin O'Rourke, *Health Care Ethics: A Theological Analysis*, 4th ed. (Washington, DC: Georgetown University Press, 1996), 191–3; Thomas J. O'Donnell, *Medicine and Christian Morality*, 2nd ed. (New York: Alba House, 1991), 26–30.

21 Eike-Henner W. Kluge, "Severely Disabled Newborns," in Helga Kuhse and Peter Singer eds., *A Companion to Bioethics* (Oxford: Blackwell Publishers, 1998), 246–7.

22 John Paul II, *Evangelium Vitae*, N. 65.

23 Helga Khuse, "A Modern Myth: That Letting Die is not the Intentional Causation of Death," in Kuhse and Singer eds., *A Companion to Bioethics*, 255–68; Singer, *Practical Ethics*, 207–13; Helga Kuhse and Peter Singer, *Should the Baby Live? The Problem of Handicapped Infants* (Oxford: University Press: 1985), 18–47.

24 Paul Tournier, *The Meaning of Persons* (London: SCM Press, 1957), 43–5, 185–93, 200–4, to whom I owe these thoughts.

25 "Pastoral Constitution of the Church," *Vatican II*, N. 43.

26 Tournier, *Meaning of Persons*, 201.

27 J. J. Paris and F. E. Reardon, "Moral, Ethical, and Legal Issues in the Intensive Care Unit," *Journal of Intensive Care Medicine* 6/4 (1991): 175–7.

28 J. S. Mill, *On Liberty*, 3rd ed., London 1864

29 *Report of the Select Committee on Medical Ethics of the House of Lords* (London: HMSO, 1994), para. 237.

Chapter 4 The Human Embryo

1   See Norman Ford SDB, "When Does Human Life Begin? Science, Government, Church," *Pacifica* 1/3 (1988): 298–327.

2   A. Henry Sathananthan et al., *Atlas of Fine Structure of Human Sperm Penetration, Eggs and Embryos Cultured In Vitro* (New York: Praeger Publishers, 1986), 85.

3   Ford, "When Does Human Life Begin?," 298–327; Norman M. Ford, *When Did I Begin? Conception of the Human Individual in History, Philosophy and Science* (Cambridge: University Press, 1988); S. Buckle et al., "The Syngamy Debate: When Precisely does a Human Life Begin?," in Peter Singer et al., eds., *Embryo Experimentation* (Cambridge: University Press, 1990), 213–25.

4   *Acta Apostolicae Sedis* 80/1 (1988): 78, note: "zygotum est cellula orta a fusione duorum gametum." It is to be noted that "orta" is a past participle.

5   Health Council of the Netherlands: Committee on In Vitro fertilization. *IVF-related Research* (Rijswijk: 1998, pub. no. 1998/08E), 10, 28–9.

6   Ford, *When Did I Begin?*, 155.

7   Andràs Nagy et al., "Derivation of Completely Cell Culture-derived Mice from Early-Passage Embryonic Stem Cells," *Proceedings of the National Academy of Science, USA*, 90 (1993): 8424–8.

8   Alan Trounson, "Why Do Research on Human Pre-Embryos?," in Singer et al., eds., *Embryo Experimentation*, 15.

9   Trounson, "Why Do Research on Human Pre-embryos?," 8–9.

10 A. J. Wilcox et al., "Incidence of Early Loss of Pregnancy," *New England Journal of Medicine* 319 (1988): 189–94.

11   Trounson, "Why Do Research on Human Pre-embryos?," 17.

12   Gayle M. Jones et al., "The Factors Affecting the Success of Human Blastocyst Development and Pregnancy Following IVF and Embryo Transfer," *Fertility & Sterility* 70/6 (1998), 1024.

13   D. Wells and Joy Delhanty, "Comprehensive Chromosomal Analysis of Human Preimplantation Embryos Using Whole Genome Amplification and Single Cell Comparative Genomic Hybridization," *Molecular Human Reproduction* 6 (2000): 1055–62.

14   Health Council, *IVF-related Research*, 38–9; A. Trounson and M. Pera, "Potential Benefits of Cell Cloning for Human Medicine," *Journal of Reproduction, Fertility and Development* 110 (1998), 122–3.

15   E. Van den Abbeel et al., "Embryo Freezing After Intracytoplasmic Sperm Injection," *Molecular & Cellular Endocrinology* 169/1–2 (2000): 49–54; Karen Dawson, *Reproductive Technology: The Science, the Ethics, the Law and the Social Issues* (Melbourne: VCTA Publishing, Macmillan Education Australia, 1995), 49.

16   Jacques Testart, "Safety of Embryo Cryopreservation: Statistical Facts and Artefacts. Episcientific Aspects of the Epigenetic Factors in Artificial Procreation," *Human Reproduction* 13 (1998): 783–8.

17   Karen Dawson, "Introduction: An Outline of Scientific Aspects of Human Embryo Research," in Singer et al., eds., *Embryo Experimentation*, 6–8.

18   Trounson, "Why Do Research on Human Pre-embryos?," 22.

19   Mario R. Capecchi, "Human Germline Gene Therapy: *How and Why*," in G. Stock and J. Campbell, eds., *Engineering the Human Germline* (New York: Oxford University Press, 2000), 31–42; M. Bunting et al., "Targeting Genes for Self-Excision in the Germ Line," *Genes & Development* 13 (1999): 1524–8.

20   James A. Thomson et al., "Embryonic Stem Cell Lines Derived from Human Blastocysts," *Science* 282 N. 5391 (1998): 1145–7.

21   Norman Ford, "Are All Cells Derived from an Embryo Themselves Embryos?," *Pluripotent Stem Cells: Therapeutic Perspectives and Ethical Issues*, eds. Betty Dodet and Marissa Vicari (Paris: John Libbey, Eurotext, 2001), 81–7.

22   John A. Robertson, "Ethics and Policy in Embryonic Stem Cell Research," *Kennedy Institute of Ethics Journal* 9/2 (1999): 111–12.

23   Thomson et al., "Embryonic Stem Cell Lines Derived from Human Blastocysts," 1145–7; Robertson, "Ethics and Policy in Embryonic Stem Cell Research," 109–11.

24   Benjamin E. Reubinoff et al., "Embryonic Stem Cell Lines From Human Blastocysts: Somatic Differentiation In Vitro," *Nature Biotechnology* 18 (2000): 402.

25   Dan S. Kaufman et al., "Hematopoietic Colony-forming Cells Derived from Human Embryonic Stem Cells," *Proceedings of the National Academy of Sciences USA* 98/19 (2001): 10716–21.

26   Douglas Kondziolka et al., "Transplantation of Cultured Human Neuronal Cells for Patients with Stroke," *Neurology* 55/4 (2000): 565–9.

27   Alan O. Trounson, "Cloning: Potential Benefits for Human Medicine," *Medical Journal of Australia* 167 (1997): 568–9; Alan Trounson and Kim Giliam, "What Does Cloning Offer Human Medicine?" *Today's Life Science* March/April (1999): 14; Trounson and Pera, "Potential Benefits of Cell Cloning for Human Medicine," 123–4.

28   Neil D. Theise et al., "Liver from bone Marrow in Humans," *Hepatology* 32/1 (2000): 11–16; Christopher R. Bjornson and Rodney L. Rietze et al., "Turning Brain into Blood: A Hematopoietic Fate Adopted by Adult Neural Stem Cells in Vivo," *Science* 283 (Jan. 22, 1999): 534–7. Malcolm R. Alison et al., "Hepatocytes from Non-hepatic Adult Stem Cells," *Nature* 406 (2000): 257.

29   B. E. Strauer et al., "Intracoronary, Human Autologous Stem Cell Transplantation for Myocardial Regeneration following Myocardial Infarction," *Deutsche Medizinische Wochenschrift* 126 (34–5) (2001): 932–8; Donald Orlic et al., "Bone Marrow Cells Regenerate Infarcted Myocardium," *Nature* 410 (April 5, 2001): 701–5; Neil Scolding, "The Body's Seeds of Construction," *The Tablet*, Sept. 15, 2001, pp. 1288–9.

30   Scolding, "The Body's Seeds of Construction," 1288–9.

31   News report, *New Scientist*, Feb. 23, 2001.

32   Report of the Chief Medical Officer's Expert Group, *Stem Cell Research: Medical Progress with Responsibility* (London: Department of Health, June 2000), 25; Australian Academy of Science, *On Human Cloning: A Position Statement*, 15; Trounson and Giliam, "What Does Cloning Offer Human Medicine?" 14; Wilmut, "Cloning for Medicine," 34–5.

33   Trounson and Giliam, "What Does Cloning Offer Human Medicine?" 12; Australian Academy of Science, *On Human Cloning: A Position Statement* (Canberra: 1999), 4.

34   I. Wilmut et al., "Viable Offspring Derived from Fetal and Adult Mammalian Cells," *Nature* 385 (1997): 810–13.

35   Jose B. Cibelli et al., "Somatic Cell Nuclear Transfer in Humans: Pronuclear and Early Embryonic Development," *e-biomed: The Journal of Regenerative Medicine* 2 (2001): 25–31.

36   David Humphreys et al., "Epigenetic Instability in ES Cells and Cloned Mice," *Science*, 293 (2001): 95–7.

37   Trounson and Giliam, "What Does Cloning Offer Human Medicine?" 12–14; Trounson, "Cloning: Potential Benefits for Human Medicine," 568–9.

38   Megan J. Munsie et al., "Isolation of Pluripotent Embryonic Stem Cells from Reprogrammed Adult Mouse Somatic Cell Nuclei," *Current Biology* 10 (2000): 989–92.

39   Trounson, "Why Do Research on Human Pre-Embryos?," 18–19 and P. Braude et al., "Human Gene Expression First Occurs Between the

Four- And Eight-Cell Stage of Preimplantation Development," 332 *Nature* (1988): 459–61.

40 A. J. Muggleton-Harris et al., "Biopsy of the Human Blastocyst and Polymerase Chain Reaction (PCR) Amplification of the B-Globin Gene and a Dinucleotide Repeat Motif from 2–6 Trophectoderm Cells," *Human Reproduction* 8 (1993): 2197–205.

41 Frances A. Flinter, *Editorial*, "Preimplantation Genetic Diagnosis," *British Medical Journal* 322 (2001): 1008–9; J. C. Harper, "Preimplantation Diagnosis of Inherited Disease by Embryonic Biopsy: An Update of the World Figures," *Journal of Assisted Reproduction and Genetics* 13/2 (1996): 90–5.

42 K. Hardy et al., "Human Preimplantation Development In Vitro is Not Adversely Affected by Biopsy at the 8-Cell Stage," *Human Reproduction* 5 (1990): 708–14.

43 Health Council of the Netherlands, *IVF-related research*, 24, 28.

44 A. M. Nagy et al., "Scientific and Ethical Issues of Preimplantation Diagnosis," *Annals of Medicine* 30/1 (1998): 1–6; Sozos J. Fasouliotis and Joseph G. Schenker, "Preimplantation Genetic Diagnosis Principles and Ethics," *Human Reproduction* 13/8 (1998): 2238–45.

45 J. Milliez and C. Sureau "Pre-implantation Diagnosis and the Eugenics Debate: Our Responsibility to Future Generations," in *Ethical Dilemmas in Assisted Reproduction*, eds. F. Shenfield and C. Sureau (New York: Parthenon Publishing Group, 1997), 59.

46 Joy D. A. Delhanty and Joyce C. Harper, "Pre-implantation Genetic Diagnosis," *Bailliére's Clinical Obstetrics and Gynaecology* 14 (2000): 693.

47 G. M. Jones et al., "Evolution of a Culture Protocol for Successful Blastocyst Development and Pregnancy," *Human Reproduction* 13 (1998): 169–77.

48 Flinter, "Preimplantation Genetic Diagnosis," 1009.

49 Deborah Josefson, News reports, *British Medical Journal* 321 (2000): 917–18.

50 Ian Findlay et al., "Fluorescent PCR: A New Technique for PGD of Sex and Single-Gene Defects," *Journal of Assisted Reproduction and Genetics* 13/2 (1996): 96–102.

51 Delhanty and Harper, "Pre-implantation," 691–4.

52 Joseph D. Schulman and R. G. Edwards, "Preimplantation Diagnosis is Disease Control, Not Eugenics," *Human Reproduction* 11 (1996): 463–4.

53 Congregation for the Doctrine of the Faith, *Declaration on Procured Abortion*, ed. A. Flannery, *Vatican Council II: More Postconciliar Documents* (Dublin: Dominican Publications, 1982), 443.

54 "Pastoral Constitution of the Church in the Modern World," *Vatican II: The Conciliar and Post Conciliar Documents*, ed. A. Flannery (Dublin: Dominican Publications, 1975), N. 51; *Acta Synodalia Sacrosanti Concilii Oecumenici Vaticani II*, vol. IV, Pars VII (Rome: Vatican Polyglot Press,

1978), 501, where it is clear that the text does not refer to the time of ensoulment.

55 Antoine Suarez, "Hydatidiform Moles and Teratomas Confirm the Human Identity of the Preimplantation Embryo," *Journal of Medicine and Philosophy* 15 (1990): 627–35.

56 See W. Jerome Bracken, "Is the Early Embryo a Person?," *Linacre Quarterly* 68/1 (2001): 49–70.

57 Michael Tooley, "Personhood," in Kuhse and Singer, *A Companion to Bioethics*, 122.

58 Massimo Reichlin, "The Argument from Potential," *Bioethics* 11 (1997): 12–23.

59 For more views on the status of the embryo see the series of articles published in *The Tablet* beginning Feb. 24, 1990. The authors were Oliver Pratt, Nigel M. de S. Cameron, Richard A. McCormick, Anne McLaren, and John Marshall.

60 Werner Wolbert, "The Potentiality Argument in the Debate relating to the Beginning of Personhood," *Human Reproduction and Genetic Ethics* 6/2 (2000): 19–26.

61 Germain Grisez, "When do People Begin?," in Stephen J. Heaney, ed., *Abortion: A New Generation of Catholic Responses* (Braintree, Mass.: The Pope John Center, 1993), 3–27; W. May, "The Moral Status of the Embryo," *Linacre Quarterly* 59/4 (1992): 76–83.

62 Norman Ford, "The Human Embryo as Person in Catholic Teaching," *The National Catholic Bioethics Quarterly* 1/2 (2001): 155–60; Ford, *When Did I Begin?*, 68–84.

63 Pope John Paul II, *Encyclical Letter, Evangelium Vitae* (Vatican City: Libreria Editrice Vaticana, 1995), N. 60. This translation has been modified to be more faithful to the official Latin text in *Acta Apostolicae Sedis*, 87/2 (1995), N. 60, 468–9.

64 F. Shenfield and C. Sureau, "Ethics of Embryo Research," in *Ethical Dilemmas in Assisted Reproduction*, eds. Shenfield and Sureau, 15.

65 Ford, *When Did I Begin?*, 132–82; Norman Ford, "Fetus," *The Encyclopedia of Applied Ethics*, vol. 2, ed. Ruth Chadwick (San Diego: Academic Press, 1998); Jason T. Eberl, "The Beginning of Personhood: A Thomistic Biological Approach," *Bioethics* 14/2 (2000): 134–57.

66 For a contrary critical view see John Finnis, "Abortion and Health Care Ethics," in Helga Khuse and Peter Singer, eds., *Bioethics – An Anthology* (Oxford: Blackwell Publishers, 1999) 13–15, and other references, 19.

67 R. L. Gardner, "Specification of Embryonic Axes Begins Before Cleavae in Normal Mouse Development," *Development* 128/6 (2001): 839–47; K. Piotrowska et al., "Blastomeres Arising from the First Cleavage Division have Distinguishable Fates in Normal Mouse Development," *Development* 128/19 (2001): 3739–48.

68 See Lewis Wolpert, *The Triumph of the Embryo* (Oxford: University Press, 1991), 31–2, 37–40, 84, 199–202.

69 Wolpert, *The Triumph of the Embryo*, 199–200.

70 Peter J. Cataldo, "Human Rights and the Human Embryo," *Ethics & Medics* 26/12 (2001): 1–2; Peter Singer and Karen Dawson, "IVF Technology and the Argument from Potential," in Singer et al., eds., *Embryo Experimentation*, 87–8.

71 Stephen Buckle, "Arguing from Potential," in Singer et al., eds., *Embryo Experimentation*, 99–101.

72 Mary Anne Warren, "On the Moral and Legal Status of Abortion," in *The Ethics of Abortion: Pro-Life vs Pro-Choice*, eds. Robert M. Baird and Stuart E. Resenbaum (Buffalo, NY: Prometheus, 1993), 232; see also *Report of the Committee of Inquiry into Human Fertilisation and Embryology*, Chairman Dame Mary Warnock, Dept. of Health and Social Security (London: HMSO, 1984), 63, 90.

73 David B. Resnik, "The Commodification of Human Reproductive Materials," *Journal of Medical Ethics* 24 (1998), 391–2.

74 Dave Wendler, "Understanding the 'Conservative' View on Abortion," *Bioethics* 13 (1999): 32–55.

75 Peter Singer, *Rethinking Life and Death: The Collapse of Our Traditional Ethics* (Melbourne: The Text Publishing Company, 1994 and Oxford: Oxford University Press, 1995), 217, 130.

76 Peter Singer, *Practical Ethics*, 2nd ed. (Cambridge: University Press, 1993), 171; Singer, *Rethinking*, 217.

77 See Singer, *Practical Ethics*, 95–100.

78 H. Kuhse and P. Singer, "Individuals, Humans and Persons: The Issue of Moral Status," Singer et al., eds., *Embryo Experimentation*, 73.

79 Mary Warnock, "Do Human Cells Have Rights?," *Bioethics* 1 (1987): 6–11.

80 Mary Warnock "Experimentation on Human Embryos and Fetuses," in Kuhse and Singer, eds., *A Companion to Bioethics*, 393–6.

81 Mary Warnock, "Green College Lecture – Ethical Challenges in Embryo Manipulation," *British Medical Journal* 304 (1992): 1045–7. For an excellent analysis of the issues see Health Council of the Netherlands, *IVF-related Research*, 49–64.

82 Mary Warnock, "Green College Lecture," 1047.

83 United Nations Educational, Scientific and Cultural Organization, *Universal Declaration on the Human Genome and Human Rights* 1997, art. 1.

84 Robert Williamson, "Human Reproductive Cloning is Unethical Because it Undermines Autonomy: Commentary on Savulescu," *Journal of Medical Ethics* 25 (1999): 96–7.

85 The Australian Academy of Science agrees, *On Human Cloning*, 6, 13; Chief Medical Officer, *Stem Cell Research*, Recommendation, 7, 47.

86 *Universal Declaration on the Human Genome*, art. 11.

87   *Herald-Sun* newspaper, Melbourne Oct. 10, 2000, revealed this was done three years earlier.

88   Udo Schüklenk and Richard Ashcroft, "The Ethics of Reproductive and Therapeutic Cloning (Research)," *Monash Bioethics Review* 19/2 (2000): 33–44.

89   Julian Savulescu, "Should We Clone Human Beings? Cloning as a Source of Tissue for Transplantation," *Journal of Medical Ethics* 25 (1999): 94; see also J. Savulescu "The Ethics of Cloning and Creating Embryonic Stem Cells as a Source of Tissue for Transplantation: Time to Change the Law in Australia," *Australian and New Zealand Journal of Medicine* 30 (2000): 492–8.

90   Michael Tooley, "The Moral Status of Cloning Humans," *Human Cloning* (Biomedical Ethics Reviews), eds. James M. Humber and Robert Almeder (Totowa, NJ: Humana Press, 1998), 67–101.

91   John Harris, "'Goodby Dolly?' The Ethics of Human Cloning," *Journal of Medical Ethics* 23 (1997): 353–60; David McCarthy, "Persons and their Copies," *Journal of Medical Ethics* 25 (1999): 98–104.

92   Chief Medical Officer, *Stem Cell Research*, Recommendation 1, 45; Geron Ethics Advisory Board, "Research with Human Embryonic Stem Cells: Ethical Considerations," *Hastings Center Report* 29/2 (1999): 31–6; ibid. see commentaries by Glenn McGee and Arthur L. Caplan, Lori P. Knowles, Gladys B. While, Carol A. Tauer, and Lisa Sowle Cahill; Australian Academy of Science, *On Human Cloning: A Position Statement*, 6, 13, 17.

93   John Paul II, Address to the 18th International Congress of the Transplantation Society, *L'Osservatore Romano*, Weekly Edition in English, Aug. 30, 2000.

94   Robertson, "Ethics and Policy in Embryonic Stem Cell Research," 112–13.

95   President Bush's "Address on Federal Funding of Embryonic Stem-Cell Research," *Origins* 31/12 (2001): 215–16.

96   Chief Medical Officer, *Stem Cell Research*, 44–5.

97   *Origins* 31/12 (2001): 214.

98   The Ethics Committee of the American Society of Reproductive Medicine, "Sex Selection and Preimplantation Genetic Diagnosis," *Fertility and Sterility* 72/4 (1999): 595–8.

99   Glannon, "Genes, Embryos, and Future People," 187–205, 209–10; Fasouliotis and Schenker, "Preimplantation Genetic Diagnosis Principles and Ethics," 2241.

100 Heather Draper and Ruth Chadwick, "Beware! Preimplantation Genetic Diagnosis May Solve Some Old Problems But It Also Raises New Ones," *Journal of Medical Ethics* 25 (1999): 11–12.

101 Dorothy C. Wertz et al., *Guidelines on Ethical Issues in Medical Genetics and the Provision of Genetics Services* (Geneva: World Health Organization Hereditary Diseases Programme, 1995), 70.

102 David S. King, "Preimplantation Genetic Diagnosis and the 'New' Eugenics," *Journal of Medical Ethics* 25 (1999): 176–82.

103 Milliez and Sureau, "Pre-implantation Diagnosis," 61–3.

104 Pope John Paul II, *Evangelium Vitae*, N. 63.
105 Nelson A. Wivel and LeRoy Walters, "Germline Gene Modification and Disease Prevention: Some Medical and Ethical Perspectives," *Science*, 262 (1993): 533–8.
106 Capecchi, "Human Germline Gene Therapy: *How and Why*," 38.
107 Marc Lappé, "Ethical Issues in Manipulating the Human Germ Line," in Khuse and Singer, eds., *Bioethics – An Anthology*, 155–64; John Harris, "Is Gene Therapy a form of Eugenics?," ibid., 165–70.

Chapter 5 The Pregnant Woman and her Fetus

1 Stephanie Brown and Judith Lumley, "Antenatal Care: A Case of the Inverse Care Law?," *Australian Journal of Public Health* 17 (1993): 95–103.
2 Deborah A. Turnbull, "Women's Role and Satisfaction in the Decision to Have a Caesarean Section," *Medical Journal of Australia* 170 (1999): 580–3.
3 See Constance Hoenk Shapiro, *Infertility and Pregnancy Loss* (San Francisco: Jossey-Bass Publishers, 1988), 155–86.
4 Allen J. Wilcox et al., "Incidence of Early Loss of Pregnancy," *New England Journal of Medicine* 319 (1988): 189–94.
5 R. J. McKinlay Gardner and Grant R. Sutherland, *Chromosome Abnormalities and Genetic Counselling* (Oxford: Oxford University Press, 1996), 313; I. Young, "Incidence and Genetics of Congenital Malformations," in David J. Brock et al., eds., *Prenatal Diagnosis and Screening* (Edinburgh: Churchill Livingstone, 1992), 173.
6 James H. Harger, "Recurrent Spontaneous Abortion and Pregnancy Loss," in Thomas R. Moore et al., eds., *Gynecology and Obstetrics: A Longitudinal Approach* (New York: Churchill Livingstone, 1993), 247–8.
7 Wilcox et al., "Incidence," 191.
8 Allen Wilcox et al., "Time of Implantation of the Conceptus and Loss of Pregnancy," *New England Journal of Medicine* 340 (1999): 1796–9.
9 Wilcox, "Incidence," 191.
10 P. Braude et al., "Mechanisms of Early Embryonic Loss in Vivo and in Vitro," in M. Chapman et al., eds., *The Embryo: Normal and Abnormal Development and Growth* (London: Springer-Verlag, 1991), 2.
11 Braude et al., "Mechanisms of Early Embryonic Loss," 3–8; Allen Wilcox et al., "Post-ovulatory Ageing of the Human Oocyte and Embryo Failure," *Human Reproduction* 13/2 (1998): 394–7.
12 Michelle Plachot "Chromosome Analysis of Oocytes and Embryos," *Preimplantation Genetics*, eds. Y. Verlinsky and A. Kuliev (New York: Planum Press, 1991), 109–10.

13 Mark V. Sauer et al., "In *vivo* Blastocyst Production and Ovum Yield among Fertile Women," *Human Reproduction* 2 (1987): 701–3.

14 John D. Biggers, "In Vitro Fertilization and Embryo Transfer in Human Beings," *New England Journal of Medicine* 304 (1981): 339.

15 Plachot, "Chromosome Analysis of Oocytes and Embryos," 109; I. Young, "Incidence and Genetics of Congenital Malformations," in Brock, *Prenatal*, 174–5; E. Hook, "Prevalence, Risks and Recurrence," in Brock, *Prenatal*, 360; S. Knowles, "Spontaneous Abortion and the Pathology of Early Pregnancy," in *Fetal and Neonatal Pathology*, ed. J. W. Keeling, 2nd ed. (London: Springer-Verlag, 1993), 87–90 and also N. M. Ford, *When Did I Begin?: Conception of the Human Individual in History Philosophy and Science* (Cambridge: Cambridge University Press, 1988, 1991), 180 and notes.

16 See Ming-Hseng Wang and Frederick S. vom Saal, "Maternal Age and Traits in Offspring," *Nature* 407 (2000): 469–70; Jean Golding, "Epidemiology of Fetal and Neonatal Death," in Keeling, ed., *Fetal and Neonatal Pathology*, 171–2; The Consultative Council on Obstetric and Paediatric Mortality and Morbidity, *Annual Report for the Year 1998*, Melbourne, 2000, 17–20, 39–41; R. G. Edwards, "Causes of Early Embryonic Loss in Human Pregnancy," *Human Reproduction* 1 (1986): 185–98.

17 Donald L. Fylstra "Tubal Pregnancy: A Review of Current Diagnosis and Treatment," *Obstetrical & Gynecological Survey* 53/5 (1998): 320.

18 Lee R. Hickok and Phillip E. Patton, "Ectopic Pregnancy," in Moore et al., eds., *Gynecology & Obstetrics: A Longitudinal Approach*, 271–2.

19 Judith H. Ford, Lesley MacCormac, and Janet Hiller, "PALS (Pregnancy and Lifestyle Study) Association between Occupational and Environmental Exposure to Chemicals and Reproductive Outcome," *Mutation Research* 313 (1994): 153–64.

20 Ibid., 153–64.

21 Ibid., 158.

22 Anthony D. Milner et al., "Effects of Smoking in Pregnancy on Neonatal Lung Function," *Archives of Disease in Children Fetal Neonatal Edition*, 80 (1999): F8–F14, and Jean Golding's research on 14,893 pregnant women in the Avon area in 1991 and 1992 in the *Report of the Institute of Child Health*, University of Bristol, Feb. 1994; Mark A. Klebanoff et al., "Maternal Serum Paraxanthine, a Caffeine Metabolite, and the Risk of Spontaneous Abortion," *New England Journal of Medicine* 341 (1999): 1639–44; R. P. K. Ford et al., "Heavy Caffeine Intake in Pregnancy and Sudden Infant Death Syndrome," *Archives of Diseases in Childhood* 78 (1998): 9–13.

23 Dorthe Hansen et al., "Serious Life Events and Congenital Malformations: A National Study With Complete Follow-up," *Lancet* 356 (2000): 875–80.

24 Bonnie Steinbock, "Mother–Fetus Conflict," in Helga Kuhse and Peter Singer, eds., *A Companion to Bioethics* (Oxford: Blackwell Publishers, 1998), 141.

25 Roger V. Short, "Contraceptive Strategies for the Future," *Population – the Complex Reality: A Report of the Population Summit of the World's Scientific Academies*, ed. Sir Francis Graham-Smith (London: The Royal Society, 1994), 327.

26 R. A. Hatcher et al., *Contraceptive Technology*, 17th ed. (New York: Ardent Media, 1998), 680–2.

27 *An Information Paper on Termination of Pregnancy in Australia* (Canberra: Australian Government Publishing Service, 1996), 36.

28 Ibid., 37.

29 Pamela L. Adelson et al., "A Survey of Women Seeking Termination of Pregnancy in New South Wales," *Medical Journal of Australia* 163 (1995): 419–22.

30 Jacques Suaudeau, "Contraception and Abortion, Foes or Friends?," *Linacre Quarterly* 67/2 (2000): 57–84.

31 I. Z. MacKenzie, "Pregnancy Termination," in Brock, *Prenatal*, 677–9; R. C. Henshaw and A. Templeton, "Methods Used in First Trimester Abortion," *Current Obstetrics and Gynaecology* 3 (1993): 11–16.

32 Diana Webster et al., "A Comparison of 600 and 200 mg Mifepristone Prior to Second Trimester Abortion with the Prostaglandin Misoprostol," *British Journal of Obstetrics and Gynecology*, 103/7 (1996): 706–9.

33 MacKenzie, "Pregnancy Termination," 680–3; Robert M. Ford, "Vaginally Administered 16,16-Dimethyl-PGE1-Methyl Ester (Gemeprost) to Induce Termination of Pregnancy after the First Trimester," *Australian and New Zealand Journal of Obstetrics and Gynaecology* 28 (1988): 169–71.

34 Hazem El-Refaey and Allan Templeton, "Induction of Abortion in the Second Trimester by a Combination of Misopistol and Mifepristone: A Randomized Comparison between Two Misopristol Regimens," *Human Reproduction* 10/2 (1995): 475–8.

35 Sjef Gevers, "Third Trimester Abortion for Fetal Abnormality," *Bioethics* 13 (3/4): (1999): 306–13.

36 Willard Cates Jr. and Charlotte Ellertson, "Abortion," in *Contraceptive Technology*, ed. Hatcher et al., 688–9; Suzanne Daley, *The New York Times*, Oct. 5, 2000.

37 Task Force on Postovulatory Methods of Fertility Regulation, "Comparison of Three Single Doses of Mifepristone as Emergency Contraception: A Randomized Trial," *Lancet* 353 (1999): 697–702.

38 R. M. Sharp et al., "Absence of hCG Like Activity in the Blood of Women Fitted with Intra-Uterine Contraceptive Devices," *Journal of Clinical Endocrinology & Metabolism*, 43 (1977): 496–9. This study showed that when IUDs were used embryos did not develop to the blastocyst stage where they are capable of secreting measurable amounts of hCG.

39 Maria Elena Ortiz and Horacio B. Croxatto, "The Mode of Action of IUDs," *Contraception*, 36 (1987): 11–22; *Mechanism of action, safety and efficacy of intrauterine devices*, Report of a WHO Scientific Group (Geneva: World Health Organization, 1987), 12–17; 68–71.

40 James Trussell et al., "The Yuzpe Regimen of Emergency Contraception: How Long After the Morning After?," *Obstetrics and Gynecology* 88 (1996): 150–4. For evidence that inhibition of ovulation does not entirely account for ECPs' effectiveness see James Trussell and Elizabeth G Raymond, "Statistical Evidence about the Mechanism of the Yuzpe Regimen of Emergency Contraception," *Obstetrics & Gynecology* 93 (1999): 872–6.

41 Paul F. A. Van Look and Felicia Stewart, "Emergency Contraception," in Hatcher et al., *Contraceptive Technology*, 281.

42 Task Force on Postovulatory Methods of Fertility Regulation, "Randomised Controlled Trial of Levonorgestrel versus the Yuzpe Regimen of Combined Oral Contraceptives for Emergency Contraception," *Lancet* 352 (1998): 428–33.

43 James Trussell et al., "The Effectiveness of the Yuzpe Regimen of Emergency Contraception," *Family Planning Perspectives*, 28/2 (1996): 58–64, 87.

44 Task Force, "Randomised Controlled Trial of Levonorgestrel," 431.

45 World Health Organization, "A Prospective Multicentre Trial of the Ovulation Method of Natural Family Planning. III. Characteristics of the Menstrual Cycle and of the Fertile Phase," *Fertility and Sterility* 40 (1983): 773–8.

46 Wilcox et al., "Incidence," 190; Ian S. Fraser and Edith Weisberg, "Fertility Following Discontinuation of Different Forms of Fertility Control," *Contraception*, 1982; 26:4: 389–415 at 390.

47 Allen Wilcox et al., "Timing of Sexual Intercourse in Relation to Ovulation," *New England Journal of Medicine* 333 (1995): 1517–21.

48 Allen Wilcox et al., "The Timing of the "Fertile Window" in the Menstrual Cycle: Day Specific Estimates from a Prospective Study," *British Medical Journal* 321 (2000): 1259–62.

49 D. S. Settlage et al., "Sperm Transport from the External Cervical Os to the Fallopian Tubes in Women: A Time and Quantitation Study," *Fertility and Sterility* 24 (1973): 655–61; D. F. Hawkins and M. G. Elder, *Human Fertility Control: Theory and Practice* (London: Butterworths, 1979), 421.

50 Anna Glasier, "Emergency Postcoital Contraception," *New England Journal of Medicine* 337/15 (1997): 1063.

51 Fabienne Grou and Isabel Rodrigues, "The Morning-after Pill – How Long After?," *American Journal of Obstetrics and Gynecology* 171 (1994): 1529–34.

52 Margaret F. McCann and Linda S. Potter, "Progestin-only Oral Contraception: A Comprehensive Review," *Contraception* 50 (1994; Suppl. Dec.

1): S14–S21; Hatcher et al., *Contraceptive Technology*, 468–9; John Guillebaud, *The Pill and Other Hormones for Contraception*, 4th ed. (Oxford: University Press, 1991), 208; Fraser and Weisberg, "Fertility Following Discontinuation of Different Forms of Fertility Control," 395.

53 McCann and Potter, "Progestin-only Oral Contraception," S34–35.

54 McCann and Potter, "Progestin-only Oral Contraception," S19–S21; Tonti-Filippini, "The Pill: Abortifacient or Contraceptive?, A Literature Review," *Linacre Quarterly* 62/1 (1995): 9; K. Fotherby, "The Progestogen-only Pill," *Contraception*, eds. Filshie and Guillebaud, 102; D. R. Mishell "Contraceptive Use and Effectiveness," in Mishell, *Infertility*, 846.

55 John Guillebaud, "Combined Hormonal Contraception," in *Handbook of Family Planning and Reproductive Health Care*, eds. Nancy Loudon et al. (Edinburgh: Churchill Livingstone, 1995): 44–5; Hatcher et al., *Contraceptive Technology*, 406.

56 McCann and Potter, "Progestin-only Oral Contraception," S34–35; A. Kubba and J. Guillebaud, "Combined Oral Contraceptives: Acceptability and Effective Use," *British Medical Bulletin* 49/1 (1993): 142–3.

57 Howard J. Tatum and Frederick H. Schmidt, "Contraceptive and Sterilization Practices and Extrauterine Pregnancy: A Realistic Perspective," *Fertility and Sterility*, 28 (1977): 414–17.

58 J. Coste et al., "Risk Factors for Ectopic Pregnancy: A Case-control Study in France, with a Special Focus on Infectious Factors," *American Journal of Epidemiology*, 133/9 (1991): 839–49.

59 Walter L. Latimore and Randy Alcorn, "Using the Birth Control Pill is Ethically Unacceptable," in John Kilner et al., eds., *The Reproductive Revolution: A Christian Appraisal of Sexuality, Reproductive Technology and the Family* (Grand Rapids, Mich.: Wm. B. Eerdmans, 2000), 183–4.

60 Stephen G. Somkuti et al., "The Effect of Oral Contraceptive Pill on Markers of Endometrial Receptivity," *Fertility and Sterility*, 65 (1996): 488.

61 John Wilks, "The Role of the Pill at the Time of Implantation of the Human Embryo – New Research Findings," *Ethics and Medicine* 16/1 (1999): 15–22.

62 S. J. Segal et al., "Norplant Implants: The Mechanism of Contraceptive Action," *Fertility and Sterility* 56/2 (1991): 273–7.

63 Mamdouh M. Shaaban et al., "Sonographic Assessment of Ovarian and Endometrial Changes During Long-Term Norplant Use and the Correlation with Hormonal Levels," *Fertility and Sterility* 59 (1993): 998–1002.

64 Latimore and Alcorn, "Using the Birth Control Pill is Ethically Unacceptable," 180–3.

65 MacKenzie, "Pregnancy Termination," 683–4; T. T. Lao and L. F. Ho, "Induced Abortion is not a Cause of Subsequent Preterm Delivery in Teenage Pregnancies," *Human Reproduction* 13/3 (1998): 759–61.

66 MacKenzie, "Pregnancy Termination," 685; *An Information Paper on Termination of Pregnancy in Australia*, 23–33.

67 Theresa Marteau and Elizabeth Anionwu, "Evaluating Carrier Testing: Objectives and Outcomes," in Theresa Marteau and Martin Richards eds., *The Troubled Helix: Social and Psychological Implications of the New Human Genetics* (Cambridge: Cambridge University Press, 1996), 134; Josephine Green and Helen Statham, "Psychosocial Aspects of Prenatal Screening and Diagnosis," ibid. 151–2.

68 S. Iles and D. Garth, "Psychiatric Outcome of Termination of Pregnancy for Foetal Abnormality," *Psychological Medicine*, 23 (1993): 407–13; T. Kitamura et al., "Psychological and Social Correlates of the Onset of Affective Disorders among Pregnant Women," *Psychological Medicine*, 23 (1993): 967–75.

69 Anne C. Gilchrist et al., "Termination of Pregnancy and Psychiatric Morbidity," *British Journal of Psychiatry*, 167 (1995): 243–8; Helen Statham, "Professional Understanding and Parents' Experience of Termination," Brock, *Prenatal*, 697–702.

70 See Patricia R. Casey, "Psychological Effects of Abortion," *Catholic Medical Quarterly* (Feb. 1996): 18; Paul K. B. Dagg, "The Psychological Sequelae of Therapeutic Abortion – Denied and Completed," *American Journal of Psychiatry* 148 (1991): 578–85; G. Zolese and C. V. R. Blacker, "The Psychological Complications of Therapeutic Abortion," *British Journal of Psychiatry*, 160 (1992): 742–9.

71 Mika Gissler et al., "Suicides after Pregnancy in Finland, 1987–94: Register Linkage Study," *British Medical Journal*, 313 (1996): 1431–4.

72 See Ronan O'Rahilly and Fabiola Müller, *Human Embryology and Teratology* (New York: Wiley-Liss, 1992), 285–7; "Neuralation in the Normal Human Embryo," in *Neural Tube Defects*, ed. Gregory Bock and Joan Marsh (Chichester: Wiley–Ciba Foundation Symposium 181, 1994), 70–89; Keith L. Moore and T. V. N. Persaud, *The Developing Human: Clinically Oriented Embryology*, 6th ed. (Philadelphia: W. B. Saunders, 1998), 418–19, 463–4; The Medical Task Force on Anencephaly, "The Infant with Anencephaly," in *The New England Journal of Medicine* 322 (1990): 669–73.

73 Task Force, "The Infant with Anencephaly," 670.

74 O'Rahilly and Müller, "Neuralation in the Normal Human Embryo," 80.

75 Eva Alberman and Joan M. Noble, "Commentary: Food Should Be Fortified with Folic Acid," *British Medical Journal* 319 (1999): 93; N. Ward and C. Bower, "Folic Acid, Pernicious Anaemia and Prevention of Neural Tube Defects," *Lancet* 307 (1994): 343; N. J. Wald, "Folic Acid and Neural Tube Defects," in *Neural Tube Defects – CIBA Foundation Symposium* (Chichester: Wiley, 1994), 192–211.

76 Task Force, "The Infant with Anencephaly," 669–70; N. J. Wald and M. P. Gilbertson, "Folic Acid in Prevention of Neural Tube Defects,"

Lancet 345 (1995): 389–90; Gary M. Shaw et al., "Risks of Orofacial Clefts in Children Born to Women Using Multivitamins Containing Folic Acid Periconceptually," *Lancet* 345 (1995): 393–6.

77 Task Force, "The Infant with Anencephaly," 671.

78 *Perinatal Deaths 1975* (Canberra: Australian Bureau of Statistics, 1977), ref. no. 4.29, 28.

79 Ibid., 24.

80 *Perinatal Deaths Australia*, from 1988 to 1993 (Canberra: Australian Bureau of Statistics, 1989–94), cat. no. 3304.0 and *Causes of Death Australia*, 1994 and 1995 (Canberra: Australian Bureau of Statistics), cat. no. 3303.0.

81 *Congenital Malformations Australia 1993 and 1994*, eds. Paul Lancaster et al. (Sydney: Australian Institute of Health and Welfare, National Perinatal Statistics Unit, 1997), 37–8.

82 D. J. Henderson-Smart, "Low Birth-weight Babies: Where to Draw the Line?," in *Trends in Biomedical Regulation*, ed. H. Caton (Sydney: Butterworth, 1990), 146.

83 William H. Kitchen et al., "Live-born Infants of 24 to 28 Weeks' Gestation: Survival and Sequelae at Two Years of Age," in Ciba Foundation Symposium 115 *Abortion: Medical Progress and Social Implications* (London: Pitman, 1985), 122–35.

84 J. Edgar Morison, *Foetal and Neonatal Pathology*, 2nd ed. (London: Butterworths, 1963), 114, with data from the 1940s; L. Cussen et al., "Mean Organ Weights of an Australian Population of Fetuses and Infants," *Journal of Paediatrics and Child Health* (1990): 26, 102.

85 Alan R. Fleichman et al., "The Physician's Moral Obligations to the Pregnant Woman, the Fetus and the Child," *Seminars in Perinatology* 22 (1998): 186–7.

86 Judith M. Lumley, "Attitudes to the Fetus among Primigravidae," *Australian Paediatric Journal* 18 (1982): 106–9.

87 Christopher Belshaw, "Abortion, Value and the Sanctity of Life," *Bioethics* 11/2 (1997): 130–50.

88 Aristotle, *Politics*, 1335b.

89 R. M. Hare, "Abortion and the Golden Rule," in Helga Khuse and Peter Singer, eds., *Bioethics – An Anthology* (Oxford: Blackwell Publishers, 1999), 58–68.

90 Laura M. Purdy, "Are Pregnant Women Fetal Containers?," in Khuse and Singer, eds., *Bioethics – An Anthology*, 72.

91 Mary Anne Warren, "Abortion," in Helga Kuhse and Peter Singer, eds., *A Companion to Bioethics* (Oxford: Blackwell Publishers, 1998), 127–8.

92 Mary Anne Warren, "On the Moral and Legal Status of Abortion," *The Ethics of Abortion: Pro-Life vs Pro-Choice*, ed. Robert M. Baird and Stuart E. Resenbaum (Buffalo, NY: Prometheus Books, 1993), 231.

93   Judith Jarvis Thompson, "A Defence of Abortion," *Philosophy and Public Affairs*, 1 (1971): 47–66.

94   Judith Jarvis Thompson, "Abortion," *Boston Review* 20/3 (1996): 47.

95   Ibid., 47.

96   Ibid., 47.

97   Ibid., 48.

98   See Michael Banner, *Christian Ethics and Contemporary Moral Problems* (Cambridge: Cambridge University Press, 1999), 86–135; *Abortion: A New Generation of Catholic Responses*, ed. Stephen J. Heaney (Braintree, Mass.: The Pope John Center, 1992); James J. Mulligan, *Choose Life* (Baintree, Mass.: The Pope John Center, 1991).

99   John Paul II, Encyclical Letter *Evangelium Vitae* (Vatican City: Libreria Editrice Vaticana, 1995), 62.

100 Dave Wendler, "Understanding the "Conservative" View on Abortion," *Bioethics* 13 (1999): 32–55.

101 Janet Podell, "The Right to Choose Life . . ." *Australian Jewish News*, Sydney edition (Sept. 15, 1995), 1475.

102 Don Marquis, "Why Abortion is Immoral?," in Khuse and Singer, eds., *Bioethics – An Anthology*, 46–57.

103 Gevers, "Third Trimester Abortion for Fetal Abnormality," 306–13.

104 Rebecca J. Cook, "Legal Abortion: Limits and Contributions to Human Life," in *Abortion: Medical Progress and Social Implications*, 222–3.

105 See John Finnis, "Abortion and Health Care Ethics," in Khuse and Singer, eds., *Bioethics – An Anthology*, 16–17.

106 Benedict Ashley and Kevin O'Rourke, *Health Care Ethics: A Theological Analysis*, 4th ed. (Washington, DC: Georgetown University Press, 1997), 253–4.

107 John R. Higgins and Shaun Brennecke, "Pre-eclampsia – Still a Disease of Theories?," *Current Opinions in Obstetrics and Gynecology* 10 (1998): 129–33; Y. M. Dennis Lo, "Fetal DNA in Maternal Plasma: Biology and Diagnositc Applications," *Clinical Chemistry* 46/12 (2000): 1903–6.

108 Harriette L. Hampton, "Care of the Woman Who Has Been Raped," *New England Journal of Medicine* 332/4 (1995): 234.

109 Van Look and Stewart, "Emergency Contraception," in Hatcher et al., *Contraceptive Technology*, 281.

110 Finnis, "Abortion and Health Care Ethics," 17.

111 *Ethical and Religious Directives for Catholic Health Care Services*, 24/27 *Origins* (1994 Dec. 24): 456. The UK Bishops said much the same, Joint Committee on Bioethical Issues Statement, "Use of the 'Morning-After Pill' in Cases of Rape," *Origins* 15/39 (1986): 634–8; Ashley and O'Rourke, *Health Care Ethics: A Theological Analysis*, 305–6.

112 Thomas Boyle III, "The Licitness (According to Roman Catholic Premises) of Inducing the Non-viable Anencephalic Fetus: Reflections on Professor Drane's Policy Proposals," *H.E.C. Forum* 4/2 (1992): 126–33; D. A.

Shewmon, "Caution in the Definition and Diagnosis of Infant Brain Death," in D. C. Thomasma and J. F. Monagle, eds., *Medical Ethics: A Guide for Health Professionals* (Rockville, Md.: Aspen Systems Corp., 1987), 38–57.

113 Boyle, "The Licitness," 125–6.

114 Jean deBlois, "Anencephaly and the Management of Pregnancy," *Health Care Ethics USA Fall* 1/4 (1993): 2–3.

115 J. F. Drane, "Anencephaly and the Interruption of Pregnancy: Policy Proposals for HECs," *H.E.C. Forum* 4/2 (1992): 103–19.

116 Cook, "Legal Abortion," 211–17.

117 Joel Feinberg, *Harm to Others* (New York: Oxford University Press, 1984), 101; "Wrongful Life and the Counterfactual Element in Harming," in Joel Feinberg, *Freedom and Fulfilment* (Princeton: Princeton University Press, 1992), 22; see a critique of his views in Bonnie Steinbock and Ron McClamrock, "When is Birth Unfair to the Child," *Hastings Center Report* 24/6 (1994): 15–21; Philip P. Reilly, "Medicolegal Aspects," in Brock, *Prenatal*, 762–5.

118 Henry Davis, *Moral and Pastoral Theology*, vol. 2 (London: Sheed and Ward, 1959), 167–8; T. J. O'Donnell, *Medicine and Christian Morality* (New York: Alba House, 1991), 177–8.

119 Karin Clark et al., "Early Induction of Labor: Legal and Ethical Considerations," *Linacre Quarterly* 66/2 (1999): 7–25.

120 Kevin O'Rourke, "Ethical Opinions in Regard to the Question of Early Delivery of Anencephalic Infants," *Linacre Quarterly*, 63/3 (1996): 55–9.

Chapter 6 Infertility and Artificial Reproductive Technology

1 Tara Hurst et al., *Assisted Conception, Australia and New Zealand, 1997*. AIHW cat. no. PER 10 (Sydney: Australian Institute of Health and Welfare National Perinatal Statistics Unit, 1999, Assisted Conception Series no. 4), 1.

2 See Karen Dawson, *Reproductive Technology: The Science, the Ethics, the Law and the Social Issues* (Melbourne: VCTA Publishing, Macmillan Education Australia, 1995); D. M. Saunders and L. J. Satchwell, *Assisted Reproductive Technology: What the doctor should know* (New York & London: The Parthenon Publishing Group, 1995); Donald Evans and Neil Pickering, eds., *Creating the Child: The Ethics, Law and Practice of Assisted Procreation* (The Hague: Martinus Nijhoff Publishers, 1996).

3 Egbert te Velde et al., "Variation in Couple Fecundity and Time to Pregnancy, An Essential Concept of Human Reproduction," *Lancet* 355 (2000): 1928–9.

4   Ibid., 1928–9; J. Yovich and G. Grundzinskas, "The Spectrum of Infertility," *The Management of Infertility: A Manual of Gamete Handling Procedures* (Oxford: Heinemann, 1990), 5–11.

5   Dawson, *Reproductive Technology*, 1–2.

6   D. R. Mishell and V. Davajan, "Evaluation of the Infertile Couple," in D. R. Mishell et al., *Infertility, Contraception and Reproductive Endocrinology*, 3rd ed. (Boston: Blackwell Scientific Publications, 1991), 557–9.

7   Egbert te Velde and Bernard J. Cohlen, "The Management of Infertility," *New England Journal of Medicine* 340 (1999): 224.

8   Hurst et al., *Assisted Conception*, 41.

9   Ibid., 9, 41.

10   *Human Fertilization and Embryology Authority (HF&EA). Seventh Annual Report & Accounts 1998*, 8.

11   Peter T. Ellison, "Human Ovarian Function and Reproductive Ecology: New Hypotheses," *American Anthropologist* 92/4 (1990): 933–52.

12   Mishell, "Evaluation of the Infertile Couple," 562; Dawson, *Reproductive Technology*, 1, 5–15.

13   Louise Vandelac and Marie-Hélène Bacon, "Will We Be Taught By Our Clones? The Mutations of the Living, From Endocrine Disruptors to Genetics," *Baillière's Clinical Obstetrics and Gynaecology* 13/4 (1999): 581–3; Alfred Spira and Luc Multigner, "The Effect of Industrial and Agricultural Pollution on Human Spermatogenesis," *Human Reproduction* 13/8 (1998): 2041–2.

14   Michael Joffe, "Time Trends in Biological Fertility in Britain," *Lancet* 355 (2000): 1961–5.

15   E. L. Yong et al., "Male Infertility and the Androgen Receptor: Molecular, Clinical and Therapeutic Aspects," *Reproductive Medicine Review*, 6 (1997): 113–31; M. Auroux, "Age of the Father and Development," *Contraception, Fertilité, Sexualité* 21 (1993): 382–5.

16   Juan J. Tarín et al., "Long-term Effects of Delayed Parenthood," *Human Reproduction* 13/9 (1998): 2371–6; A. J. Wyrobek et al., "Mechanisms and Targets Involved in Maternal and Paternal Effects on Numerical Aneuploidy," *Environmental and Molecular Mutagenesis* 28/3 (1996): 254–64.

17   See *Infertility: Guidelines for Practice, Fertility Committee of the Royal College of Obstetricians and Gynaecologists* (London: RCOG Press 1992).

18   Swren Holm, "Infertility, Childlessness and the Need for Treatment," in Evans and Pickering, *Creating the Child*, 65–78; R. G. Edwards, "Human Conception *in vitro* 1995, a Summing Up," *Human Reproduction* 11 Suppl 1 (1996): 199–211.

19   David S. Guzick et al., "Efficacy of Superovulation and Intrauterine Insemination in the Treatment of Infertility," *New England Journal of Medicine* 340 (1999): 177–83; te Velde and Cohlen, "The Management of Infertility," 225.

20 Michael G. R. Hull and Charlotte F. Fleming, "Tubal Surgery Versus Assisted Reproduction: Assessing their Role in Infertility Therapy," *Current Opinions in Obstetrics and Gynecology* 7 (1995): 161.

21 Dawson, *Reproductive Technology*, 9.

22 Dawson, *Reproductive Technology*, 49.

23 Gayle M. Jones et al., "The Factors Affecting the Success of Human Blastocyst Development and Pregnancy Following IVF and Embryo Transfer," *Fertility & Sterility* 70/6 (1998): 1022–9.

24 Dawson, *Reproductive Technology*, 51–2. A. Laws-King et al., "Fertilization of Human Oocytes by Microinjection of a Single Spermatozoon under the Zona Pellucida," *Fertility and Sterility* 48 (1987): 395–401.

25 Saunders and Satchwell, *Assisted Reproductive Technology*, 72–3.

26 Mark V. Sauer and Richard J. Paulson, "Oocyte and Embryo Donation," *Current Opinion in Obstetrics and Gynecology* 7 (1995): 193–8.

27 Debra A. Gook and David H. Edgar, "Cryopreservation of the Human Female Gamete: Current and Future Issues," *Human Reproduction* 14/12 (1999): 2938–40; Carl E. Wood et al., "Cryopreservation of Ovarian Tissue: Potential 'Reproductive Insurance' for Women at Risk of Early Ovarian Failure," *Medical Journal of Australia* 166 (1997): 366–9.

28 Tae K. Yoon et al., "Pregnancy and Delivery of Healthy Infants Developed from Vitrified Oocytes in a Stimulated In Vitro Fertilization Embryo Transfer Program," *Fertility and Sterility* 74 (2000): 180–1; E. Porcu, "Freezing of Oocytes," *Current Opinions in Obstetrics and Gynecology* 11/3 (1999): 297–300.

29 Y. Yokota, "Successful Pregnancy Following Blastocyst Vitrification," *Human Reproduction* 15 (2000): 1802–3.

30 Gook and Edgar, "Cryopreservation of the Human Female Gamete," 2939; Wood et al., "Cyropreservation of Ovarian Tissue," 369.

31 Dawson, *Reproductive Technology*, 76–7.

32 Roger Dobson, "Ovarian Transplant Raises Hope for Women Facing Cancer Treatment," News, *British Medical Journal* 319 (1999): 871.

33 Kamal A. Jaroudi et al., "Embryo Development and Pregnancies from In Vitro Matured and Fertilized Human Oocytes," *Human Reproduction* 14/7 (1999): 1749–51; Health Council of the Netherlands: Committee on In Vitro Fertilization. *IVF-related research* (Rijswijk, 1998; pub. no. 1998/08E): 11, 41–4.

34 A. Brzezinski and J. G. Schenker, "Induction of Ovulation and Risk of Breast Cancer: An Overview and Perspectives," *Gynecological Endocrinology* 11 (1997): 357–64; Alison Venn et al., "Breast and Ovarian Cancer Incidence after Infertility and In Vitro Fertilisation," *Lancet* 346 (1995): 995–1000; Mary Anne Rossing et al., "Ovarian Tumors in a Cohort of Infertile Women," *New England Journal of Medicine*, 331 (1994): 771–6.

35 Guzick et al., "Efficacy of Superovulation," 177–83.

36   Gianpiero D. Palermo, "Intracytoplasmic Sperm Injection: A Powerful Tool to Overcome Fertilization Failure," *Fertility and Sterility* 65 (1996): 899–908; A. C. Van Steirteghem et al., "High fertilization and Implantation Rates after Intracytoplasmic Sperm Injection," *Human Reproduction*, 8/7 (1993): 1061–6. The clinical pregnancy rate was 35.3 percent per started cycle and the total pregnancy rate was 49.6 percent per embryo transfer.

37   *HF&EA, Seventh Annual Report 1998*, 1998, 10.

38   Hurst et al., *Assisted Conception*, 32, 33, 35.

39   Seang-Lin Tan et al., "Pregnancy and Birth Rates of Live Infants after In Vitro Fertilization in Women With and Without Previous In Vitro Fertilization Pregnancies: A Study of Eight Thousand Cycles at One Center," *American Journal of Obstetrics and Gynecology* 170 (1994): 34–40.

40   J. de Mouzon and P. Lancaster, "World Collaborative Report on In Vitro Fertilization: Preliminary data for 1995," *Journal of Assisted Reproduction and Genetics*, 14/5 (1997): (Supplement): 253S, 263S–264S; Edwards, "Human Conception *In Vitro* 1995, a Summing Up," 202.

41   *HF&EA, Seventh Annual Report*, 1998, 12.

42   Hurst et al., *Assisted Conception*, 30.

43   *HF&EA, Seventh Annual Report*, 1998, 14.

44   Hurst et al., *Assisted Conception*, 39, 55–6.

45   Mark V. Sauer et al., "In *Vivo* Blastocyst Production and Ovum Yield Among Fertile Women," *Human Reproduction* 2 (1987): 701–3.

46   Hurst et al., *Assisted Conception*, 54; Peter Day et al., *Australia's Mothers and Babies 1997*, AIHW cat. no. PER 12 (Sydney: AIHW National Perinatal Statistics Unit: Perinatal Statistics Series N. 9, 1999), 92.

47   Hurst et al., *Assisted Conception*, 54; Day et al., *Australia's Mothers and Babies 1997*, 93.

48   *HF&EA, Seventh Annual Report 1998*, 12.

49   Hurst et al., *Assisted Conception*, 47, 63; Day et al., *Australia's Mothers and Babies 1997*, 15, 62; Ashi Daftary and Steve N. Caritis, "Preterm Labor and Delivery," in Thomas R. Moore et al., eds., *Gynecology and Obstetrics: A Longitudinal Approach* (New York: Churchill Livingstone, 1993), 511.

50   Hurst et al., *Assisted Conception* 49, 63; Day et al., *Australia's Mothers and Babies 1997*, 80.

51   Ayse Aytoz et al., "Obstetric Outcome of Pregnancies after Transfer of Cryopreserved and Fresh Embryos Obtained by Conventional In-Vitro Fertilization and Intracytoplasmic Sperm Injection," *Human Reproduction* 14 (1999): 2619–24.

52   Lee R. Hickok and Phillip E. Patton, "Ectopic Pregnancy," in Moore et al., eds, *Gynecology and Obstetrics: A Longitudinal Approach*, 263; Hurst et al., *Assisted Conception*, 46, 62.

53 Hurst et al., *Assisted Conception*, 54, 67; *Congenital Malformations Australia 1995 and 1996*, AIHW cat. no. PER 8 (Sydney: Australian Institute of Health and Welfare National Perinatal Statistics Unit, 1999), 1, 12.

54 M. Bonduelle et al., "Commentary: Major Defects are Overestimated," *British Medical Journal* 315 (1997): 1265–6.

55 M. Bonduelle et al., "Seven Years of Intracytoplasmic Sperm Injection and Follow-up of 1987 Subsequent Children," *Human Reproduction* 14 Suppl 1(1999): 243–64; M. Bonduelle et al., "Incidence of Chromosomal Aberrations in Children Born after Assisted Reproduction Through Intracytoplasmic Sperm Injection," *Human Reproduction* 13/4 (1998): 781–2.

56 Mark D. Johnson, "Genetic Risks of Intracytoplasmic Sperm Injection in the Treatment of Male Infertility: Recommendations for Genetic Counselling and Screening," *Fertility and Sterility* 70/3 (1998): 397–411; Howard W. Jones Jr., "New Reproductive Technologies," *Baillière's Clinical Obstetrics and Gynaecology* 13/4 (1999): 484–5; Vandelac and Bacon, "Will We Be Taught by Our Clones? The Mutations of the Living, From Endocrine Disruptors to Genetics," 585; A. Van Steirteghem et al., "Ethical Considerations of Intracytoplasmic Sperm Injection," *Ethical Dilemmas in Assisted Reproduction*, eds. F. Shenfield and C. Sureau (New York and London: Parthenon Publishing Group, 1997), 51–6.

57 M. Bonduelle, et al., "Incidence of Chromosomal Aberrations in Children," 781–2; E. te Veld et al., "Sex Chromosomal Abnormalities and Intracytoplasmic Sperm Injection," *Lancet* 346 (1995): 773.

58 U. B. Wennerholm et al., "Incidence of Congenital Malformations in Children Born after ICSI," *Human Reproduction* 15 (2000): 944–8; Govaerts et al., "Comparisons of Pregnancy Outcome after Intracytoplasmic Sperm Injection and In-vitro Fertilization," *Human Reproduction* 13/6 (1998): 1514–18.

59 Lucinda L. Veeck, "Significantly Enhanced Pregnancy Rates Per Cycle Through Cryopreservation and Thaw of Pronuclear Stage Oocytes," *Fertility and Sterility* 59/6 (1993): 1202; Michael J. Tucker et al., "Cryopreservation of Human Embryos and Oocytes," *Current Opinion in Obstetrics and Gynecology* 7 (1995): 188–192.

60 Jacques Testart, "Episcientific Aspects of the Epigenetic Factors in Artificial Procreation," *Human Reproduction* 13/4 (1998): 783–5.

61 H. Laverge et al., "Flourescent In-Situ Hybridization on Human Embryos Showing Cleavage Arrest after Freezing and Thawing," *Human Reproduction* 13/2 (1998): 425–9.

62 F. L. Gibson et al., "Development, Behaviour and Temperament: A Prospective Study of Infants Conceived Through In-Vitro Fertilization," *Human Reproduction* 13/6 (1998): 17–32.

63 Kerry Saunders et al., "Growth and Physical Outcome of Children Conceived by In Vitro Fertilization," *Pediatrics* 97 (1996): 688–92.

64 See Lancaster, "Assisted Conception: Health Services Evaluation," 494; National Health and Medical Research Council, *Long-term Effects on Women from Assisted Conception* (Canberra: Australian Government Publishing Service, 1995), 34–5.

65 Human Fertilization and Embryology Authority, *The Patients' Guide to DI and IVF Clinics*, London, 1995, 10.

66 *House of Commons Hansard Debates*, May 6, 1998, col. 657.

67 Bradley J. Van Voorhis et al., "Cost-effective Treatment of the Infertile Couple," *Fertility and Sterility* 70/6 (1998): 998.

68 See Commonwealth Department of Health and Family Services, *Medicare Benefits Schedule Book* (Canberra: Australian Government Publications, Nov. 1998), 98.

69 For an informative ethical overview see Jones Jr, "New Reproductive Technologies," 473–90.

70 See Maurizio Mori, "Is a 'Hands Off' Policy to Reproduction Preferable to Artificial Intervention?," in Evans and Pickering, *Creating the Child*, 99–110, and Neil Pickering, "Naturally Conceived," ibid., 111–25.

71 Tony Hope et al., "An Ethical Debate: Should Older Women be Offered *In Vitro* Fertilization?," in Helga Khuse and Peter Singer, eds., *Bioethics – An Anthology* (Oxford: Blackwell Publishers, 1999), 116–19.

72 Editorial, *Lancet* 341 (1993): 345.

73 David B. Resnik, "The Commodification of Human Reproductive Materials," *Journal of Medical Ethics* 24 (1998): 388–93; G. M. Lockwood, "Donating Life: Practical and Ethical Issues in Gamete Donation," in Shenfield and Sureau, eds., *Ethical Dilemmas in Assisted Reproduction*, 23–30.

74 R. G. Gosden, "Transplantation of Fetal Germ Cells," *Journal of Assisted Reproduction* (US) 9 (1992): 118–23.

75 Susan Golombok, "New Families, Old Values: Considerations Regarding the Welfare of the Child," *Human Reproduction* 13/9 (1998): 2342–7; Bambi E. S. Robinson, "Birds do it. Bees do it. So Why not Single Women and Lesbians?," *Bioethics* 11/3&4 (1997): 217–27.

76 Golombok, "New Families, Old Values," 2346.

77 Eva M. Durna et al., "Donor Insemination: Attitudes of Parents Towards Disclosure," *Medical Journal of Australia* 167 (1997): 256–9.

78 Roy Eccleston, "Dear Dad (whoever your are. . .)," *The Australian Magazine*, Aug. 18–19, 1998: 12–17; Ruth Landau, "The Management of Genetic Origins: Secrecy and Openness in Donor Assisted Conception in Israel and Elsewhere," *Human Reproduction* 13/11 (1998): 3268–73; Eric Blyth and Jennifer Hunt, "Sharing Genetic Origins Information in Donor Assisted Conception: Views from Licensed Centres on H&EFA Donor Information Form (91)4," *Human Reproduction* 13/11 (1998): 3274–7.

79 A. J. Turner and A. Coyle, "What Does It Mean to Be a Donor Offspring? The Identity Experiences of Adults Conceived by Donor Insemination and

the Implications for Counselling and Therapy," *Human Reproduction* 15 (2000): 2041–51.

80 See Jean-Marie Thevoz, "The Rights of Children to Information Following Assisted Conception," in Evans and Pickering, *Creating the Child*, 195–209.

81 Laura M. Purdy, "Assisted Reproduction," in Helga Kuhse and Peter Singer, eds., *A Companion to Bioethics* (Oxford: Blackwell Publishers, 1998), 168–71.

82 Laura M. Purdy, "Surrogate Mothering: Exploitation or Empowerment?," in Khuse and Singer, eds., *Bioethics*, 103–10.

83 V. English et al., "Surrogacy," in Shenfield and Sureau, eds., *Ethical Dilemmas in Assisted Reproduction*, 31–40.

84 Max Charlesworth, *Bioethics in a Liberal Society* (Cambridge: University Press, 1993), 63–88.

85 Robyn Rowland, *Living Laboratories: Women and Reproductive Technologies* (Sydney: Pan Macmillan, 1992), 190.

86 See Susan Dodds and Karen Jones, "A Response to Purdy," in Khuse and Singer, *Bioethics*, 113–15.

87 Anna Stokes, "Surrogate Motherhood: Is it Now Legal in Australia?," *Caroline Chisholm Centre for Health Ethics Bulletin*, 2/1 (1996): 6–9.

88 Hugh V. McLachlan, "Defending Commercial Surrogate Motherhood Against Van Niekerk and Van Zyl," *Journal of Medical Ethics* 23 (1997): 344–8.

89 John Harris, " 'Goodby Dolly?' The Ethics of Human Cloning," *Journal of Medical Ethics* 23 (1997): 353–60.

90 Michael Tooley, "The Moral Status of the Cloning of Humans," *Monash Bioethics Review* 18/1 (1999): 27–49.

91 Gregory Pence, "Ethics, Cloning, and Persons," *Monash Bioethics Review* 18/1 (1999): 50–3.

92 David McCarthy, "Persons and their Copies," *Journal of Medical Ethics* 25 (1999): 98–104.

93 Julian Savulescu, "Should we Clone Human Beings? Cloning as a Source of Tissue for Transplantation," *Journal of Medical Ethics* 25 (1999): 87–95.

94 See Victoria's *Infertility Treatment Act*, Victoria, 1995, clause 5, where the welfare of the child is "paramount"; *Human Fertilisation and Embryology Act 1990*, s. 13(5).

95 Ruth Weston and Jody Hughes, "Family Forms – Family Well-being," *Family Matters* (N.53 Winter 1999), 14–20.

96 C. L. Ten, "A Child's Right to a Father," *Monash Bioethics Review* 19/4 (2000): 33–7; Loane Skene, "Voices in the ART Access Debate," *Monash Bioethics Review* 20/1 (2001): 9–23.

97 *Truth and the Child 10 Years On: Information Exchange in Donor Assisted Conception*, eds. Eric Blyth et al. (Birmingham: British Association of Social Workers, 1998).

98 Demetrio Neri, "Child or Parent Oriented Controls of Reproductive Technologies," in Evans and Pickering, *Creating the Child*, 145–56.

99 Claes Gottlieb et al., "Disclosure of Donor Insemination to the Child: The Impact of Swedish Legislation on Couples' Attitudes," *Human Reproduction* 15 (2000): 2052–6; *Infertility Treatment Act 1995*, Victoria, clause 80.

100 Roy Eccleston, "Procreators Anonymous," *The Australian Magazine*, April 18–19, 1998: 12–17.

101 Timothy F. Murphy, "Sperm Harvesting and Post-Mortem Fatherhood," *Bioethics* 9/5 (1995): 380–98.

102 Carson Strong et al., "Ethics of Sperm Retrieval After Death or Persistent Vegetative State," *Human Reproduction* 15 (2000): 739–45.

103 *Human Fertilization and Embryology Authority, Fourth Annual Report 1995*, London, p. 19.

104 *Status of Children (Amendment) Act*, 1984, Victoria, clause 10(E).

105 Group of Advisers on the Ethical Implications of Biotechnology, *Journal of Medical Ethics* 23 (1997): 352.

106 National Health and Medical Research Council, *Long-term Effects on Women from Assisted Conception*, 42–3.

107 Ibid., 37–42.

108 Ibid., 37; Human Fertilization and Embryology Authority, *Code of Practice*, 4th ed. (London: July 1998): 28.

109 Van Steirteghem et al., "Ethical Considerations of Intracytoplasmic Sperm Injection," 54–5.

110 Donald Evans, "The Clinical Classification of Infertility," in Evans and Pickering, eds., *Creating the Child*, 60–1.

111 "Pastoral Constitution of the Church in the Modern World," *Vatican II. The Conciliar and Post Conciliar Documents*, ed. A Flannery (Dublin: Dominican Publications, 1975), N. 48; *Code of Canon Law*, Canons 1055 no. 1 and 1057 no. 2.

112 Ibid., N. 50.

113 Congregation for the Doctrine of the Faith, *Instruction on Respect for Human Life in its Origin and on the Dignity of Procreation. Replies to Certain Questions of the Day* (Vatican City: Polyglot Press, 1987), II 1; Bishops' Committee on Bioethics, *Assisted Human Reproduction* (Dublin: Veritas Publications, 2000).

114 John Paul II, Encyclical Letter *Evangelium Vitae* (Vatican City: Libreria Editrice Vaticana, 1995), N. 14.

115 *Instruction*, I, 6.

116 Stephen Mason, "Abnormal Conception," *The Australian Law Journal* 56 (1982): 348–9.

117 Jones, "New Reproductive Technologies," 480.

118 *Instruction* II, 5.

119 Ibid., I, 6 and II, 4–5.

120 Ibid., II, 6.

121 W. Wolbert, "The Catholic Attitude towards Intervention in Reproduction," in Geoffrey M. H. Waites et al., eds., *Current Advances in Andrology* (Bologna: Monduzzi Editore, 1997), 408–9; Agneta Sutton, *Infertility and Assisted Conception – What you Should Know: Answers to Questions about Medical Techniques of Assisted Conception* (London: The Catholic Bishops' Joint Committee on Bioethical Issues, 1993), 24–48.

122 *Instruction*, II, B, 5.

123 Ibid., II, B, 5.

124 Laura M. Purdy, "What Can Progress in Reproductive Technology Mean for Women?," *Journal of Medicine and Philosophy*, 21/5 (1996): 499–514; Anne Donchin, "Feminist Critiques of New Fertility Technologies: Implications for Social Policy," ibid. 475–98.

125 Emmanuel Dulioust et al., "Embryo Cryopreservation and Development: Facts, Questions and Responsibility," *Human Reproduction* 14/5 (1999): 1144.

Chapter 7 Prenatal Screening and Diagnosis

1 Peter Thorogood, "The Relationship Between Genotype and Phenotype: Some Basic Concepts," in *Embryos, Genes and Birth Defects*, ed. Peter Thorogood (Chichester: John Wiley & Sons, 1997), 1–16.

2 The Consultative Council on Obstetric and Paediatric Mortality and Morbidity. *Annual Report for the Year 1998, Incorporating the 37th Survey of Perinatal Deaths in Victoria* (Melbourne, 2000), 39.

3 Tara Hurst et al., *Congenital Malformations Australia 1995 and 1996. AIHW cat. no. Per.8* (Sydney: Australian Institute of Health and Welfare and National Perinatal Statistics Unit, Birth Defects Series N.3, 1999), 12, 32.

4 Michael Connor and Malcolm Ferguson-Smith, *Essential Medical Genetics* (Oxford: Blackwell Science, 1997), 118.

5 M. Riley et al., "Congenital Malformations in Victoria, Australia, 1983–95: An Overview of Infant Characteristics," *Journal of Paediatrics and Child Health* 34 (1998): 236.

6 *Genetic Screening: Ethical Issues* (London: Nuffield Council on Bioethics, 1993), 1–10, 107–14.

7 Dorothy C. Wertz, et al., *Guidelines on Ethical Issues in Medical Genetics and the Provision of Genetics Services* (Geneva: World Health Organization Hereditary Diseases Program, 1995), 61. For more ethical discussions, see 52–70.

8 R. J. McKinlay Gardner and Grant R. Sutherland, *Chromosome Abnormalities and Genetic Counselling* (New York: Oxford University Press, 1996), 327.

9   Connor and Ferguson-Smith, *Essential Medical Genetics*, 118.
10 Ibid.
11 E. Hook, "Prevalence, Risks and Recurrence," in David J. Brock et al., eds., *Prenatal Diagnosis and Screening* (Edinburgh: Churchill Livingstone, 1992), 364; Eric Jauniaux et al., "What Invasive Procedure to Use in Early Pregnancy?," *Baillière's Clinical Obstetrics and Gynaecology* 14 (2000): 658.
12 C. Bernadette Modell, "Screening as Public Policy," in Brock, *Prenatal*, 612–13.
13 Judith Searle, "Fearing the Worst – Why do Pregnant Women Feel 'At Risk'?," *Australian and New Zealand Journal of Obstetrics and Gynaecology* 36 (1996): 279–86.
14 Jeronima M. A. Teixeira, Nicholas M. Fisk, and Vivette Glover, "Association between Maternal Anxiety in Pregnancy and Increased Uterine Artery Resistance Index: Cohort Based Study," *British Medical Journal* 318 (1999): 153–7.
15 Searle, "Fearing the Worst," 282.
16 Ibid., 284.
17 John C. Fletcher and Mark I. Evans, "Ethical Issues in Reproductive Genetics," *Seminars in Perinatology* 22/3 (1998): 190.
18 Wertz et al., *Guidelines on Ethical Issues in Medical Genetics*, 61.
19 Josephine Green and Helen Statham, "Psychosocial Aspects of Prenatal Screening and Testing," Theresa Marteau and Martin Richards, eds., *The Troubled Helix: Social and Psychological Implications of the New Human Genetics* (Cambridge: University Press, 1996), 147.
20 Ibid., 156.
21 Nuffield, *Genetic Screening*, 3.
22 For more information see Report of the RCOG Working Party, *Ultrasound Screening for Fetal Abnormalities* (London: RCOG, 1997); Report of a Joint Working Party of the Royal College of Paediatrics and Child Health and the Royal College of Obstetricians and Gynaecologists, *Fetal Abnormalities: Guidelines for Screening, Diagnosis and Management* (London, 1997).
23 Lachlan de Crespigny et al., *Prenatal Testing: Making Decisions in Pregnancy* (Ringwood, Vic.: Penguin Books, 1998), 99–104; Nuffield, *Genetic Screening*, 24–5, 112.
24 James E. Haddow, "Antenatal Screening for Down's Syndrome: Where Are We and Where Next?," *Lancet* 352 (1998): 336–7; Nicholas J. Wald et al., "Prenatal Screening for Down's Syndrome Using Inihibin-A as a Serum Marker," *Prenatal Diagnosis* 16 (1996): 143–53, at 151; de Crespigny, *Prenatal Testing*, 102.
25 Carole Webley and Jane Halliday, eds., *Report on Prenatal Diagnostic Testing in Victoria 1999* (Melbourne: The Murdoch Institute, 2000), 13.

26 Mateu Serra-Prat et al., "Trade-offs in Prenatal Detection of Down Syndrome," *American Journal of Public Health* 88 (1998): 551–5; Howard Cuckle, "Rational Down Syndrome Screening Policy," ibid. 559.

27 Nuffield, *Genetic Screening*, 24.

28 H. Harris et al., "Cystic Fibrosis Carrier Testing in Early Pregnancy by General Practitioners," 306 *British Medical Journal* (1993): 1580–3.

29 E. K. Watson et al., "Psychological and Social Consequences of Community Carrier Screening Programme for Cystic Fibrosis," *Lancet* 340 (1992): 217–20.

30 Sally MacIntyre and Anne Sooman, "Non-paternity and Prenatal Genetic Screening," *Lancet* 338 (1991): 869–71; Marie-Gaelle Le Roux et al., Letters, *Lancet* 340 (1992): 607.

31 Nuffield, *Genetic Screening*, 22.

32 RCOG Working Party, *Ultrasound Screening for Fetal Abnormalities*, 14.

33 George Makrydas and Dimitrios Lolis, Letter, "Nuchal Translucency," *Lancet* 350 (1997): 1630–1.

34 De Crespigny et al., *Prenatal Testing*, 104–6.

35 N. J. Wald and A. K. Hackshaw, "Advances in Antenatal Screening cor Down Syndrome," *Baillière's Clinical Obstetrics and Gynaecology* 14 (2000): 570; Haddow, "Antenatal screening," *Lancet* 352 (1998): 336–7.

36 RCOG Working Party, *Ultrasound Screening for Fetal Abnormalities*, 5–6.

37 Judith Lumley, "Uncertainty and Ultrasound Diagnosis," in John McKie, ed., *Ethical Issues in Prenatal Diagnosis and the Termination of Pregnancy* (Melbourne: Monash University Centre for Human Bioethics, 1994), 26–7; Nuffield, *Genetic Screening*, 23, 115.

38 P. A. Boyd et al., "6-year Experience of Prenatal Diagnosis in an Unselected Population in Oxford, UK," *Lancet* 352 (1998): 1577–81; Nuffield, *Genetic Screening*, 23, 115.

39 Rebecca Smith-Bindman et al., "Second-trimester Ultrasound to Detect Fetuses with Down Syndrome: A Meta-analysis," *Journal of the American Medical Association* 285/8 (2001): 1044–55.

40 Boyd, "6-year Experience of Prenatal Diagnosis," 1577–81; Nuffield, *Genetic Screening*, 23, 115.

41 Robin Heise Steinhorn, "Prenatal Ultrasonography: First Do No Harm?," *Lancet* 352 (1998): 1568–9.

42 Leonie C. Stranc et al., "Chorionic Villus Sampling and Amniocentesis for Prenatal Diagnosis," *Lancet* 349 (1997): 711–14.

43 Eric Jauniaux et al., "What Invasive Procedure to Use in Early Pregnancy?," *Baillière's Clinical Obstetrics and Gynaecology* 14/4 (2000): 651–62; M. E. Pembrey, "Genetic Factors in Disease," in D. J. Weatherall et al., eds., *Oxford Textbook of Medicine*, 3rd ed., vol. I (Oxford: University Press, 1996), 136.

44 V. R. Collins et al., "Fetal Outcome and Maternal Morbidity after Early Amniocentesis," *Prenatal Diagnosis* 18 (1998): 767–72.

45 Connor and Ferguson-Smith, *Essential Medical Genetics*, 118; Jane Wheatley, "What if . . . ," *HQ* (March–April 1997), 44.
46 See E. Pergament and B. Fine "The Current Status of 46.2250 Chorionic Villus Sampling," in R. G. Edwards, ed., *Preconception and Preimplantation Diagnosis of Human Genetic Disease* (Cambridge: Cambridge University Press, 1993): 145–9.
47 Barbara Katz Rothman, *The Tentative Pregnancy: Prenatal Diagnosis and the Future of Motherhood* (New York: Viking Press, 1986), 101–11.
48 L. H. Kornman et al., "Women's Opinions and the Implications of First-versus Second-Trimester Screening for Fetal Down's Syndrome," *Prenatal Diagnosis* 17/11 (1997): 1011–18.
49 H. V. Firth et al., "Analysis of Limb Reduction Defects in Babies Exposed to Chorionic Villus Sampling," *Lancet* 343 (1994): 1069–71.
50 Jauniaux et al., "What Invasive Procedure to Use in Early Pregnancy?," *Baillière's Clinical Obstetrics and Gynaecology* 14 (2000): 656, 658; Stranc et al., "Chorionic Villus Sampling," 711–14; Pembrey, "Genetic Factors in Disease," 136.
51 E. Pergament and B. Fine, "The Current Status of Chorionic Villus Sampling," in Edwards, *Preconception*, 148.
52 Connor and Ferguson-Smith, *Essential Medical Genetics*, 118.
53 Jane Halliday et al., "Comparison of Women Who Do and Do Not Have Amniocentesis or Chorionic Villus Sampling," *Lancet* 345 (1995): 704–9.
54 Wolfgang Holzgreve and Sinuhe Hahn, "Fetal Cells in Cervical Mucus and Maternal Blood," *Baillière's Clinical Obstetrics and Gynaecology* 14 (2000): 709–22; J. L. Simpson and S. Elias, "Fetal Cells in the Maternal Circulation," in *Fetal Medicine: Basic Science and Clinical Practice*, eds. Charles H. Rodeck and Martin J. Whittle (London: Churchill Livingstone, 1999), 409–16.
55 Y. M. Dennis Lo, "Fetal DNA in Maternal Plasma: Biology and Diagnositc Applications," *Clinical Chemistry* 46/12 (2000): 1903–6.
56 M. Buscaglia et al., "Percutaneous Umbilical Cord Sampling: Indication Changes and Procedure Loss Rate in a Nine Years' Experience," *Fetal Diagnosis & Therapy* 11/2 (1996): 103–13.
57 M. Jayne Freitag-Koontz, "Prevention of Hepatitis B and C Transmission during Pregnancy and the First Year of Life," 10/2 *Journal of Perinatal & Neonatal Nursing* (1996): 40–55.
58 Laura E. Riley and Michael Greene, "Elective Cesarean Delivery to Reduce the Transmission of HIV," *New England Journal of Medicine*, 340 (1999): 1032.
59 Frank D. Johnstone, "HIV and Pregnancy," *British Journal of Obstetrics and Gynaecology* 103 (1996): 1184–90.
60 Winit Phuarpradit, "Timing and Mechanism of Perinatal Human Immunodeficiency Virus-1 Infection," *Australian and New Zealand Journal of Obstetrics and Gynaecology* 38/3 (1998): 296.

61 Lynne M. Mofenson and James A. McIntyre, "Advances and Research Directions in the Prevention of Mother-to-Child HIV-1 Transmission," *Lancet* 355 (2000): 2237–44.

62 Amnon Botchan et al., "Sperm Separation for Gender Preference: Methods and Efficacy," *Journal of Andrology* 10/2 (1997): 107–8; R. G. Edwards and Helen K. Beard, "Sexing Human Spermatozoa to Control Sex Ratios at Birth is Now a Reality" [Editorial], *Human Reproduction* 10/4 (1995): 977–8.

63 E. F. Fugger et al., "Birth of Normal Daughters After Microsort Sperm Separation and Intrauterine Insemination, *In Vitro* Fertilization, or Intracytoplasmic Sperm Injection," *Human Reproduction* 13 (1998): 3350–6.

64 Y. Verlinsky and N. Ginsberg, "A Brief History of Prenatal Diagnosis," Edwards, *Preconception*, 138–40.

65 See Joshua A. Copel and Charles S. Kleinman, "Fetal Arrhythmias," in *Fetal Therapy: Invasive and Transplacental*, eds. Nicholas M. Fisk and Kenneth J. Moise Jr. (Cambridge: Cambridge University Press, 1997), 184–98.

66 Steinhorn, "Prenatal Ultrasonography," 1568–9.

67 The European Collaborative Study, "Therapeutic and Other Interventions to Reduce the Risk of Mother-to-child Transmission of HIV-1 in Europe," *British Journal of Obstetrics and Gynaecology* 105/7 (1998): 704–9.

68 Phuarpradit, "Timing and Mechanism of Perinatal Human Immunodeficiency Virus-1 Infection," 293–6.

69 Samuel Kaplan and Helene Cohen, Letters, *New England Journal of Medicine* 327 (1992): 646, and a reply by Rhonda S. Sperling, 646–7.

70 Frank A. Chervenak and Laurence B. McCullough, "Ethics in Fetal Medicine," *Baillière's Clinical Obstetrics and Gynaecology* 13/4 (1999): 495–9.

71 Searle "Fearing the Worst – Why do Pregnant Women Feel 'At Risk'?," 282.

72 Lachlan de Crespigny, "Prenatal Diagnosis: The Australian Clinical Situation," in McKie ed., *Ethical Issues in Prenatal Diagnosis*, 13.

73 M. d'A. Crawfurd, "Ethical Guidelines in Fetal Medicine," *Fetal Therapies* 2 (1987): 178.

74 John Paul II, Encyclical Letter *Evangelium Vitae, The Gospel of Life*, N. 63. For more details of Catholic teaching on prenatal diagnosis see *Instruction on Respect for Human Life in its Origin and on the Dignity of Procreation: Replies to Certain Questions of the Day*, Congregation for the Doctrine of the Faith (Vatican City: Vatican Polyglot Press, 1987), I, 2.

75 Elio Sgreccia, *Bioetica: manuale per medici e biologi* (Milano: Vita e Pensiero, 1986), 149.

76 Pope John Paul II, *Evangelium Vitae*, N. 63.

77 Paquita de Zulueta "The Ethics of Anonymised HIV Testing of Pregnant Women: A Reappraisal," *Journal of Medical Ethics* 26/1 (2000): 16–21; 22–4.

78 H. Bekker et al., "Uptake of Cystic Fibrosis Testing in Primary Care: Supply Push or Demand Pull?' *British Medical Journal* 306 (1993): 1584–6.

79 Susan Michie and Theresa Marteau, "Genetic Counselling: Some Issues of Theory and Practice," in Theresa Marteau and Martin Richards, eds., *The Troubled Helix: Social and Psychological Implications of the New Human Genetics* (Cambridge: Cambridge University Press, 1996), 104–22.

80 Mary Terrell White, "Making Responsible Decisions: An Interpretative Ethic for Genetic Decision making," *Hasting Center Report* 29/1 (1999): 14–21.

81 Wertz et al., *Guidelines on Ethical Issues in Medical Genetics and the Provision of Genetics Services*, 26. See pp. 52–70 for a good discussion of relevant ethical issues.

82 Theresa M. Marteau, "Towards Informed Decisions about Prenatal Testing: A Review," *Prenatal Diagnosis* 15 (1995): 1215–18.

83 Helen Statham and Josephine Green, "Serum Screening for Down's Syndrome: Some Women's Experiences," *British Medical Journal*, 307 (1993): 174; Letter by Helen Statham, Josephine Green, and Clare Snowdon, 306 *British Medical Journal* (1993): 858–9.

84 Wertz et al., *Guidelines on Ethical Issues in Medical Genetics*, 17–18; 22.

85 Helen Statham et al., "Prenatal Diagnosis of Fetal Abnormality: Psychological Effects on Women in Low-risk Pregnancies," *Baillière's Clinical Obstetrics and Gynaecology* 14 (2000): 731–47; Statham and Green, "Serum Screening for Down's Syndrome," 174–6.

86 Lenore Abramsky et al., "What Parents are Told After Prenatal Diagnosis of a Sex Chromosome Abnormality: Interview and Questionnaire Study," *British Medical Journal* 322 (2001): 463–6.

87 Crawfurd, "Ethical Guidelines in Fetal Medicine," *Fetal Therapies*, 176; John M. Thorp Jr. and Watson A. Bowes Jr., "Pro-life Perinatologist – Paradox or Possibility?," *New England Journal of Medicine* 326 (1992): 1217–19.

88 Chris Goodey et al., "The Ethical Implications of Antenatal Screening for Down's Syndrome," *Bulletin of Medical Ethics* 147 (1999): 14.

89 K. L. Garver and B. Garver "The Human Genome Project and Eugenic Concerns," *American Journal of Human Genetics* 54/1 (1994): 148–58.

90 John Paul II in *Evangelium Vitae*, N. 63.

91 John Finnis "Abortion and Health Care Ethics," in Helga Khuse and Peter Singer, eds., *Bioethics – An Anthology* (Oxford: Blackwell Publishers, 1999): 18.

92 C. Mansfield et al., "Termination Rates After Prenatal Diagnosis of Down Syndrome, Spina Bifida, Anencephaly, and Turner and Klinefelter Syndromes: A Systematic Literature Review," in the European Concerted Action: DADA (Decision Making after a Fetal Abnormality), *Prenatal Diagnosis* 19/9 (1999): 808–12.

93 Jane Wheatley, "What if . . . ," *HQ* (March–April 1997): 44.

94 De Crespigny et al., *Prenatal Testing*, 130.

95 Webley and Halliday, *Report on Prenatal Diagnostic Testing in Victoria 1999*, 11.

96 E. Watson et al., "Screening for Genetic Carriers of Cystic Fibrosis Through Primary Health Care Services," *British Medical Journal* 303 (1991): 504–7.

97 Webley and Halliday, *Report on Prenatal Diagnostic Testing in Victoria 1999*, 8; see also Fletcher and Evans, "Ethical Issues in Reproductive Genetics," *Seminars in Perinatology*, 22/3 (1998): 191, where it is stated positive results do not usually exceed 4 percent.

98 The editorial "Screening for Cystic Fibrosis," *Lancet* 340 (1992): 209–10.

99 Wertz et al., *Guidelines on Ethical Issues in Medical Genetics*, 37.

100 The Canon Law Society of Great Britain and Ireland, *The Canon Law, Letter & Spirit*, (Alexandria: E. J. Dwyer, 1995), Can. 1091, 607–8.

101 See Laura M. Purdy, "Genetics and Reproductive Risk: Can Having Children be Immoral," in Helga Khuse and Peter Singer, eds., *Bioethics – An Anthology* (Oxford: Blackwell Publishers, 1999), 123–9.

102 Mary Anne Warren, "Sex Selection: Individual Choice or Cultural Coercion," in Khuse and Singer, eds., *Bioethics – An Anthology*, 137–42.

103 Julian Savulescu, "Sex Selection: The Case For," *Medical Journal of Australia* 171 (1999): 373–5.

104 Wolfram Henn, "Consumerism in Prenatal Diagnosis: A Challenge for Ethical Guidelines," *Journal of Medical Ethics* 26 (2000): 444–6.

105 Giuseppe Benagiano and Paola Bianchi, "Sex Preselection: An Aid to Couples or a Threat to Humanity," *Human Reproduction* 14/4 (1999): 868–70.

106 Wertz et al., *Guidelines on Ethical Issues in Medical Genetics*, 57–60; Jonathan M. Berkowitz and Jack W. Snyder, "Racism and Sexism in Medically Assisted Conception," 12 *Bioethics* (1998): 25–44; Bernard M. Dickens, "Conflict Between Protecting and Respecting Women: The Prohibition of Sex-selected Birth," *Human Health Care International* 13/2 (1997): 14–15.

107 Jonathan M. Berkowitz, "Sexism and Racism In Preconceptive Trait Selection," *Fertility and Sterility* 71/3 (1999): 415–17; J. A. Nisker and M. Jones, "The Ethics of Sex Selection," *Ethical Dilemmas in Assisted Reproduction*, eds. F. Shenfield and C. Sureau (New York and London: Parthenon Publishing Group, 1997), 41–50.

108 Quoted in Jonathan M. Berkowitz and Jack W. Snyder, "Racism and Sexism in Medically Assisted Conception," 12 *Bioethics* (1998): 43.

109 Wertz et al., *Guidelines on Ethical Issues in Medical Genetics*, 52–70.

110 Liz Hepburn, "Genetic Counselling: Parental Autonomy or Acceptance of Limits?," *Concilium* 2 (1998): 40.

111 Goodey et al., "The Ethical Implications of Antenatal Screening for Down's Syndrome," 16.

112 Christopher Newell, "The Social Nature of Disability, Disease and Genetics: A Response to Gillam, Persson, Holtug, Draper and Chadwick," *Journal of Medical Ethics* 25 (1999): 174.

113 Ibid., 174.

114 Ani B. Satz, "Prenatal Genetic Testing and Discrimination Against the Disabled: A Conceptual Analysis," *Monash Bioethics Review* 18/4 (1999): 11–22.

115 Lynn Gillam, "Prenatal Diagnosis and Discrimination Against the Disabled," *Journal of Medical Ethics* 25 (1999): 163–71.

116 Wertz et al., *Guidelines on Ethical Issues in Medical Genetics*, 61.

117 Deborah Kaplan, "Prenatal Screening and its Impact on Persons with Disabilities," in Khuse and Singer, eds., *Bioethics – An Anthology*, 135.

118 Paul Robinson, "Prenatal Screening, Sex Selection and Cloning," in Helga Kuhse and Peter Singer, eds., *A Companion to Bioethics* (Oxford: Blackwell Publishers, 1998), 173–85.

119 See Wertz et al., *Guidelines on Ethical Issues in Medical Genetics*, 19–21, 54, 79.

Chapter 8 The Fetus

1 Kevin C. Pringle, "In Utero Surgery," in John A. Mannick, ed., *Advances in Surgery* (Chicago: Yearbook Medical Publishers, 1986), vol. 19, 106–8; "Fetal Surgery, Old Controversies about New Therapies," in *Perinatal Genetics: Diagnosis and Treatment*, eds. I. H. Porter, N. H. Hatcher, and A. M. Willey (Orlando: Academic Press, 1986), 125–31.

2 Caroline A. Crowther, "Respiratory Distress Syndrome," in Nicholas M. Fisk and Kenneth J. Moise Jr., eds., *Fetal Therapy: Invasive and Transplacental* (Cambridge: Cambridge University Press, 1997), 72–83.

3 M. R. Harrison et al., "Management of the Fetus with a Correctable Defect," *Journal of the American Medical Association*, 246/7 (1981): 775.

4 Ibid., 775.

5 Jeffrey A. Kuller and Mitchell S. Golbus, "Fetal Therapy," in David J. Brock et al., eds., *Prenatal Diagnosis and Screening* (Edinburgh: Churchill Livingstone, 1992), 703–15.

6 See C. H. Rodeck and E. Letsky, "How the Management of Erythroblastosis Fetalis has Changed," *British Journal of Obstetrics and Gynaecology* 96 (1989): 760.

7 Ibid., 761.

8 Ibid., 761.

9 Kuller and Golbus, "Fetal Therapy," 705.

10 D. L. Farmer, "Fetal Surgery: A Brief Review," *Pediatric Radiology* 28/6 (1998): 409–13; Ross Milner and N. Scott Adzick, "Perinatal Management of Fetal Malformations Amenable to Surgical Correction," *Current Opinions in Obstetrics and Gynecology* 11 (1999): 177–83.

11 Alan W. Flake and Michael R. Harrison, "Fetal Surgery," *Annual Review of Medicine*, 46 (1995): 67–78.

12 Henry E. Rice and Michael R. Harrison, "Open Fetal Surgery," *Fetal Therapy: Invasive and Transplacental*," 27–8; Michael R. Harrison, "Fetal Surgery," "Fetal Medicine [Special Issue]," *The Western Journal of Medicine* 159 (1993): 341–2.

13 Michael R. Harrison, "The Rationale for Fetal Treatment: Selection, Feasibility, and Risk," in Michael R. Harrison et al., eds., *The Unborn Patient: The Art and Science of Fetal Therapy* (Philadelphia: W. B. Saunders Company, 2001), 39–42.

14 Rice and Harrison, "Open Fetal Surgery," 31.

15 Harrison, "Fetal Surgery," 342–4.

16 T. M. Quinn and N. S. Adzick, "Fetal Surgery," *Obstetrics and Gynecology Clinics of North America*, 24/1 (1997): 143–57.

17 Pringle, "In Utero Surgery," 116.

18 David C. Merrill and Carl P. Weiner, "Urinary Tract Obstruction," in *Fetal therapy*, eds. Fisk and Moise, 280–1.

19 Harrison, "The Rationale for Fetal Treatment," 42.

20 Ibid., 42; H. T. Hounsley and M. R. Harrison, "Fetal Urinary Tract Abnormalities: Natural History, Pathophysiology, and Treatment," *Urolologic Clinics of North America* 25/1 (1998): 63–73.

21 N. Scott Adzick and Marc H. Hedrick, "Other Surgical Conditions," in *Fetal Therapy*, eds. Fisk and Moise, 306–7; Harrison, "Fetal Surgery," 344–6.

22 N. S. Adzick et al., "Fetal Lung Lesions: Management and Outcomes," *American Journal of Obstetrics & Gynecology*, 179/4 (1998): 884–9.

23 Harrison, "Fetal Surgery," 346; Michael R. Harrison et al., "Congenital Diaphragmatic Hernia: An Unsolved Problem," in Adzick and Harrison, *Seminars in Paediatric Surgery*, 2/2 (1993): 109–12.

24 Harrison, "The Rationale for Fetal Treatment," 45, 49; M. R. Harrison et al., "Correction of Congenital Diaphragmatic Hernia In Utero VII: A Prospective Trial," *Journal of Pediatric Surgery* 32/11 (1997): 1637–42.

25 W. D. Andrew Ford, "Diaphragmatic Hernia," in *Fetal Therapy*, eds. Fisk and Moise, 290–4.

26 Harrison, "The Rationale for Fetal Treatment" 46; Adzick and Hedrick, "Other surgical conditions," 310–11; Harrison, "Fetal Surgery," 347; Pringle, "In Utero Surgery," 112–15 and Pringle, "Fetal Surgery," 127.

27 N. Scott Adzick, "Successful Fetal Surgery for Spina Bifida," Letter, *Lancet* 352 (1998): 1675–6.

28 Thomas Kohl et al., "Fetoscopic and Open Transumbilical Fetal Cardiac Catheterisation in Sheep: Potential Approaches for Human Fetal Cardiac Intervention," *Circulation* 95/4 (1997): 1048–53.

29 C. T. Albanese and M. R. Harrison, "Surgical Treatment for Fetal Disease: The State of the Art," *Annals of the New York Academy of Sciences* 847 (1998): 74–85; Rodolfo Montemagno and Peter Soothill, "Invasive Procedures," in *Fetal therapy*, eds. Fisk and Moise, 12–13; Rice and Harrison, "Open Fetal Surgery," 31–2; Harrison, "Fetal Surgery," 348.

30 Harrison et al., "Correction of Congenital Diaphragmatic Hernia In Utero IX," 1017–22 and Discussion, 1022–3.

31 For an overview see D. R. Jones and T. H. Bui, "Fetal Therapy: Prospects for Transplantation Early in Pregnancy. In Utero Stem Cell Transplantation and Gene Therapy: Second International Meeting, Nottingham, UK, Sept. 1–2, 1997," *Molecular Medicine Today*, 4/1 (1998): 10–11.

32 Harrison, "The Rationale for Fetal Treatment," 46.

33 Jean-Louis Touraine, "In Utero Transplantation of Fetal Liver Stem Cells into Human Fetuses," *Journal of Hematotherapy* 5/2 (1996): 195–9; Alan Flake and Esmail D. Zanjani, "In Utero Hematopoietic Cell Transplantation: A Status Report," *Journal of the American Medical Association*, 278/11 (1997): 932–7; Harrison, "Fetal Surgery," 348; Kuller and Golbus, "Fetal Therapy," 714–15; Maria Michejda, "Fetal Tissue Transplantation: Miscarriages and Tissue Banks," *The Fetal Tissue Issue: Medical and Ethical Aspects*, eds. Peter J. Castaldo and Albert S. Moraczewski (Braintree, Mass.: The Pope John Center, 1994), 6–8.

34 Helmut Pschera, "Stem Cell Therapy In Utero," *Journal of Perinatal Medicine* 28 (2000): 347–8.

35 F. Golfier et al., "Fetal Bone Marrow as a Source of Stem Cells for in Utero or Postnatal Transplantation," *British Journal of Haematology* 109/1 (2000): 173–81.

36 Flake and Zanjani, "In Utero Hematopoietic Cell Transplantation," 932–7.

37 Pschera, "Stem Cell Therapy In Utero," 348–50; Touraine, "In Utero Transplantation of Fetal Liver Stem Cells into Human Fetuses," 195–9.

38 Touraine, "In Utero Transplantation of Fetal Liver Stem Cells into Human Fetuses," 195–9.

39 Touraine, "Stem Cell Transplantation," in *Fetal therapy*, eds. Fisk and Moise, 321–6.

40 Harrison, "The Rationale for Fetal Treatment," 46–7.

41 Harrison, "Fetal Surgery," 348; Crombleholme et al., "Transplantation of Fetal Cells," *American Journal of Obstetrics & Gynecology* 164/1 (1991): 218–30.

42 Esmail D. Zanjani and W. French Anderson, "The Fetus with a Genetic Defect Correctable by Gene Therapy," in Harrison et al., *The Unborn Patient*, 630, 632–3.

43 Edmung Y. Yang et al., "Prospects for Fetal Gene Therapy," *Seminars in Perinatology* 23/6 (1999): 524–34; Zanjani and Anderson, "The Fetus with a Genetic Defect Correctable by Gene Therapy," 633.

44 K. H. Andy Choo, "Engineering Human Chromosomes for Gene Therapy Studies," *Trends in Molecular Biology* 7/6 (June 2001): 235–7.

45 Nell Boyce, "Catch Them Young," *New Scientist*, June 27, 1998.

46 J. Milliez and C. Sureau, "Pre-implantation Diagnosis and the Eugenics Debate: Our Responsibility To Future Generations," in *Ethical dilemmas in Assisted Reproduction*, eds. F. Shenfield and C. Sureau (New York and London: Parthenon Publishing Group, 1997), 60–1; James D. Goldberg, "Gene Therapy," in *Fetal Therapy*, eds. Fisk and Moise, 330–6.

47 Yang, "Prospects for Fetal Gene Therapy," 526–32.

48 See Goldberg, "Gene Therapy," 330–6.

49 Philip Cohen's news report, "The Greater Good: Fetuses Destined for Abortion May Be Used to Test Gene Therapy," *The New Scientist*, Oct. 10, 1998.

50 Chris D. Porada et al., "In Utero Gene Therapy: Transfer and Long-term Expression of the Bacterial Neo(r) Gene in Sheep After Direct Injection of Retoviral Vectors into Preimmune Fetuses," *Human Gene Therapy* 9/11 (1998): 1571–85.

51 See Mark I. Evans et al., "Selective Termination," in Brock, *Prenatal*, 689–95; MacKenzie, "Pregnancy Termination," 683.

52 Harrison, "The Rationale for Fetal Treatment," 45.

53 *Fetal therapy*, ed. Fisk and Moise, 240–1.

54 Ibid., 240–1.

55 See Harrison, "Fetal Surgery," 347; Kuller and Golbus, "Fetal Therapy," 713–14.

56 See Evans et al., "Selective Termination," Brock, *Prenatal*, 689–95.

57 Shlomo Lipitz et al., "A Prospective Outcome of Triplet Pregnancies Managed Expectantly or by Multifetal Reduction to Twins," *American Journal of Obstetrics and Gynecology* 170/3 (1994): 874–9.

58 A. Benshushan et al., "Multifetal Pregnancy Reduction: Is It Always Justified?," *Fetal Diagnosis and Therapy* 8/3 (1993): 214–20; Alison Hall, "Selective Reduction of Pregnancy: A Legal Analysis," *Journal of Medical Ethics* 22 (1996): 304–8.

59 Jean-Louis Touraine, "Perinatal Fetal-cell and Gene Therapy," *International Journal of Immunopharmacology* 22/12 (2000): 1033–44; Touraine, "Stem Cell Transplantation," 317–21.

60 Crombleholme et al., "Transplantation of Fetal Cells," 227.

61 Pablo Rubinstein et al., "Outcomes among 562 Recipients of Placental-blood Transplants from Unrelated Donors," *New England Journal of Medicine* 339/22 (1998): 1565–77.

62 Crombleholme et al., "Transplantation of Fetal Cells," 225–6.

63   Crombleholme et al., "Transplantation of Fetal Cells," 226–7; Michejda, "Fetal Tissue Transplantation: Miscarriages and Tissue Banks," *The Fetal Tissue Issue* 3.

64   O. Lindvall, "Update on Fetal Transplantation: The Swedish Experience," *Movement Disorders* 13 Suppl 1 (1998): 83–7.

65   Curt R. Freed et al., "Transplantation of Embryonic Dopamine Neurons for Severe Parkinson's Disease," *New England Journal of Medicine* 344/10 (2001): 710–19.

66   Gerald D. Fischbach and Guy M. McKhann, editorial, ibid., 765.

67   Pschera, "Stem Cell Therapy In Utero," 351; Michejda, "Fetal Tissue," 6–9; Daniel J. Garry et al., "Are There Really Alternatives to the Use of Fetal Tissue From Elective Abortions in Transplantation Research?," *New England Journal of Medicine* 327 (1992): 1592–5.

68   G. B. Mychaliska et al., "The Biology and Ethics of Banking Fetal Liver Hematopoietic Stem Cells for In Utero Transplantation," *Journal of Pediatric Surgery* 33/2 (1998): 394–9.

69   S. J. Fasouliotis and J. G. Schenker, "Human Umbilical Cord Blood Banking and Transplantation: A State of the Art," *European Journal of Obstetrics & Gynecology Reproductive Biology* 90/1 (2000): 13–25; S. B. Cohen "Blood Money," *Biologist* (London), 47/5 (2000): 280; Michejda, "Fetal Tissue," 10–11.

70   Media Conference (April 11, 2001) of Anthrogenesis Corporation in New Jersey.

71   Stuart W. G. Derbyshire, "Locating the Beginnings of Pain," *Bioethics* 13 (1999): 19, 27.

72   David Benatar and Michael Benatar, "A Pain in the Fetus: Toward ending Confusion about Fetal Pain," *Bioethics* 15 (2001): 57–76.

73   J. A. Burgess and S. A. Tawia, "When did you first begin to feel it? – Locating the Beginning of Human Consciousness," *Bioethics* 10 (1996): 1–26.

74   The Royal College of Obstetricians and Gynaecologists, *Fetal Awareness: Report of a Working Party* (London: RCOG Press, 1997), 7–13 at 4; Stuart W. G. Derbyshire, Ann Furedi, Vivette Glover, Nicholas Fisk, Zbigniew Szawarski, Adrian R. Lloyd-Thomas, Maria Fitzgerald in the debate "Do Fetuses Feel Pain?," *British Journal of Medicine* 313 (1996): 795–8; Maria Fitzgerald, "Fetal Pain: An Update Of Current Scientific Knowledge," A Paper for the Department of Health, London, 1995.

75   Singer, *Practical Ethics*, 2nd ed. (Cambridge: University Press, 1993), 149–52; 165.

76   Peter McCullagh, "Fetal Sentience and Fetal Surgery," in *Recent Advances in Anaesthesia and Analgesia*, eds. A. P. Adams and J. N. Cashman (Edinburgh: Churchill Livingstone, 1998), 107.

77   McCullagh, "Fetal Sentience and Fetal Surgery," 116.

78 D. Alan Shewmon et al., "The Use of Anencephalic Infants as Organ Sources," *Journal of the American Medical Association* 261 (1989): 1776.

79 David Lamb, *Organ Transplants and Ethics* (Aldershot: Avebury, 1996), 99–100; McCullagh, "Brain Absence," 155.

80 Shewmon et al., "The Use of Anencephalic Infants as Organ Sources," 1776; Peter McCullagh, *Brain Dead, Brain Absent, Brain Donors – Human Subjects or Objects?* (Chichester: John Wiley & Sons, 1993), 117–25; 63–4, 133, 135–9, 155.

81 "Fetal Sentience: The All Party Parliamentary Pro-Life Group," *Catholic Medical Quarterly*, Nov. 1996, 6–12; *Human Sentience Before Birth – A Report by the Commission of Inquiry into Fetal Sentience*, London: Her Majesty's Stationery Office, 1996; Peter McCullagh, "Determining Foetal Sentience," *Hospital Update*, Jan. 1996, 5–6.

82 McCullagh "Fetal Sentience and Fetal Surgery," 111.

83 McCullagh, "Determining Foetal Sentience," 6.

84 McCullagh, "Fetal Sentience and Fetal Surgery," 113.

85 Alan R. Fleischman et al., "The Physician's Moral Obligations to the Pregnant Woman, the Fetus and the Child," *Seminars in Perinatology* 22/3 (1998): 184–8.

86 John R. Friend, "Some Current Obstetric and Gynaecological Problems," *Ballière's Clinical Obstetrics and Gynaecology* 13/4 (1999): 456–7; Steinbock, "Mother–Fetus Conflict," in Helga Kuhse and Peter Singer, eds., *A Companion to Bioethics* (Oxford: Blackwell Publishers, 1998), 141–4.

87 Cathy Hammerman et al., "Does Pregnancy Affect Medical Ethical Decision Making?," *Journal of Medical Ethics* 24 (1998): 409–13.

88 Harrison, "The Rationale for Fetal Treatment," 48.

89 Ibid., 39–49.

90 Fletcher and Jonsen, "Ethical Considerations," 14–24.

91 John C. Fletcher, "The Fetus as Patient: Ethical Issues," *Journal of the American Medical Association* 246/7 (1981): 772–3; M. R. Harrison et al., "Management of the Fetus with a Correctable Congenital Defect," ibid., 774–7; W. Barclay et al. "The Ethics of *In Utero* Surgery," *Journal of the American Medical Association* 246/14 (1981): 1550–5.

92 Harrison, "The Rationale for Fetal Treatment," 48.

93 Kevin C. Pringle, "Ethical Issues in Fetal Surgery," in *Surgery and Support of the Premature Infant*, ed. Prem Puri (Dublin: Karger, 1985), 190–201; "The Ethical Implications of Fetal Surgery," *Controversies in Paediatric Surgery*, ed. Benjy Frances Brooks (Austin: University of Texas Press, 1984), 214–20; "Fetal Surgery," 125–31; "In Utero Surgery," 109–14.

94 Barclay et al., "The Ethics of *In Utero* Surgery," 1550–5.

95 A. T. Thein and P. Soothill, "Antenatal Invasive Therapy," *European Journal of Pediatrics* 157 Suppl 1 (1998): S2–S6.

96   John Keown, "The Polkinghorne Report on Fetal Research: Nice Recom-
     mendations, Shame About the Reasoning," *Journal of Medical Ethics* 19
     (1993): 116–17.
97   Flake and Zanjani, "In Utero Hematopoietic Cell Transplantation,"
     932–7.
98   Peter J. Cataldo and Thomas Murphy Goodwin, "The Determination of
     Fetal Death in Miscarriage: Its Ethical Significance for Fetal Tissue Trans-
     plantation," in *The Fetal Tissue Issue: Medical and Ethical Aspects*, eds.
     Peter J. Castaldo and Albert S. Moraczewski (Braintree, Mass.: The Pope
     John Center, 1994), 95–6, 117; Lamb, *Organ Transplants and Ethics*,
     73–81.
99   J. C. Polkinghorne, *Review of the Guidance on the Research Use of Fetuses
     and Fetal Material* (London: HMSO, 1989), sec. 3.7 – known as the
     Polkinghorne Report after its chairman.
100 Polkinghorne, *Review*, 7.
101 See the Polkinghorne Report, *Review*, 9–12; Mychaliska et al., "The
     Biology and Ethics of Banking Fetal Liver Hematopoietic Stem Cells,"
     394–9.
102 *Review*, 1–24; R. C. Cefalo and H. T. Engelhart Jr., "The Use of Fetal and
     Anencephalic Tissue for Transplantation," *Journal of Medicine and
     Philosophy* 14/1 (1989): 25–43.
103 Robert C. Cefalo et al., "The Bioethics of Human Fetal Tissue Research
     and Therapy: Moral Decision Making of Professionals," *American Journal
     of Obstetrics and Gynecology* 170/1 (1994): 12–19.
104 Jerome P. Kassirer and Marcia Angell, "The Use of Fetal Tissue in Research
     on Parkinson's Disease," *New England Journal of Medicine* 327 (1992):
     1591.
105 See Antonio G. Spagnolo, *L'Osservatore Romano*, Weekly Edition in
     English, Feb. 8, 1995; Hadley Arkes, "Fetal Tissue and the Question of
     Consent," in Castaldo and Moraczewski, *Fetal Tissue*, 15–31; and Bopp,
     "Fetal Tissue Transplantation and Moral Complicity with Induced Abor-
     tion," *Fetal Tissue*, 71–6.
106 Benedict M. Ashley and Kevin D. O'Rourke, *Health Care Ethics: A The-
     ological Analysis*, 4th ed. (Washington DC: Georgetown University Press,
     1997), 338–9.
107 Yang et al., "Prospects for Fetal Gene Therapy," 532; D. V. Surbek et al.,
     "Haematopoietic Stem Cell Transplantation and Gene Therapy in the
     Fetus: Ready for Clinical Use?," *Human Reproduction Update* 7/1 (2001):
     85–91.
108 I. M. Burger and B. S. Wilfond, "Limitations of Informed Consent for
     In Utero Gene Transfer Research: Implications for Investigators and
     Institutional Review Boards," *Human Gene Therapy* 11/7 (2000): 1057–
     63.
109 Kuller and Golbus, "Fetal Therapy," 713.

110 See I. Nisand and F. Shenfield, "Multiple Pregnancies and Embryo Reduction: Ethical and Legal Issues," in *Ethical Dilemmas in Assisted Reproduction*, eds. Shenfield and Sureau, 67–74.

111 See Frank A. Chervenak et al., "Selective Termination to a Singleton Pregnancy is Ethically Justified," *Ultrasound in Obstetrics and Gynecology* 2 (1992): 84–7; "Selective Fetal Reduction," Editorial, *The Lancet* (1988): i, 773–5; M. I. Evans et al., "Ethical Problems In Multiple Gestations: Selective Termination," in Mark I. Evans et al., eds., *Fetal Diagnosis and Therapy: Science, Ethics and the Law* (Philadelphia: J. B. Lippincott, 1989), 266–76.

112 Evans et al., "Selective Termination," 694–5.

113 National Health and Medical Research Council, *Australian Code of Practice for the Care and Use of Animals for Scientific Purposes*, 6th ed. (Canberra: Commonwealth Dept. of Health and Family Services, 1997), 28.

Chapter 9 Newborns

1 Roger V. Short, "What the Breast Does for the Baby, and What the Baby Does for the Breast," *Australian and New Zealand Journal of Obstetrics and Gynaecology* 34/3 (1994): 262–4; "Breast Feeding," *Scientific American* (April 1984): 35–41.

2 Louise Vandalic and Marie-Halloween Bacon, "Will We Be Taught by Our Clones? The Mutations of the Living, From Endocrine Disruptors to Genetics," *Bailière's Clinical Obstetrics and Gynaecology* 13/4 (1999): 576–8.

3 Peter Day et al., *Australia's mothers and babies 1997*, AIHW Cat. No. Per. 12. (Sydney: AIHW National Perinatal Statistics Unit [Perinatal Statistics Series N. 9], 1999), 5–6.

4 Day et al., *Australia's mothers and babies 1997*, 5–6

5 See D. J. Henderson-Smart, "Low Birth-weight Babies: Where to Draw the Line?," in H. Caton, ed., *Trends in Biomedical Regulation* (Sydney: Butterworth, 1990), 145–7.

6 Calculated from neonatal deaths of all persons, *Perinatal Deaths 1975* (Canberra, 1977, Ref. no. 4.29), 3; Australian Bureau of Statistics, *Causes of Death Australia 3303.0–1998* (Canberra, 1999), 61.

7 Australian Bureau of Statistics, *Causes of Death Australia 3303.0–1998*, 57–8, 64; Malcolm I. Levene et al., *Essentials of Neonatal Medicine*, 3rd ed. (Oxford: Blackwell Science, 2000), 2–3; Jean Golding "Epidemiology of Fetal and Neonatal Death," in Jean W. Keeling, ed., *Fetal and Neonatal Pathology*, 2nd ed. (London: Springer-Verlag, 1993), 173.

8   Levene et al., *Essentials of Neonatal Medicine*, 1–2; for the breakdown of infants' birthweights see Day et al., *Australia's Mothers and Babies 1997*, 81.

9   Day et al., *Australia's Mothers and Babies 1997*, 42, 81.

10 L. Cussen et al., "Mean Organ Weights of an Australian Population of Fetuses and Infants," *Journal of Paediatrics and Child Health* 26 (1990): 102.

11 William B. Pittard III, "Classification of the Low-Birth Weight Infant," in Marshall H. Klaus and Avroy A. Fanaroff, *Care of the High-Risk Neonate*, 4th ed. (Philadelphia: W. B. Saunders, 1993), 90.

12 Enrique M. Ostrea Jr. et al., "Mortality Within the First 2 Years in Infants Exposed to Cocaine, Opiate, or Cannabinoid during Gestation," *Pediatrics* 100/1 (1997): 79–83.

13 Pittard, "Classification," 89–90.

14 Gillian Batcup, "Prematurity," in Keeling, ed., *Fetal and Neonatal Pathology*, 199–205.

15 See also Victor Y. H. Yu and E. Carl Wood, eds., *Prematurity* (Edinburgh: Churchill Livingstone, 1987).

16 Henderson-Smart, "Low Birth-weight Babies: Where to Draw the Line?," 146.

17 Douglas Richardson et al., "Risk Adjustment for Quality Improvement," *Pediatrics* 103/1 Suppl E (1999): 255–65.

18 Forrest C. Bennett and David T. Scott, "Long-Term Perspective on Premature Infant Outcome and Contemporary Investigation Issues," *Seminars in Perinatology. Outcomes of Low Birthweight Premature Infants* 21/3 (1997): 190.

19 Jonathan Muraskas et al., "Neonatal Viability in the 1990s: Held Hostage by Technology," *Cambridge Quarterly of Healthcare Ethics* 8 (1999): 162.

20 Nicholas S. Wood et al., "Neurologic and Developmental Disability after Extremely Preterm Birth," *New England Journal of Medicine* 343 (2000): 378–84.

21 Lex Doyle et al., "Why Do Preterm Infants Die in the 1990s?," *Medical Journal of Australia* 170 (1999): 528–32.

22 L. W. Doyle et al., "Changing Mortality and Causes of Death in Infants 23–27 Weeks' Gestational Age," *Journal of Paediatric and Child Health* 35 (1999): 255–9.

23 Bennett and Scott, "Long-Term Perspective on Premature Infant Outcome and Contemporary Investigation Issues," 190–2.

24 Victorian Infant Collaborative Group, "Improved Outcome into the 1990s for Infants Weighing 500–999 g at Birth," *Archives of Disease in Childhood* 77 (1997): F91–F94.

25 Lex Doyle, for the Victorian Infant Collaborative Study Group, "Outcome to Five Years of Age of Children Born at 24–26 Weeks Gestational Age in Victoria," *Medical Journal of Australia*, 163 (1995): 13.

26 Michael D. Kaplan and Linda C. Mayes, "Introduction," *Seminars in Perinatology. Outcomes of Low Birthweight Premature Infants* 21/3 (1997): 161.

27 Wood et al., "Neurologic and Developmental Disability after Extremely Preterm Birth," 379.

28 Betty R. Vohr and Michael Msall, "Neuropsychological and Functional Outcomes of Very Low Birth Weight Infants," *Seminars in Perinatology. Outcomes of Low Birthweight Premature Infants* 21/3 (1997): 202–3.

29 A. L. Stewart et al., "Brain Structure and Neurocognitive and Behavioural Function in Adolescents who were Born Very Preterm," *Lancet* 353 (1999): 1653–6.

30 N. R. C. Roberton, "Should We Look After Babies Less Than 800 g?," *Archives of Disease in Childhood* 68 (1993): 328.

31 Victorian Infant Collaborative Study Group, "The Cost of Improving the Outcome for Infants of Birthweight 500–999 g in Victoria," *Journal of Paediatrics and Child Health* 29 (1993): 56–62; Victor Y. H. Yu et al., "Outcome of Infants at Less than 26 Weeks Gestation," *Current Topics in Neonatology* no. 1, eds. Thomas N. Hansen and Neil McIntosh (London: W.B. Saunders, 1996), 78.

32 The Victorian Infant Collaborative Group, "Economic Outcome for Intensive Care of Infants of Birthweight 500–999 g Born In Victoria in the Post Surfactant Era," *Journal of Paediatrics and Child Health* 33 (1997): 202–8.

33 See Laura E. Riley and Michael Greene, "Elective Cesarean Delivery to Reduce the Transmission of HIV," *New England Journal of Medicine* 340 (1999): 1032.

34 Craig V. Towers et al., "A 'Bloodless Cesarean Section' and Perinatal Transmission of the Human Immunodeficiency Virus," 179/3 Pt 1 *American Journal of Obstetrics and Gynecology* (1998): 708–14.

35 Jeffrey Stringer et al., "Prophylactic Caesarean Delivery for the Prevention of Perinatal Human Immunodeficiency Virus Transmission: The Case for Restraint," *Journal of the American Medical Association* 281/20 (1999): 1946–9.

36 See Thomas A. Grubert et al., "Complications after Caesarean Section in HIV-1-Infected Women Not Taking Antiretroviral Treatment," Research Letter, *Lancet* 354 (1999): 1612–13; Stringer et al., "Prophylactic Caesarean Delivery," 1946–1949.

37 See Trinh Duong et al., "Vertical Transmission rates for HIV in the British Isles: Estimates Based on Surveillance Data," *British Medical Journal* 319 (1999): 1227–9.

38 Paul D. Losty, Recent advances – "Paediatric surgery," *British Medical Journal* 318 (1999): 1668–72.

39 Donoghue and Cust, *Australian and New Zealand Neonatal Network 1998*, 22.

40 See James Wilkinson, "A Cardiologist's Perspective," in K. Sanders and B. Moore, eds., *Anencephalics, Infants and Brain Death: Treatment Options and the Issue of Organ Donation, Proceedings of Consensus Development Conference* (Melbourne, 1991): 100–6.

41 Peter McCullagh, "Brain Absence: Use of the Anencephalic Infant in Transplantation," in Peter MCullagh, *Brain Dead, Brain Absent, Brain Donors – Human Subjects or Objects* (Chichester: John Wiley & Sons, 1993), 143–8.

42 R. E. Chinnock, "Pediatric Heart Transplantation at Loma Linda: 1985–1996," *Clinical Transplants* (1996): 145–51.

43 F. Dapper et al., "Clinical Experience with Heart Transplantation in Infants," *European Journal of Cardio-Thoracic-Surgery* 14/1 (1998): 1–5; discussion 5–6.

44 S. A. Webber, "Newborn and Infant Heart Transplantation," *Current Opinions in Cardiology* 11/1 (1996): 68–74.

45 W. Middlesworth and R. P. Altman, "Biliary Atresia," *Current Opinion in Pediatrics* 9/3 (1997): 265–9.

46 W. J. Van der Werf et al., "Infant Pediatric Liver Transplantation Results Equal Those for Older Pediatric Patients," *Journal of Pediatric Surgery* 33/1 (1998): 20–3.

47 H. Bonatti et al., "Hepatic Transplantation in Children Under 3 Months of Age: A Single Center's Experience," *Journal of Pediatric Surgery* 32/3 (1997): 486–8.

48 Arthur B. Zinn "Inborn Errors of Metabolism," in Avroy A. Farnaroff and Richard J. Martin, ed., *Neonatal – Perinatal Medicine; Diseases of the Fetus and Infant* (St. Louis: Mosby Year Book, 5th ed., 1992), 1129, 1149.

49 McCullagh, "Brain Absence," 144–6.

50 R. W. Johnson et al., "Outcome of Pediatric Cadaveric Renal Transplantation: A 10 Year Study," *Kidney International* – Supplement 53 (1996): S72–S76.

51 J. M. Cecka et al., "Pediatric Renal Transplantation: A Review of the UNOS Data. United Network for Organ Sharing," *Pediatric Transplantation* 1/1 (1997): 55–64.

52 Patrick Kelly et al., "Umbilical Cord Blood Stem Cells: Application for Treatment of Patients with Hemoglobinopathies," *Journal of Pediatrics* 130/5 (1997): 695–703.

53 A. M. Will, "Umbilical Cord Blood Transplantation," *Archives of Disease in Childhood*, 80 (1999): 3–5.

54 John E. Wagner et al., "Allogeneic Sibling Umbilical-Cord-Blood Transplantation in Children with Malignant and Non-malignant Disease," *Lancet* 346 (1995): 214–19.

55 Joseph M. Wiley and Jeffrey A. Kuller, "Storage of Newborn Stem Cells for Future Use," *Obstetrics & Gynecology* 89/2 (1997): 300–3; L. Lazzari et al., "The Milan Cord Blood Bank and the Italian Cord Blood Network," *Journal of Hematotherapy*, 5/2 (1996): 117–22.

56　Stephen Ashwal, "Brain Death in the Newborn," *Clinics in Perinatology* 24/4 (1997): 8860–1; Mark S. Scher et al., "Clinical Examination Findings in Neonates with the Absence of Electrocerebral Activity: An Acute or Chronic Encephalopathic State?," *Journal of Perinatology* 16/6 (1996): 455–60.

57　*Diagnosis of Brain Stem Death in Infants and Children*, A Working Party Report of the British Paediatric Association, November 1991; for the first week also see *Working Party on Organ Transplantation in Neonates. Conference of Medical Colleges and their Faculties in the United Kingdom*, Report (London: Department of Health and Social Security, 1988).

58　*Working Party on Organ Transplantation in Neonates*, 8.

59　For details of the Loma Linda project see Joyce L. Peabody et al., "Experience with Anencephalic Infants as Prospective Organ Donors," *New England Journal of Medicine* 321 (1989): 345; for a review see D. Alan Shewmon et al., "The Use of Anencephalic Infants as Organ Sources: A Critique," *Journal of the American Medical Association* 261 (1989): 1773–4; Peter McCullagh, "Brain Absence," 143–4; 148–58.

60　The Catholic Bishops' Joint Committee on Bioethical Issues, *Care of the Handicapped Newborn: Parental Responsibility and Medical Responsibility* (London: Catholic Media Office, 1986), 6–7.

61　John S. Wyatt, "Neonatal Care: Withholding or Withdrawal of Treatment in the Newborn Infant," *Bailière's Clinical Obstetrics and Gynaecology* 13/4 (1999): 506.

62　Ibid., 507.

63　John Colin Partridge and Stephen N. Wall, "Analgesia for Dying Infants Whose Life Support is Withdrawn or Withheld," *Pediatrics* 99/1 (1997): 76–9.

64　M. Cuttini et al., "End-of-life Decisions in Neonatal Intensive Care: Physicians' Self-Reported Practices in Seven European Countries," *Lancet* 355 (2000): 2112–18.

65　Peter Singer, *Practical Ethics*, 2nd ed. (Cambridge: Cambridge University Press, 1993), 184, 211–12, 342–3.

66　Sonia Le Bris and Lori Luther, "Alternative Regulatory Perspectives of Obstetrics and Gynaecology," *Bailière's Clinical Obstetrics and Gynaecology* 13/4 (1999): 517–31.

67　Peter M. Dunn, "Appropriate Care of the Newborn: Ethical Dilemmas," *Journal of Medical Ethics*, 19 (1993): 84.

68　Eike-Henner W. Kluge, "Severely Disabled Newborns," in Helga Kuhse and Peter Singer, eds., *A Companion to Bioethics* (Oxford: Blackwell Publishers, 1998), 248.

69　Dorothy C. Wertz et al., *Guidelines on Ethical Issues in Medical Genetics and the Provision of Genetics Services* (Geneva: World Health Organization Hereditary Diseases Program, 1995), 70.

70 Wyatt, "Neonatal Care: Withholding or Withdrawal of Treatment in the Newborn Infant," 505; David K. Stevenson and Amnon Goldworth, "Ethical Dilemmas in the Delivery Room," *Seminars in Perinatology. Ethical Issues in Perinatal Medicine* 22/3 (1998): 199–204.

71 Michael Norup, "Limits of Neonatal Treatment: A Survey of Attitudes in the Danish Population," *Journal of Medical Ethics* 24 (1998): 201–3.

72 Deborah A. Turnbull et al., "Women's Role and Satisfaction in the Decision to have a Caesarean Section," *Medical Journal of Australia* 170 (1999): 580–3.

73 Senate Community Affairs References Committee, *Rocking the Cradle, A Report into Childbirth Procedures* (Canberra: Commonwealth of Australia, 1999), 107; Day et al., *Australia's Mothers and Babies 1997*, 20, 66.

74 Caroline M. de Costa, "Caesarean Section: A Matter of Choice?," editorial, *Medical Journal of Australia* 170 (1999): 572–3. John R. Friend "Some Current Obstetric and Gynaecological Problems," *Bailière's Clinical Obstetrics and Gynaecology* 13/4 (1999): 461–2.

75 Riley and Greene, "Elective Cesarean Delivery to Reduce the Transmission of HIV," 1033.

76 Trin Duong et al., "Vertical Transmission Rates for HIV in the British Isles," 1228.

77 B. W. Levin et al., "The Treatment of Non-HIV Related Conditions in Newborns at Risk for HIV: A Survey of Neonatologists," *American Journal of Public Health*, 85/11 (1995): 1507–13.

78 The Catholic Bishops' Joint Committee on Bioethical Issues, *Care of the Handicapped Newborn*, 6. Norman Ford, "Moral Dilemmas in the Care of the Dying," *Australasian Catholic Record* 73 (1996): 479–90. Norman Ford, "Ethical Dilemmas in Treatment Decisions at the End of Life," in Ford, ed., *Ethical Aspects of Treatment Decisions at the End of Life* (East Melbourne: Caroline Chisholm Centre for Health Ethics, 1997), 65–86.

79 Stevenson and Goldworth "Ethical Dilemmas in the Delivery Room," 199–204.

80 Kathy Kinlaw, "The Changing Nature of Neonatal Ethics in Practice," *Clinics in Perinatology* 23/3 (1996): 426.

81 L. T. Singer et al., "Maternal Psychological Distress and Parenting Stress After the Birth of a Very Low-birth-weight Infant," *Journal of the American Medical Association* 281/9 (1999): 799–805; Pam Hefferman and Steve Heilig, "Giving 'Moral Distress' a Voice: Ethical Concerns among Neonatal Intensive Care Unit Personnel," *Cambridge Quarterly of Healthcare Ethics* 8 (1999): 173–8.

82 Kluge, "Severely Disabled Newborns," 242–5.

83 Steven Gross et al., "Impact of Family Structure and Stability on Academic Outcome in Preterm Children at 10 Years of Age," *Journal of Pediatrics* 138 (2001): 169–75.

84 John Paul II, Encyclical Letter *Evangelium Vitae* (Vatican City: Libreria Editrice Vaticana, 1995), N. 65.

85 Henderson-Smart, "Low Birth-weight Babies," 148–151; Victor Y. H. Yu, "Selective Non-treatment of Newborn Infants," *Medical Journal of Australia* 161 (1994): 627–9; V. Y. H. Yu, "The Extremely Low Birth-weight Infant: Ethical Issues in Treatment," *Australian Paediatric Journal* 23 (1987): 97–103.

86 Stevenson and Goldworth, "Ethical Dilemmas in the Delivery Room," 198–9.

87 C. de Garis, et al., "Attitudes of Australian Neonatal Paediatricians to the Treatment of Extremely Preterm Infants," *Australian Paediatric Journal* 23 (1987): 223–6.

88 Ernest N. Kraybill, "Ethical Issues in the Care of Extremely Low birth Weight Infants," *Seminars in Perinatology, Ethical Issues in Perinatal Medicine* 22/3 (1998): 207.

89 Joyce L. Peabody and Gilbert I. Martin, "From How Small is Too Small to How Much is Too Much: Ethical Issues at the Limits of Neonatal Viability," *Clinics in Perinatology* 23/3 (1996): 481.

90 Muraskas et al., "Neonatal Viability in the 1990s: Held Hostage by Technology," 166; Yu et al., "Outcome of Infants at Less than 26 Weeks Gestation," 70, 78.

91 Muraskas et al., "Neonatal Viability in the 1990s: Held Hostage by Technology," 166–7; Yu et al., "Outcome of Infants at Less than 26 Weeks Gestation," 70, 78; Kraybill, "Ethical Issues in the Care of Extremely Low birth Weight Infants," 207.

92 Doyle et al., "Why Do Preterm Infants Die in the 1990s?," 529; Muraskas et al., "Neonatal Viability in the 1990s: Held Hostage by Technology," 162, 166–7; Yu et al., "Outcome of Infants at Less than 26 Weeks Gestation," 70, 78.

93 Norup, "Limits of Neonatal Treatment: A Survey of Attitudes in the Danish Population," 202–3.

94 Robert D. Troug and John C. Fletcher, "Anencephalic Newborns: Can Organs be Transplanted before Brain Death?," *New England Journal of Medicine* 321 (1989): 388–90; Peabody et al., "Experience with Anencephalic Infants as Prospective Organ Donors," 344–50; F. K. Beller and J. Reeve, "Brain Life and Brain Death – The Anencephalic as an Explanatory Example. A Contribution to Transplantation," *Journal of Medicine and Philosophy* 14 (1989): 5–23; T. E. Mandel, "Future Directions in Transplantation," *Medical Journal of Australia*, 158 (1993): 269–73; C. Strong, "Fetal Tissue Transplantation: Can It be Morally Insulated from Abortion?," *Journal of Medical Ethics* 17 (1991): 70–6.

95 See McCullagh, "Brain Absence," 143–77; F. Ahmad, "Anencephalic Infants as Organ Donors: Beware the Slippery Slope," in *Canadian Medical Association Journal*, 146 (1992): 236–44; Shewmon et al., "The Use of

Anencephalic Infants," 1773–81; Donald M. Mediaris Jr. and Lewis B. Holmes, "On the Use of Anencephalic Infants as Organ Donors," *New England Journal of Medicine* 321 (1989): 391–3.

96 John Paul II, *L'Osservatore Romano*, in English, June 6, 1991.

97 Yu, et al., "Outcome of Infants at Less than 26 Weeks Gestation," 78–9.

Glossary

This glossary generally contains terms which have not been explained when they were first introduced in the book.

adenomatoid: resembling an adenoma, i.e. a benign tumor on internal or external cellular surfaces.

adenovirus: any of a large group of viruses that cause disease in the upper respiratory tract and the membrane lining the eyelids and covering the eyeball.

allogenic: pertains to different gene constitution within the same species.

alveolus: pl., alveoli: a small saclike structure in the lung.

autologous: belonging to the same organism.

autosomal trisomies: trisomies not involving a sex chromosome.

biochemical pregnancy: a pregnancy that is diagnosed by the presence of the hormone HCG in the blood or urine.

blastocyst: a human embryo at four days after fertilization when it appears as a hollow ball of cells, filled with fluid, just before implantation begins.

bradycardia: slowness of the heart beat.

chimera (chimerism): an organism formed naturally or artificially by aggregating cells from different genotypes.

chorion: outermost of the cellular extraembryonic membranes.

chorionic villi: finger-like projections of the chorion which act as vascular processes and help form the placenta. They allow fetal and maternal blood to come in close vessels proximity without actually mixing.

chromosome: a linear thread of DNA that transmits genetic information through genes spaced along its entire length. In the human somatic cell there are 23 sets of chromosomes including two (XX or XY) that determine the sex of the individual. Sperm and egg normally have one set of chromosomes.

cilia: motile hair-like extensions of a surface cell which by their movement produce locomotion.

congenital: existing at birth.

cryopreserve: freeze.

cytogenetic: pertaining to the origin and development of a cell.

diaphragmatic hernia: protrusion of part of the stomach through an opening in the diaphragm.

DNA: deoxyribonucleic acid, the primary constituent of chromosomes and the basis of the genetic code and inherited traits.

dopamine: a hormone derived form amino acids which acts as a neurotransmitter in the central nervous system.

dystocia: difficult labor caused by an obstruction or constriction of the birth passage.

ecogenic: a structure or tissue that is capable of producing echoes.

embryo: the developing organism from fertilization (conception), the zygote stage for about eight weeks; also until the completion of implantation.

embryonic stem cell: pluripotent cultured cells derived from the inner cell mass of a blastocyst.

endometriosis: occurrence of endometrial tissue outside the uterus.

endometrium: the mucous membrane lining the uterus.

endoscope: instrument for examining the interior of a large hollow organ.

estrogen: one of a group of hormonal steroid compounds that renders the female tract suitable for fertilization, implantation and nutrition of the embryo.

fertilization: the process beginning with the penetration of an ovum by a sperm and completed by the union of the male and female pro-nuclei to form a zygote.

fetoscopy: a procedure for directly observing a fetus in utero.

fetus: the developing human young in the uterus from about eight weeks after fertilization; also from the completion of implantation, 14–15 days after fertilization.

fluorescent *in situ* hybridization (FISH): a method for annealing nucleic acid probes to cellular DNA and using fluorescent detection systems.

gene: a hereditary factor composed of DNA.

genome: the complete set of genes in the chromosomes derived from one parent; also the complete set of genes in the chromosomes of each cell of an organism.

hematopoiesis: the normal formation and development of blood cells in the bone marrow;

hematopoietic stem cells: precursors of mature blood cells.

hemolysis: breaking down or destruction of red blood cells resulting in the liberation of hemoglobin.

hemophilia: a group of hereditary bleeding disorders in which there is a deficiency of one of the factors necessary for coagulation of the blood.

hyaline membrane disease: a respiratory distress disorder in newborns, usually premature, characterized by the formation of a glass-like membrane and caused by a lack of pulmonary surfactant.

hydrocephaly: pathological condition marked by excessive accumulation of fluid resulting in dilation of the cerebral ventricles and raised intracranial pressure.

hydronephrosis: dilation of the pelvis and calices of one or both kidneys resulting from obstruction to the flow of urine.

hydrops: gross abnormal accumulation of serous fluid in body tissues or cavities.

hypothermia: abnormal and dangerous condition in which the body temperature is below 95°F (33°C), respiration slow, heart rate faint, and the person may appear to be dead.

hypoxia: reduction of the supply of oxygen to a tissue below normal physiological levels despite adequate perfusion of the tissue by blood.

hysterectomy: excision of the uterus.

hysterotomy: incision in the uterus.

intraperitoneal: within the walls of the abdomen and pelvic cavities.

lysomal storage disease: an inborn error of metabolism characterized by a defect in the lysomal hydrolase.

meiosis: cell division during the maturation of the sex cells whereby in the human each daughter nucleus receives half the number of 46 chromosomes typical of the somatic cells so that sperm and egg have each 23 genetically unique chromosomes.

miscarriage: spontaneous abortion before viability.

mitochondrion: (pl. -ia) a minute self-replicating granule in living cells with its own source of extranuclear DNA, is the main source of cellular energy and functions in respiration.

monochorionic: having a single outermost cellular extraembryonic membrane.

necrotizing enterocolitis: inflammation of the small intestine and colon which causes cells to die.

oligohydramnios: an abnormally small amount of amniotic fluid.

ontological individual: a single concrete entity that exists as a distinct being and is not an aggregation of smaller things nor merely a part of a greater whole; hence its unity is said to be intrinsic.

ontological: refers to what exists in reality as distinct from in one's mind.

organochlorins: any of a large group of persistent chemical compounds containing chlorine which are harmful to all animal and human life, are used as pesticides and accumulate in the food chain.

oxytocin: a hormone that is used to induce labor or stimulation of contractions.

parenteral: not through the alimentary canal, e.g. injection.

peritoneal: pertaining to the abdominal cavity and viscera.

periventricular: pertaining to small cavities in the brain or heart, e.g. brain or lung ventricles.

phenylketonuria: an inborn error of metabolism marked by an inability to convert phenylalanine into tyrosine thereby causing an accumulation of phenylalanine, resulting in mental retardation neurologic manifestations unless treated by a diet low in phenylalanine.

pluripotency: is actual capacity of the progeny of one or more embryonic cells to form all types of cells, but not an entire embryo or fetus; pluripotent. These cells are also called pluripotent stem cells.

polar body: one of the minute cells produced during the two meiotic divisions in the maturation of the ovum; it is nonfunctional and is not capable of being fertilized.

polycystic ovary syndrome: an abnormal condition characterized by enlarged ovaries, anovulation amenorrhea and infertility.

progestogen (also progestagen): any natural or synthetic hormone that prepares the uterus for the reception of an early embryo.

prostaglandin: one of several potent hormone like unsaturated fatty acids that may be used to terminate a pregnancy.

retrovirus: any of the family of RNA (ribonucleic acid) viruses containing reverse transcriptase which, during replication, enables the viral DNA to become integrated into the DNA of the host cell.

somatic cell: a cell of the body that is not a germ cell.

stem cell: a precursor cell which may divide to reproduce itself as well as a more specialized cell type.

surfactant: an agent that reduces the surface tension of pulmonary fluids and helps make pulmonary tissue elastic.

teratogen, teratogenic: anything that interferes with normal prenatal development and thereby causes a fetal abnormality.

thalassemia: any of a group of inherited disorders of hemoglobin metabolism causing anemia.

totipotency: the actual potential of a cell or cluster of cells to produce the blastocyst, placental tissues and entire offspring; totipotent.

trisomy: an abnormality in which the cells of an individual have an additional (third) chromosome.

xeno-estrogens: estrogens from a nonhuman source, e.g. water in rivers, environment, etc.

zygote: the diploid cell that results from the union of a sperm and egg.

Select
Bibliography

Books

Ashley, Benedict and Kevin O'Rourke, *Health Care Ethics: A Theological Analysis*, 4th ed., Washington: Georgetown University Press, 1997.

Baird, Robert M. and Stuart E. Resenbaum (eds.), *The Ethics of Abortion: Pro-Life vs Pro Choice*, Buffalo, NY: Prometheus Books, 1993.

Banner, Michael, *Christian Ethics and Contemporary Moral Problems*, Cambridge: University Press, 1999.

Beauchamp, Tom L. and James F. Childress, *Principles of Biomedical Ethics*, 5th ed., New York: Oxford University Press, 2001.

Bishops' Committee on Bioethics, *Assisted Human Reproduction*, Dublin: Veritas Publications, 2000.

Blyth, Eric et al. (eds.), *Truth and the Child 10 Years On: Information Exchange in Donor Assisted Conception*, Birmingham: British Association of Social Workers, 1998.

Castaldo, Peter J. and Albert S. Moraczewski (eds.), *The Fetal Tissue Issue: Medical and Ethical Aspects*, Braintree, Mass.: The Pope John Center, 1994.

Catholic Bishops' Joint Committee on Bioethical Issues, *Care of the Handicapped Newborn: Parental Responsibility and Medical Responsibility*, London: Catholic Media Office, 1986.

Congregation for the Doctrine of the Faith, *Instruction on Respect for Human Life in its Origin and on the Dignity of Procreation. Replies to Certain Questions of the Day*, Vatican City: Polyglot Press, 1987.

Correa, Juan de dios Vial and Elio Sgreccia (eds.), *Identity and Statute of Human Embryo*, Città del Vaticano: Libreria Editrice Vaticana, 1998.

Dawson, Karen, *Reproductive Technology: The Science, the Ethics, the Law and the Social Issues*, Melbourne: VCTA Publishing, Macmillan Education Australia, 1995.

Evans, Donald and Neil Pickering (eds.), *Creating the Child: The Ethics, Law and Practice of Assisted Procreation*, The Hague: Martinus Nijhoff Publishers, 1996.

Evans, Donald (ed.), *Conceiving the Embryo*, The Hague: Martinus Nijhoff Publishers, 1996.

Finnis, John, *Moral Absolutes: Tradition, Revision and Truth*, Washington, DC: Catholic University of America Press, 1991.

Fisk, Nicholas M. and Kenneth J. Moise Jr. (eds.), *Fetal Therapy: Invasive and Transplacental*, Cambridge: Cambridge University Press, 1997.

Ford, Norman, *When Did I Begin? Conception of the Human Individual in History, Philosophy and Science*, Cambridge: University Press, 1988, p/b 1991.

Ford, Norman, *Quando Comincio Io? Il Concepimento nella Storia, nella Filosofia e nella Scienza*. Milano: Baldini and Castoldi, 1997. An updated Italian translation of *When Did I Begin?* by Rodolfo Rini, with replies to critiques in Appendix V.

George, R., *In Defence of Natural Law*, Oxford: Oxford University Press, 1991.

Gula, Richard M., *Reason Informed by Faith: Foundations of Catholic Morality*, Mahwah, NJ: Paulist Press, 1989.

Hansen, Thomas N. and Neil McIntosh (eds.), *Current Topics in Neonatology* no. 1, London: W. B. Saunders, 1996.

Harrison, Michael R. et al. (eds.), *The Unborn Patient: The Art and Science of Fetal Therapy*, Philadelphia: W. B. Saunders Company, 2001.

Health Council of the Netherlands: Committee on In Vitro fertilization. *IVF-related Research*. Rijswijk, 1998; pub. no. 1998/08E.

Heaney, Stephen J. (ed.), *Abortion: A New Generation of Catholic Responses*, Braintree, Mass.: The Pope John Center, 1992.

Humber, James M. and Robert Almeder (eds.), *Human Cloning*, Biomedical Ethics Reviews, Totowa, NJ: Humana Press, 1998.

Jansen, Robert and David Mortimer (eds.), *Towards Reproductive Certainty: Fertility and Genetics beyond 1999*, New York: Parthenon, 1999.

John Paul II, *Veritatis Splendor*, Encyclical Letter, Vatican City: Libreria Editrice Vaticana, 1993.

John Paul II, *Evangelium Vitae*, Encyclical Letter, Vatican City: Libreria Editrice Vaticana, 1995.

Kilner, John F., Nigel M. de S. Cameron, and David L. Schiedermayer (eds.), *Bioethics and the Future of Medicine: A Christian Appraisal*, Grand Rapids, Mich.: Wm. B. Eerdemans, 1995.

Kuhse, Helga and Peter Singer, *Should the Baby Live? The Problem of Handicapped Infants*, Oxford: Oxford University Press: 1985, 18–47.

Kuhse, Helga and Peter Singer (eds.), *A Companion to Bioethics*, Oxford: Blackwell Publishers, 1998.

Lamb, David, *Organ Transplants and Ethics*, Aldershot: Avebury, 1996, 69–73.

Marteau, Theresa and Martin Richards (eds.), *The Troubled Helix: Social and Psychological Implications of the New Human Genetics*, Cambridge: Cambridge University Press, 1996.

McCormick, Richard A., *The Critical Calling: Reflections on Moral Dilemmas since Vatican II*, Washington, DC: Georgetown University Press, 1989.

McCormick, Richard A. and Paul Ramsay (eds.), *Doing Evil to Achieve Good*, Chicago: Loyola University Press, 1978.

Nuffield Council on Bioethics, *Genetic Screening: Ethical Issues*, London: 1993.

Pellegrino, Edmund D. and Alan I. Faden (eds.), *Jewish and Catholic Bioethics: An Ecumenical Dialogue*, Washington, DC: Georgetown University Press, 1999.

Polkinghorne, J. C., *Review of the Guidance on the Research Use of Fetuses and Fetal Material*, London: HMSO, 1989.

Reich, Warren Thomas, *Bioethics, Sex, Genetics and Human Reproduction*, New York: Macmillan Library Reference USA, 1995.

Rothman, Barbara Katz, *The Tentative Pregnancy: Prenatal Diagnosis and the Future of Motherhood*, New York: Viking Press, 1986.

Royal College of Obstetricians and Gynaecologists, *Fetal Awareness: Report of a Working Party*, London: RCOG Press, 1997.

Seminars in Perinatology. *Ethical Issues in Perinatal Medicine* 22, 1998.

Shannon, Thomas A., *Surrogate Motherhood: The Ethics of Using Human Beings*, New York: Crossroad, 1988.

Shannon, Thomas A. (ed.), *Bioethics*, Mahwah, NJ: Paulist Press, 1993.

Shannon, Thomas A. and Lisa Sowle Cahill, *Religion and Artificial Reproduction*, New York: Crossroad, 1988.

Shapiro, Constance Hoenk, *Infertility and Pregnancy Loss*, San Francisco: Jossey-Bass, 1988.

Shenfield, F. and C. Sureau (eds.), *Ethical Dilemmas in Assisted Reproduction*, New York and London: Parthenon Publishing Group, 1997.

Singer, Peter, *Practical Ethics*, 2nd ed., Cambridge: Cambridge University Press, 1993.

Singer, Peter, *Rethinking Life and Death: The Collapse of Our Traditional Ethics*, Melbourne: The Text Publishing Company, 1994 and Oxford: Oxford University Press, 1995.

Singer, Peter et al. (eds.), *Embryo Experimentation*, Cambridge: Cambridge University Press, 1990.

Stock, Gregory and John Campbell (eds.), *Engineering the Human Germline*, New York: Oxford University Press, 2000.

Tournier, Paul, *The Meaning of Persons*, London: SCM Press, 1957, 1974.

Waters, Brent, *Reproductive Technology: Towards a Theology of Procreative Stewardship*, London: Darton, Longman and Todd, 2001.

Wertz, Dorothy C. et al., *Guidelines on Ethical Issues in Medical Genetics and the Provision of Genetics Services*, Geneva: World Health Organization Hereditary Diseases Program, 1995.

Wildes, Kevin Wm., SJ, *Infertility: A Crossroad of Faith, Medicine and Technology*, Dordrecht: Kluwer Academic Publishers, 1997.

Wolpert, Lewis, *The Triumph of the Embryo*, Oxford: Oxford University Press, 1991.

Articles

Benagiano, Giuseppe and Paola Bianchi, Debate: Gender selection. "Sex prese-lection: an aid to couples or a threat to humanity," *Human Reproduction* 14/4 (1999): 868–70.

Berkowitz, Jonathan M., "Sexism and racism in preconceptive trait selection," *Fertility and Sterility* 71/3 (1999): 415–17

Boyle, Joseph, "An absolute rule approach," in Kuhse and Singer, eds., *A Companion to Bioethics*, 76–7.

Cuttini, M. et al., "End-of-life decisions in neonatal intensive care: physicians' self-reported practices in seven European countries," *Lancet* 355 (2000): 2112–18.

Doyle, Lex et al., "Why do preterm infants die in the 1990s?," *Medical Journal of Australia* 170 (1999): 528–532.

Draper, Heather and Ruth Chadwick, "Beware! Preimplantation genetic diag-nosis may solve some old problems but it also raises new ones," *Journal of Medical Ethics* 25/2 (1999): 114–20.

Durna, Eva M. et al., "Donor insemination: attitudes of parents towards dis-closure," *Medical Journal of Australia*, 167 (1997): 256–9.

Ford, Norman, SDB, "When does human life begin? Science, government, church," *Pacifica* 1 (1988): 298–327.

Ford, Norman, "Fetus," *The Encyclopedia of Applied Ethics*, vol. 2, ed. Ruth Chadwick, San Diego: Academic Press, 1998.

Ford, Norman, "Are all cells derived from an embryo themselves embryos?," in *Pluripotent Stem Cells: Therapeutic Perspectives and Ethical Issues*, Interna-tional Workshop organized by the Marcel Mérieux Foundation, June 21–3, 2000, eds. Betty Dodet and Marissa Vicari, Paris: John Libbey /Eurotext, 2001, 81–7.

Ford, Norman, SDB, "The human embryo as person in Catholic teaching," *The National Catholic Bioethics Quarterly* 1/2 (2001): 155–60.

Gilchrist, Anne C. et al., "Termination of pregnancy and psychiatric morbidity," *British Journal of Psychiatry*, 167 (1995): 243–8.

Golombok, Susan, "New families, old values: considerations regarding the welfare of the child," *Human Reproduction* 13/9 (1998): 2342–7.

Gross, Steven et al., "Impact of family structure and stability on academic outcome in preterm children at 10 years of age," *Journal of Pediatrics* 138 (2001): 169–75.

Hammerman, Cathy et al., "Does pregnancy affect medical ethical decision making?," *Journal of Medical Ethics* 24 (1998): 409–13.

Hefferman, Pam and Steve Heilig, "Giving 'moral distress' a voice: ethical con-cerns among neonatal intensive care unit personnel," *Cambridge Quarterly of Healthcare Ethics* 8 (1999): 173–8.

Hepburn, Liz, "Genetic counselling: parental autonomy or acceptance of limits?," *Concilium* 2 (1998): 35–42.

Joint Committee on Bioethical Issues Statement, "Use of the 'morning-after pill' in cases of rape," *Origins* 15/39 (1986): 634–8.

Keenan, James F. and Thomas R. Kopfensteiner, "Moral theology out of Western Europe," *Theological Studies* 59 (1998): 128–30.

McCann, Margaret F. and Linda S. Potter, "Progestin-only oral contraception: a comprehensive review," *Contraception* 50, Suppl 1 (Dec. 1994): S14–S21.

Moloney, Francis "Life, healing and the Bible: a Christian challenge," *Pacifica* 8 (1995): 315–34.

Muraskas, Jonathan et al., "Neonatal viability in the 1990s: held hostage by technology," *Cambridge Quarterly of Healthcare Ethics*, 8/2 (1999): 160–70.

Peabody, Joyce L. and Gilbert I. Martin, "From how small is too small to how much is too much: ethical issues at the limits of neonatal viability," *Clinics in Perinatology* 23/3 (1996): 481.

Reichlin, Massimo, "The argument from potential," *Bioethics*, 11 (1997): 12–23.

Resnik, David B., "The commodification of human reproductive materials," *Journal of Medical Ethics* 24 (1998): 391–2.

Roberton, N. R. C., "Should we look after babies less than 800g?," in *Archives of Disease in Childhood* 68 (1993): 326–9.

Savulescu, Julian, "Should we clone human beings? Cloning as a source of tissue for transplantation," *Journal of Medical Ethics* 25 (1999): 87–95.

Searle, Judith, "Fearing the worst – why do pregnant women feel 'at risk'?," *Australian and New Zealand Journal of Obstetrics and Gynaecology* 36 (1996): 279–86.

Statham, Helen et al., "Prenatal diagnosis of fetal abnormality: psychological effects on women in low-risk pregnancies," *Baillière's Clinical Obstetrics and Gynaecology*," 14 (2000): 731–47.

Trounson, Alan, and Kim Giliam, "What does cloning offer human medicine?," *Today's Life Science* (March/April 1999): 14.

Turner, A. J. and A. Coyle, "What does it mean to be a donor offspring? The identity experiences of adults conceived by donor insemination and the implications for counselling and therapy," *Human Reproduction* 15 (2000): 2041–51.

Wilcox, Allen J. et al., "Incidence of early loss of pregnancy," *New England Journal of Medicine* 319 (1988): 189–94.

Wilmut, Ian, "Cloning for medicine," *Scientific Medicine* (Dec. 1998): 30–5.

Index

This index of chapters is designed to be used in conjunction with the book's detailed Contents and Glossary. It includes entries on subjects and authors that are significant in view of the purpose of the book. Bibliographical references in the Notes give the names of authors consulted.